UP FROM THE R

GROWING A VOCAB

UP FROM THE ROOTS:
GROWING A VOCABULARY

Bob and Maxine Moore

Foreword by Molly Ivins

New Chapter Press
New York * California

Library of Congress Card Catalog Number: 92-060937

ISBN: 0-942257-20-0

Jacket and interior design by Hannah Lerner
Edited by Jill Mason
Editorial Associate — Liza Veto

10 9 8 7 6 5 4 3 2 1

First printing: July 1993

Manufactured in the United States of America

To the young people of
The Chinquapin School . . .
you who made this book
necessary

QUID PRO QUO
CHINQUAPIN
19 69

And to the supporters of
The Chinquapin School . . .
you who made it all
possible

Contents

Foreword

The reason Robert P. Moore came to teach at St. John's School in 1951 neatly sums up everything that's wrong with the public school system — Moore is not qualified to teach in it. That he is a superb teacher has nothing to do with it. That he is a splendid human being — idealistic, intelligent, and funny — matters not a whit. That he has done graduate work in English, that he knows and loves American literature, that he has the most precious of all pedagogical gifts — the ability to share his enthusiasm for his subject — none of that counts with the Texas Department of Education. Bob Moore hasn't taken 45 hours of education courses. Such courses wouldn't have taught him to teach, of course. But he might have learned to maximize personhood potentiality, to conceptualize comprehension input and to individualize curriculum facilitation. Among the many wonderful things Moore taught us was how to recognize and despise that sort of bovine intestinal effluvia.

Not long ago, I tried to imagine what one of the state's new merit pay selection committees would have made of Moore's teaching techniques. He was given to wearing an Alfred E. Neuman T-shirt under his correct St. John's garb. He threw chalk at kids who weren't paying attention. Hard. If he was really mad, he threw chairs. Sometimes he wiggled his ears just to see if anyone would notice. Sometimes he stuck a foot into the wastebasket and would then proceed to stomp around with the wastebasket stuck on his foot while he continued to lecture as though there was nothing unusual going on. Sometimes he snuck up on the class from the outside and would stand by the windows making faces at us while we took tests. I conclude that Mr. Mo' was most unlikely to have received a merit pay raise from the average coach/principal. But his classes were full of surprise and fun. We laughed all the time.

As this book reveals, Bob Moore made kids want to read. He made us keep journals and we had to produce two solid pages a week about something. And he read them all and wrote comments on them. Do you know how much work that is?

He is a man remarkable both for his energy and his intensity. He put himself into teaching wholly. He never sounded bored. He never dogged it, never gave himself an easy day. He was a serious teacher in that you never thought he wanted to be doing anything else, that there was anything more important than what he was doing.

He read all of *Long Day's Journey Into Night* to his tenth grade classes. It took three days. There was not a sound except his voice in that classroom, not a sound for three days.

He was the only teacher I ever had whose house was a hangout for his students. I couldn't think of how to describe why we went to Moore's house and what it was like until one friend said, "It was a salon. Moore ran the closest thing to a salon I ever knew." It was a place where we talked about books and ideas. I don't recall that we ever had emotional heart-to-heart talks with Moore — he is not a self-revelatory man. He was an angry man then, in the John Osborne sense, though I am told he has achieved a serenity these days.

Moore drove an Izetta, the smallest, cheapest car made. It had only three wheels and looked like a pregnant roller skate. It looked wonderfully funny parked next to Lloyd Bentsen, III's Cadillac. I though it was a comment on the materialism that afflicted St. John's — perhaps he drove it because he was a school teacher with three children.

Moore lived very close to the ideals he talked about. Teenagers are dreadfully given to searching out the gaps between what adults say and how they live. I don't think there were any with Bob Moore. But he felt them, felt there was a disjuncture between teaching the children of the over-privileged and trying to make a more just world. So he left St. John's after 18 years, when he was 48 years old, and went off to start a school of his own, a college preparatory school for kids from the ghettos and the barrios. Of all the quixotic damn fool things to do. Have you any idea how many people went off to start noble experiments in alternative education in the 1960's and how many of them failed? Moore's school is still going. Its headmaster is Bill Heinzerling, SJS Class of '64. Chinquapin School worked for two reasons. One is because Bob Moore is a phenomenally good teacher. The other is because he is one of the hardest-working sumbitches that ever walked.

—Molly Ivins
Austin, Texas

Introduction

In the late 1960s, as I neared the end of a second decade teaching English in a college preparatory school for the children of well-to-do parents, my wife and I founded — with the generous backing and encouragement of many other concerned people — a college preparatory boarding school for junior and senior high school-age kids from Houston's inner city.

Almost all of our students were ill-prepared in English language arts. Many came from families in which only Spanish was spoken, many from neighborhoods where standard English was seldom heard. We began our efforts to prepare them for college with whatever reading and vocabulary materials we could scrounge up, but none of what we examined fit our needs: a quick-fix catch-up program.

Thanks to a combination of desperation, determination, and our serendipitous discovery of a forty-five-page appendix of Indo-European roots in the 1969 edition of *The American Heritage Dictionary*, we finally found the path we had to take to solve our students' language problem. And so we began gathering the words that stemmed from one Latin root and then another and another. Over a period of two decades of intensive research (plus one hour each day of vocabulary classes for every student, along with our regular English courses in literature, grammar, and composition), we developed an extensive compilation of lists of words from more than eight hundred Latin and Greek roots.

The Chinquapin School is now in its twenty-fourth year. For the years 1990 through 1992, the average Scholastic Aptitude Test (SAT) score, verbal portion, for our students, almost all of whom are from the barrios and ghettos of Houston, was from fifty-two to eighty points above the national average, and each year our seniors are accepted at such schools as Bowdoin, Colorado College, Drake, Harvard, Middlebury, Notre Dame, Pomona, Purdue, Rice, Santa Clara, Smith, Stanford, Trinity, Vassar, and Wellesley, as well as numerous state universities. That our vocabulary system (in unison, of course, with the students' drive and determination) has been to a great extent responsible for that success is self-evident.

''The difference between the right word and the almost right word,'' Mark Twain once said, ''is the difference between lightning and the lightning bug.'' It can also be the difference between a letter of acceptance by a college and one beginning, ''We regret to inform you . . .'', for a key element in current college entrance examinations is not only being able to distinguish between antonyms and synonyms, in correctly filling in the blanks in sentence completions, and in singling out the best analogies, but in one's success in mastering the reading comprehension and mathematical word problems as well.

Voracious readers and students who have studied Latin for a year or so are more likely to know the difference between *authoritarian* and *authoritative*, *fraction* and *fractious*, and *temporize* and *extemporize* than, say, those whose principal avocation is sitting on a couch in the proximity of a picture tube. That the usual television fare does not noticeably increase one's working vocabulary is a given.

Some routes are easier than others. A friend of ours as a youth took a dictionary out into the fields where he spent long hours shepherding both sheep and words. As a result he became a veritable walking dictionary. On the other hand, we once heard an educator of some renown say that he had never once in his life opened a dictionary; it was our inescapable conclusion that either he had been born with a silver lexicon in his brain or the dictionaries in his presence had always lain open.

The shelves of bookstores and libraries are loaded with vocabulary texts of almost every description, many newspapers carry columns that feature interesting and unusual words, and page-a-day calendars entreat their users to learn 313 words a year (most have only one page for the weekend) plus a bonus word every fourth year.

The system that you will find in this book is different. All the words are grouped according to the root family from which they have sprung. The more than three thousand words that the reader will find here stem from some two hundred primarily Latin roots, all of them having been contributed to the eclectic language that we call English.

In order to understand how so many words from the ancient Greek and Roman civilizations came into the language we speak today, it will be helpful to take a brief look at a few historical occurrences that affected the development of our language.

In A.D. 43 Roman legions under Emperor Claudius crossed what we call the English Channel and managed, in time, to drive the native Celts and Picts back into the forests. The Romans stayed around for about 350 years, founding the city of London on the Thames River, setting up army posts, building walls to keep the natives at bay, bathing in the warm springs in what is now the city of Bath, and living much as they had back home.

In A.D. 410, however, the news from Rome was not at all good, and it was decreed that they had better pull out and return home to help save the tottering Roman Empire. They left behind a few native Britons who had adopted a new religion called Christianity, numerous buildings, and miles of walls, some of which are identifiable today, along with a smattering of Latin words such as *camp, colony, mountain, port, street,* and *village.* Not much in the way of thanks, it would seem, for three and a half centuries of free rent.

By the end of the fifth century, members of three German tribes, the Angles, Saxons, and Jutes, had crossed the North Sea in sufficient numbers to fill the vacuum that the Romans had left and were eventually to give the name *Englaland* (from *Angle*) to their new turf and *Englisc* to their utterances.

And then in 597 a second Latin wave washed upon England and its language. This was when Ethelbert, the Saxon king of Kent whose wife Bertha was a Christian, was baptized by St. Augustine, a missionary sent, along with forty other monks, by Pope Gregory I to convert the Anglo-Saxons to Christianity. It is recorded that in one day he baptized more than one thousand people in the River Swale. Augustine's establishing a Roman Catholic seat at Canterbury and becoming its first archbishop brought to the island a considerably larger number of Latin words, not only such clerical ones as *altar, angel, apostle, bishop, church, deacon, devil, hymn, mass, minister, minster, monk, priest, temple,* and *wine,* but also everyday household words like *cook, cup, kitchen, noon, pear, pepper, pillow, pound,* and *sock.*

However, the most far-reaching impact upon English life and its language occurred in 1066 when the Normans came calling, uninvited, from Normandy. They were the descendants of Norsemen who had conquered a large area in the north of France ages earlier. Under the leadership of William the Conquerer, they defeated the English forces at Senlac Hill near Hastings and marched on to London, where William, on Christmas Day, was crowned king of England. He and his followers spoke French, a language that was descended from Latin.

These newcomers were a highly civilized people who brought with them the language and knowledge of architecture, government, law, and the military, and, along with all that, a way of life far different from that known to the natives, a relatively uneducated and unsophisticated people of the soil. Thus the Anglo-Saxon pig of the field became the *pork* of the table, and, likewise, calf became *veal*; deer, *venison*; ox, *beef*; and sheep, *mutton*. The island was soon to become acquainted with a wide range of strange words: *army, captain, castle, court, dinner, feast, govern, honor, judge, jury, justice, mayor, navy, officer, peace, people, state, supper*, and *tower*, to mention but a sampling.

Greek words entered our language in a different way. Some became Latin words and then French and then English. Others were borrowed directly, especially those in the fields of science and technology, often seen in compound words such as *telephone, photography*, and *microscope*.

As many as half of the words in our dictionaries and vocabularies are from other tongues, and the greatest number of them by far came from Latin. One of the unique byproducts of this melting pot of languages is the richness that it has bequeathed to our speech. It is said that no other language offers so many choices. In the following list the first word is of Germanic origin, from the Anglo-Saxons and the Danes; the second from Latin-French: *bloom/flower; buy/purchase; forefather/ancestor; foretell/predict; fire/conflagration; friendly/amiable; height/altitude; lowly/humble; luck/fortune; name/appellation; offspring/descendant; outclass/surpass; outfit/equip; outlaw/criminal; scare/terrify; teach/instruct; unfriendly/hostile; unwilling/reluctant; walk/perambulate; wish/desire; withdraw/remove; work/labor*.

How To Use This Book

This book is arranged in alphabetical order by root, that is, the original word in Latin (or Greek, marked [Gk]) from which a group of English words have evolved. Words that come from the same root constitute its root family. Many of the words in a particular family, even those with different meanings, contain the same group (or groups) of letters; we call this group of letters the root's Common Base Form (CBF).

Recognizing the CBF can help you make connections among words that have similar meanings or derivations so that you can remember them more easily or even make an educated guess as to the meanings of words you've never seen before. Even though not all the words from a given root have a CBF (and a few roots have no CBF at all), you will still find it to be a handy tool that you can use to help you improve your vocabulary.

On page xv you will find a sample unit featuring *fortuna*, a Latin root meaning ''luck,'' to illustrate how each root is treated throughout the book, the format of which is as follows:

1. *Heading:* The root word is from Latin (unless marked [Gk]); it is followed by its meaning and its Common Base Form(s).

2. *Text:* In the text for each root, the words of that family are combined in sentences, making connections among them whenever possible, and using synonyms, sample sentences, and literary and historical quotations to illustrate their meanings.

3. The CBF is always in capital letters the first time a word that contains one appears in the text, and the entire word is in bold face. Note in the sample the capitalized CBF in **FORTune**; subsequent mentions of the word will be without the capital letters: ''Fortune favors the brave.''

4. All the words that stem from *fortuna* contain a CBF. This is not always the case. The CBF of *aevum*, age, the first root in this book (see page 1), is EV; it is found in **primEVal** and **mediEVal**, but not in **age** or **eternity**, both of which also stem from *aevum*. *Fortuna* has only one CBF, FORT, but *bassus*, short, low, has two: BASE and BASS (**deBASE, BASSoon**); *caedere*, to cut, has three: CIDE, CIS, CISE (**deCIDE, sCISsors, preCISE**); and *jacere*, to lie, to throw, has four:

EAS, JAC, JECT, JET (**EASy, adJACent, reJEC-Tion, JETty**).

5. *Once uPUN a time:* Puns are occasionally included to give a playful twist to the lesson.

6. *But not:* Words that look as though they might be members of the root family but are not are listed here with their own root, language (see Abbreviations below), and meaning. For example, *forte* and *fortnight* are not from *fortuna*.

7. *Combining forms:* Prefixes, suffixes, and separate words that are used in combination with a form of the root in the text are listed here with their pertinent meanings and can sometimes throw additional light upon the meaning of the word. In the sample unit, *mis-*, bad, and *un-*, not, are obviously helpful, but in *aevum* the forms *medi*, middle, and *prime*, young, when combined with the CBF, give us the whole meaning of *medieval* and *primeval*.

8. For years one of the principal sections of the verbal portion of the SAT has requested the student to "choose the word or phrase that is most nearly *opposite* in meaning to the word in capital letters." But even if the matchings of opposites were not called for on college entrance examinations, a perusal of a word's antonyms would prove fruitful: antonyms can offer a fresh slant on a word in question, as well as helping to identify an unfamiliar word by its associates. Consider, for example, these antonyms of "artist": amateur, apprentice, beginner, neophyte, novice, tyro. A person to whom, say, "neophyte" is unfamiliar now has a solid clue as to its meaning.

This is the system that has helped the students at The Chinquapin School to surpass, exceed, transcend, top, eclipse, rise above the national average on the verbal portion of the S.A.T. We believe that this book, coupled with ample helpings of drive and determination, can be of similar benefit to other aspiring students.

Bob & Maxine Moore
Minor Manor, 1993

Abbreviations

Ar	Arabic	OE	Old English
AS	Anglo-Saxon	OF	Old French
D	Dutch	ON	Old Norse
F	French	Orig.	Originally
G	German	Perh.	Perhaps
Gk	Greek	Prob.	Probably
Icel	Icelandic	?	Of uncertain origin
Inupiaq	Eskimo Indian	Russ	Russian
Ir	Irish	Scand	Scandinavian
It	Italian	Skt	Sanskrit
Lit.	Literally	Sp	Spanish
Lith	Lithuanian	Swed	Swedish
ME	Middle English	Var.	Variation
Obs.	Obsolete		

A KEY TO UNDERSTANDING OUR FORMAT

3. The CBF is capitalized throughout each unit.

1. Latin root and its meaning; Greek roots are marked ''Gk.''

FORTUNA, luck;
FORT

2. These are the ''Common Base Forms'' (CBF); they are the forms that are common to most of the words stemming from the root.

4. Each word from the root is set in bold type the first time it appears.

FORTuna was the ancient Roman goddess of **FORTune**, that aspect of life that we have little or no control over, although there are those who claim that ''Fortune favors the brave.'' For those of us not **FORTunate** enough to score high on the bravery scale, it still adds up to chance, luck, destiny, and fate. A fortune is also wealth, riches, capital, income, and circumstances. (''There certainly are not so many men of large fortune in the world, as there are pretty women to deserve them,'' Jane Austen, *Mansfield Park.*)

FORTuitous meetings or events are accidental, unintentional, unexpected, and unforeseen,) (My runing into Uncle Rich after all these years was entirely fortuitous.) A **FORTuity** is an accidental occurrence, but it is most often one on which Lady Luck or Dame Fortune has smiled.

The other side of the coin is that **misFORTune** (not Miss Fortune, *unfortunately*) is sorrow and trouble and adversity often resulting from an injury or accident or calamity. The victims then join the ranks of the **unFORTunate**.

5. Note that synonyms and an example sentence are provided here.

*☛ *Once uPUN a time* as a fisherman started out to sea, a landlubber asked him what he was going out after.
''For tuna,'' said the fisherman.
''Good fortune,'' said the landlubber.

6. Time out for a pun; they are scattered throughout the book.

9. Abbreviations are listed on page xiv.

☛ *But not:* **forte** [**fortis,** strong], one's strong point; **fortnight** [ME **fourtene niht**], two weeks.

8. Prefixes and combining forms (those used in compound words but not independently) are listed here.

☛ *Combining Forms:* **mis-,** bad; **unp,** not.

☛ *Ant.:* **fortuitous** — planned, deliberate, expected; **fortunate** — cursed, hapless, ill-fated; **fortune** — poverty, indigence, destitution, purpose, intent, design; **misfortune** — prosperity, godsend; **unfortunate** — affluent, blessed, lucky, proper, commendable, praiseworthy.

7. These words are similar in spelling or sound but do not derive from this root. The derivation of the word is in brackets.

10. Antonyms — words that are opposites in meaning — are an essential and valuable vocabulary learning tool.

A

The word **primEVal** (also **primaEVal**) refers to the first **age** or **ages** of the world, hence the primitive, pristine, antediluvian, primordial, embryonic, prehistoric era. (As we wandered through the forest, we felt as though we were in a primeval wilderness.)

The Middle Ages, the name given to the period in European history from about A.D. 500 to about 1500 (the dates vary from one history book to another) is synonymous with **mediEVal** (also **mediaEVal**), meaning literally "middle [*medi-*] age [aev]." Medieval is used informally to mean extremely old-fashioned, archaic, passé, behind the times. (When Jill was eighteen, she thought of her parents as being hopelessly medieval, completely out of touch with reality; five years later she was amazed at how sensible their ideas had become.) **CoEVal** means belonging to the same age and time as another, contemporary, coexistent, modern, up-to-date.

LongEVity is long length of life. (Longevity is a characteristic of our family line.) It is also a synonym for seniority, as in one's length of employment; having seniority is often considered a plus, especially when promotions are based on length of service, but not when **ageism** creeps in, the name given to discrimination toward persons of a certain age group. (As Henry studied the pink slip terminating his employment after forty years on the job, he suddenly realized that he was sixty years old rather than that many years young.)

In another vein, we savor the **ageless** beauty of the snow-capped mountains and the stately oak tree, enjoy the company of our **agemates**, and appreciate many of the **age-old** traditions of our society.

Poets do not always view our later years in a cheery fashion. William Butler Yeats wrote that, "An **aged** man is but a paltry thing, / A tattered coat upon a stick. . . ." And as his father lay dying, Dylan Thomas wrote, "Do not go gentle into that good night, / Old age should burn and rave at close of day; / Rage, rage against the dying of the light." The actress Billie Burke viewed it in a much lighter vein, saying that age is something "that doesn't matter unless you're a cheese," and so she lived, never seeming to grow old, even at eighty-five.

Eternity is infinity, forever, time without end, ages and ages, and eons and eons. (The minister's sermon was about the joys of eternity; it seemed to be about that long, too.) **Eternal** is everlasting, perpetual, interminable, incessant, enduring. (If you two don't quit that eternal bickering, I am going to stop the car right now and ——.) To **eternize** (also: **eternalize**) is to immortalize. (It was appropriate that the saint was eternized in Rome, the Eternal City.)

But not: coequal [*aequus*, even], equal with another in rank, etc.

Combining forms: co-, together; *long-*, long; *medi-*, middle; *prime-*, young.

AEVUM, age: EV

1

☞ *Antonyms: age* — youth, adolescence, instant, short time, second; *aged* —
green, unseasoned, immature, juvenile, unripe; *eternal* — temporary, transitory,
ephemeral, evanescent, transient, temporal, occasional, infrequent, rare,
spasmodic, irregular; *eternity* — instant, moment, mortality, the here and now;
primeval — recent, current, modern, civilized, refined, advanced, sophisticated.

AGER, field: GRI

The bird most used in falconry or hawking, the ancient sport of hunting with
the aid of a bird of prey, is the **pereGRIne** falcon. Peregrine means foreign,
roaming, migrating, and it is to that wanderlust that the bird owes its name,
for it is known over most of the globe.

To **pereGRInate** is to travel abroad, meaning away from one's land, one's
field, and, originally, on foot. Thus one's **pereGRInations** are the journeys,
odysseys, and just plain comings-and-goings that we all undertake. If we keep
a record of such travels, we call it an itinerary.

Traditionally, **pilGRIms** walked no matter the terrain or the weather or the
thinness of their soles. The object of a **pilGRImage** was most often a religious
shrine, as it was in Geoffrey Chaucer's *Canterbury Tales*, the story of an April
pilgrimage to Saint Thomas à Becket's shrine at Canterbury, then the religious
center of England.

The **air** that means appearance comes from *ager*. (There's a certain air about
that fellow that I can't stand.) So does the air that means to circulate or
publicize. (We must air that topic at the meeting this evening.) But not the
air that we breathe, even though clean air and fruitful fields would seem to
go together; it comes from the Greek **aer**, breath, atmosphere.

However, **agrarian**, relating to land, farming, and things rural, is a member
of the family. (Our schools' long summer vacations reflect the agrarian nature
of the nation's early days, when the children of the family were needed to
work in the fields.) Another member is **aGRIculture**, the science of the cultiva-
tion of fields and the raising of crops and livestock on them.

☞ *But not: grievous* [*gravis*, heavy], tragic, serious, outrageous; *integrity* [*integer*,
whole, perfect], honesty, virtue.

☞ *Combining forms: -culture*, to till; *per-*, away, beyond.

AGERE, to act, do, drive: ACT

Several dozen words with the common base form **ACT** come from this root,
and the majority of them are a staple part of our everyday vocabularies. Single
and double prefixes plus suffixes greatly increase the number of words created
from this base.

En-: To **enACT**, for example, is to make into a legislative act or statute or
enACTment. (The legislature enacted two new tax laws last session.) It also
means to act out, as on a stage. (It's preposterous for you to even consider
enacting Lady Macbeth, Alfred.) To **reenACT** is to act out again. (The two clerks
reenacted the robbery; the **reenACTment** was filmed by a TV crew.)

Ex-: An **exACT** measurement is explicit, precise, accurate, specific, and on
the nose. (They had to know the exact moment it happened and **exACTly** what

we were doing at the time.) An **exACTing** teacher is demanding, punctilious, meticulous, no-nonsense, and hardnosed; an exacting course is tough, difficult, rigorous, and trying, one requiring **exACTness** and **exACTitude** on every single assignment. Students who have a tendency to tolerate **inexACTness** are requested to forgo registering. To **redACT** is to edit. (The initial project will be to redact a technical manuscript for publication.)

Re-: How one responds to a situation is how one **reACTs**. The quickness of one's **reACTions** may determine whether one gets the job or not. A **reACTor** can be one who reacts, but it most commonly names an apparatus in which some kind of chemical or nuclear reaction takes place. A **reACTionary** is a political conservative; whether he or she is a mossback, diehard, tory, Bourbon, or standpatter depends upon the degree of "rightness" of the accused and "leftness" of the accuser.

And there are others: A pay raise that is **retroACTive** is always welcome. To **transACT** business or negotiations or activities is to carry them on or conduct them to a settlement or conclusion; a **transACTion** is a business agreement. *Counter-* as a prefix means opposite, so **counterACT** is to act in an opposite way, that is, to neutralize or thwart. (The doctor gave her a prescription for a medicine to counteract her fever.)

Several of the words in this group have antonyms created by the addition of a prefix. **ACTive** and **inACTive**, **ACTion** and **inACTion**, **ACTivate** and **deACTivate/inACTivate** (both of which mean to make ineffective, such as a bomb, but deactivate also means to disband or demobilize troops or an army).

Activate and **ACTuate** are fraternal twins. The former has a kind of start-stop meaning, that is, to turn on, put into action; its antonyms include turn off and halt. (Push the green button to activate the display; the red button will deactivate it.) Most of the synonyms of actuate have the sense of motivate, prompt, and stimulate. (It was the love of money that actuated every move that man ever made.) In one regard, however, the two are not interchangeable: when troops are mobilized, they are activated.

An **ACTivist** is a doer, an ethusiast, a partisan, an advocate, and a person who may well be active in protests, confrontations, and commitments. **ACTivism** frequently demands a fair amount of ardor, fervor, and zeal. Those who become **hyperACTive** are those most likely to be dragged away.

The job of an **ACTuary** is to mathematically compute insurance rates and premiums. **ACTual** occurrences are real, factual, and authentic; **ACTuality** is reality. ("On second thought," Smirkley said, "in actuality [truth], that is not **ACTually** [trully] what took place last night.)

But not: *didactic* [Gk *didaktikos*, instructive], instructive, preachy; *olfactory* [*olere*, to smell + *facere*, to make, do], pertaining to one's sense of smell; *practical* [GK *prattein*, to practice], pragmatic, useful.

Combining forms: *de-*, reversal; *en-*, to make; *ex-*, out; *hyper-*, above; *in-*, not; *re-*, again; *retro-*, backward.

☛ *Antonyms: act* — procrastinate, put off, inactivity; *action* — rest, complacency; *activate* — deaden, paralyze; *active* — indolent, lethargic, nonchalant, sedentary, inoperative, dull; *activist* — fencesitter, spectator; *activity* — torpor, inertia, calm; *actual* — fictional, fictitious, theoretical, probable, projected; *actuate* — deter, dampen, inhibit, hinder; *exacting* — easy-going, lax, lenient, devil-may-care, permissive; *inactive* — functional, operative, bustling, dynamic, energetic; *inexact* — accurate, precise, meticulous; *reactionary* — liberal, progressive, left-winger.

AGERE, to act, do, drive: GATE

To **castiGATE** is to criticize, rebuke, or reprimand severely. (The coach castigated the two defiant football players by suspending them for the rest of the season.)

To **divaGATE** is to wander from place to place or to digress in speech. (The speaker divagated from one topic to another.)

To **expurGATE** is to censor a work by removing words or passages that are deemed objectionable; it is to bowdlerize, excise, purge, cleanse, or abridge. (The committee voted to have the unabridged — and unexpurgated — dictionary removed from the school library.)

To **fumiGATE** is to exterminate pests such as insects by the use of fumes. (The fumigators had to spray the kitchen three times before all the roaches were gone.)

To **fustiGATE** is to beat with a club or stick or to castigate severely. (Our neighbor fustigated the dog as it started after the child.)

To **leviGATE** is to grind a substance into a powder. (The chef levigated the dried herb leaves.)

To **litiGATE** is to engage in legal proceedings, to bring before a court of law. (The order in question is now being litigated in district court.) A **litigant** is a person participating in a lawsuit; **litigation** is the process. (The suit is in litigation at the present time.) A **litigious** person is argumentative and disputatious or one who is excessively inclined to seek litigation. (Is Xerxes litigious? I'll say! This is the fifth lawsuit he's filed in the last six months!)

To **mitiGATE** is to make something, such as pain or punishment, milder and less severe, to alleviate, ameliorate, extenuate, mollify, or appease. (The principal decided to mitigate the recalcitrant students' punishment.)

To **naviGATE** is to direct a ship or airplane or to just find one's way home. (The route was shorter by way of the park, but we found it much more difficult to navigate in the dark.) A **navigable** waterway is deep and wide enough for passage; **navigation** is the art or science or directing aircraft, missiles, and ships.

To **objurGATE** is to denounce harshly, to rebuke sharply. (The major lashed out at his detractors, objurgating them with some pretty hot language.)

To **varieGATE** is to give something a varied appearance by adding different colors, especially in the form of spots and streaks. It is also to diversify. (The variegated houseplants fitted in nicely with Mamie's new decorations.)

But not: billingsgate [from the name of a London fish market where some rather foul language was common about three hundred years ago], vulgarly abusive language; *congregate* [*con-*, together + *greg*, herd], to assemble; *instigate* [*in-*, against + *stig*, to goad], to incite, goad, provoke; *obligate* [*ob-*, toward + *ligare*, to bind], to oblige or to bind legally or morally.

Combining forms: casti-, pure; *di-*, about; *ex-*, thoroughly; *fumi-*, smoke; *fusti-*, club; *jur-*, law; *levi-*, smooth; *lit-*, lawsuit; *miti-*, mild; *navi-*, a ship; *ob-*, against; *pur-*, clean; *vag-*, to wander; *vari-*, various.

Antonyms: castigate — pardon, condone, absolve, excuse; *mitigate* — magnify, aggravate, worsen, intensify, increase, exacerbate.

A **coGENt** statement or argument is a potent, convincing, and compelling one, and **coGENcy** is power, force, or strength. (The cogency of the attorney's closing argument was lost, for he couched his cogent points in legal jargon that few of the jurists understood.)

An **aGENdum** is, strictly speaking, one item on a list of items that make up an **aGENda**, which, strictly speaking, is a plural form but is usually used as a singular, with the plural being **aGENdas**. It is a program, docket, order of business, schedule, or timetable.

A travel **aGENt** works in an **aGENcy** that sometimes deals with **exiGENt** matters such as missed train connections in far-off Sri Lanka. Such predicaments are known as **exiGENcies**, and they demand immediate attention. (When Sallie lost her purse, the urgent, exigent nature of the emergency prompted a collect call home.)

An **intransiGENt** person is unwilling to compromise, remaining stubborn, resolute, and hardnosed. (The ballplayer and his agent remained intransigent, insisting that neither could face his family again for less than five million a year.) There is no "transigent."

But not: emergency [*e-*, out + *mergere*, to sink], crisis; *intelligent* [*legere*, to gather], smart; *urgent* [*urgere*, to push], very important.

Combining forms: co-, together; *ex-*, out; *in-*, not.

Antonyms: cogency — impotence, infirmity, weakness, debility; *cogent* — ineffective, irrelevant, unconvincing, weak, foolish; *exigent* — unimportant, frivolous, insignificant, trifling; *intransigent* — flexible, compromising, reconcilable, reasonable.

AGERE, to act, do, drive: GEN

The time is 1926, the book is *Winnie-the-Pooh*, and the place is chapter 4: " 'Well,' said Owl, 'the customary procedure in such cases is as follows.'

" 'What does Crustimoney Proseedcake mean?' said Pooh. 'For I am a Bear of Very Little Brain, and long words Bother me.' "

And well they should, even for those of us who are blessed with a Tad More Than a Very Little Brain. Subject these words to a bit of **coGItation** (or, if you

AGERE, to act, do, drive: GI, GU

prefer, consideration, comtemplation, deliberation, rumination, or lucubration): When we **coGItate**, we ponder, meditate, think. When we **excoGItate**, we examine mentally or consider. Now, do we really need both? Perhaps not. But isn't it nice to know that we have such a wide selection to choose from?

Excogitate on these for a few moments: While Owl was often **coGItabund** (pensive), finding many ideas and concepts to be **coGItable** (thinkable), Pooh, poor thing, was not a truly **coGItative** (thinking) being. Quite **incoGItative**, as a matter of fact. Oh, well. Pooh was certainly never **incoGItant** (inconsiderate, thoughtless), and that's certainly all to the good.

AGIlity comes in two different packages. A physically **aGIle** person is nimble, spry, supple, fleet, lithe, and volant. (That's agile? Bosh! You should see *my* daughter on the parallel bars!) One who is mentally agile is quick-witted, alert, bright, quick, clever, sharp, incisive, and perceptive.

To **aGItate** a substance is to shake, jiggle, churn, or disturb it. (The strong gusts of wind agitated the surface of the pond.) **AGItators** try to excite and stir up people, to arouse and provoke them to action, to inflame and ignite their emotions. (Those speakers certainly got to Mama; when she got home she was in a state of great **aGItation**.)

AmbiGUities are equivocal, indefinite, or unclear words or expressions or meanings. Few of us have the temerity of this Lewis Carroll character: '' 'When I use a word,' Humpty Dumpty said in rather a scornful tone, 'it means just what I choose it to mean — neither more nor less.' ''. Nothing **ambiGUous** about that! It's clear, straightforward, precise, lucid, explicit, **unambiGUous**, and downright stupid.

Blood and pudding must **coaGUlate** or in the case of blood, we bleed to death; in the case of pudding, it will be too soupy. A **coaGUlant** is a substance that produces or aids the process; a **coaGUlum** is a clot or mass.

Something that is **exiGUous** is meager, paltry, small, and scanty. (Despite their exiguous income, the elderly couple was too proud to accept anyone's help.)

☛ *But not: incognito* [*in*, not + *cognoscere*, to know], disguised; *plagiarize* [*plagium*, kidnapping], to steal another person's ideas or writings; *virgule* [F *virgule*, comma, little rod], diagonal mark (/) used to separate words and/or lines of poetry, also called diagonal, separatrix, shilling mark, slant, slash, and solidus.

☛ *Combining forms: ambi-*, around; *co-*, intensive, together; *ex-*, out.

☛ *Antonyms: agile* — clumsy, ponderous, torpid, plodding, oafish, klutzy; *agilty* — languor, lethargy, torpidity; *agitate* — soothe, allay, pacify, quiet, compose; *coagulate* — liguefy, flow, thin out, bleed; *cogitate* — ignore, disregard, neglect, overlook; *exiguous* — abundant, generous, plentiful, copious.

AGERE, to act, do, drive

To **assay** is to analyze, examine, or test. A pharmacist may assay a drug to analyze its composition and test its potency. As assay office may test ore samples to determine the quantities of gold, silver, etc., that they contain.

A wine steward may carry an assay cup to test a wine before offering it to anyone.

A **cache** is a hiding place. (Our big sister never did find our cache of Halloween goodies.) Among its synonyms are storehouse, hideaway, hoard, and repository. It is also a verb. (Emily, who is always paid in cash, caches her cash every month.)

As a verb, **essay** means to try or attempt. It has a similar meaning as a noun. (Hank made a couple of essays to throw his boomerang into the lake, but it always came back to him.) More often, an essay is a short literary composition, descriptive or expository in nature. It can also be a series of drawings or photographs. In schools it may be called a composition, paper, or theme. (Now take a sheet of paper from your notebooks and essay to write an essay using this title: ''Why and How I Spent My Summer Vacation in Timbuktu.'') An **essayist** is one who writes many of them; the late E.B. White of *The New Yorker* magazine was one of America's best.

Exams, examiners, and **examinations** are familiar to everyone; no matter what path we choose to follow, we are **examined** along the way. Answers are ''driven out'' of us, although they may not always be the desired ones. An **examen** is an examination, as of one's conscience. In such a case, it can be assumed that the **examinant** and the **examinee** are one and the same.

A **prodigal** person is wasteful, improvident, profligate, wanton, and extravagant. That is exactly what the prodigal son in the biblical parable was: after wasting his inheritance on high living, he returned home to find that his father not only forgave him but killed the fatted calf for him.

A *purge* can be a rather simple cleanup, shake-up, removal, or expulsion, but then again, it can be a reign of terror, a witch hunt, slaughter, extermination, or liquidation — sometimes all of the above. Its verb meanings range from cleanse to wipe out.

Somehow **squat** came out of *agere*, too, but the route it followed is not entirely clear. It means to sit on one's heels, to be short and thick in physical stature, or to occupy or settle on land that belongs to someone else and thus become known as a **squatter** and eventually claim to own the land through what is known as **squatter's** right.

But not: prodigious [prodigium, marvel], enormous.

Combining forms: es-, out; *ex-*, out; *pro-*, away, forth.

Antonyms: prodigal — thrifty, frugal, economical, provident, stinting, miserly, scarce, meager, miser, skinflint, tightwad.

The **AGORa** was the chief marketplace and public square of Athens in ancient Greece and the center of the city's civic and commercial life; what existed in the country's principal city was replicated in almost all of the smaller towns. Times change; today all we have left of the word is **aGORaphobia**, an abnormal dread and fear of open areas, crowds, and public places. (Ms.

AGORA [Gk], marketplace: GOR

Oberkauf's agoraphobia keeps her a prisoner behind the drawn drapes of her home.)

CateGORy originally had to do with speaking before the Agora in Athens and then evolved into a word that Aristotle needed to describe the listing of all classes of things that can be named. That qualifies the word for the coveted Twised Etymological Road award, a relatively new category at the Academy.

CateGORize has become big enough to take under its wing classify, denominate, designate, describe, catalog, pigeonhole, tag, ticket, segregate, group, rank, rate, organize, brand, and a few more of the same. The same big-growth syndrome has hit **cateGORical**. When one **cateGORically** denies ever having made a southbound turn on a northbound one-way street, he or she does so absolutely, unequivocally, unconditionally, unqualifiedly, emphatically, definitely, surely, certainly, flatly, no ifs, ands, or buts. (Senator R.W. "Rusty" Ghosh denied categorically that the $100,000,000 campaign contribution influenced his vote on the luxury-item tax bill.)

We also owe that ancient marketplace for **panegyric**, a eulogy or loftiest praise in honor of someone or something; we witness panegyrics every four years during the national political conentions, when dozens of garrulous speechifiers line up in front of the TV cameras to nominate their candidates. That is when the **panegyrist** hits those high notes that shatter the long-stemmed champagne glasses.

And finally, there is **pareGORic**, a medicine that used to be known to all the parents of children who ever had diarrhea or intestinal pain.

☞ ***But not:*** *Angora cat/goat/rabbit* [*Ankara*, capital of Turkey], soft wool of its coat.

☞ ***Combining forms:*** *cate-*, against; *-phobia*, abnormal fear or hate; *pan-*, all; *para-*, beside.

☞ ***Antonyms:*** *Categorical* — arguable, conditional, ambiguous, contingent, adventitious, vague, dubious, indefinite, qualified, hesitant, enigmatic.

ALBUS, *white:*
ALB

One of the poems we all hear or read or open our books to in school is Samuel Taylor Coleridge's *The Rime of the Ancient Mariner*, and among the more famous passages (no doubt "Water, water, every where. / Nor any drop to drink" is the most famous) is " 'God save thee, ancient Mariner! / From the fiends that plague thee thus! / Why look'st thou so?' — 'With my crossbow / I shot the **ALBatross**.' " Believing that the live bird was an omen of good luck, the mariner's shipmates hung the dead bird around his neck. Today, therefore, an albatross (besides being a large, mostly white, seabird) is a burden that is difficult to get rid of. (B.J.'s feeling of guilt for his part in the disastrous fraternity prank was an albatross that plagued him the rest of his life.)

An **ALB** is a long, traditionally white robe worn by a priest. **ALBumen** is the white of an egg. An **ALBum** was first a book of blank pages for holding photographs and later a holder for phonograph records. **Auburn** comes from albus, but as its spelling gradually changed, so did its meaning, to reddish or golden-brown.

ALBinism is the absence of certain pigments in humans and other animals; the term ''white elephant,'' an unwanted possession that is difficult to dispose of, possibly came from the King of Siam's awarding of a white elephant — **ALBino** elephants were usually natives of Thailand — to someone he didn't like, knowing that the upkeep would ruin the new owner.

ALBion is a literary name for Britain, possibly inspired by the chalk cliffs along the English Channel that were immortalized by the World War II song that prophesied, ''There'll be bluebirds over the white cliffs of Dover / Tomorrow, just you wait and see.'' ''Perfidious Albion'' (deceitful England) is a phrase that Napoleon is said to have made a buzzword during the French Revolution.

Although **ALBedo** is not likely to achieve great popularity, a Trivia Award (a gold statuette of nothing) might be in the cards; the word means not only the ratio of the light reflected by Mars (or any other planet or satellite) to that received by it, but also (drumroll, please) the white, inner rind of a citrus fruit. Cogitate that over your breakfast grapefruit.

Dealbare, the verb form of **albus**, means to whiten, [to plaster] hence **daub**. To daub a coat of plaster on a wall is not a chore requiring great skill; the object is to cover, not to create a work of art. Among its synonyms are smear, smudge, splash, and splatter. To **bedaub** is to smear with paint or mud. Thus a **daubery** is a painting that would qualify only for a Worst of Show ribbon. **Daubing** is to painting what poetastering is to poetry and scribbling is to writing.

*But not: albacore [Ar *al-bakrah*: al, the + *bakr*, young camel], a kind of tuna; *albeit* [ME *al*, all + *be*, + it], although, even if.

Keeping fueled up throughout the **adolescent** years is not always an easy task. Sufficient sustenance and support must be provided by the food and nourishment that is properly known as **ALiment**. When these are processed in the **ALimentary** canal of the digestive system, energy is produced, and with continued **ALimentation** or nourishment one is enabled to not only endure **adolescence**, but be adequately fueled to make a successful transition into **adulthood** as well.

ALERE, to feed, nourish, grow: AL

The difficulty of the growing years can be attested to by the size of the **coALition** (a growing together) of family, teachers, friends, counselors, and the fickle finger of fate that it takes to nourish one along a road littered with such intimidating detour signs as ''puerile,'' ''immature,'' ''pubescent,'' ''juvenile,'' ''sophomoric,'' ''callow,'' ''naive,'' and ''green.'' But somehow, and in time, the rough edges get smoothed out, and one **coALesces** (grows) into an **adult**, all this long before such words as divorce and **ALimony** (the supplying of sustenance and support for one's former spouse) have entered one's vocabulary.

The difficult part about getting to be a graduate of any school, college, or university is not all the years and sweat that it takes to get there nor even the pleas for money that follow; it is instead figuring out which category you will someday fit into: **ALumna**, **ALumnae**, **ALumni**, or **ALumnus**. Here's how it works: Flossie is a female grad; she is an alumna. Daisie and Maisie, twins, graduated in the same class from the same institution; their mail comes in the same envelope and the greeting is ''Dear Alumnae.'' Harvey, a male, is an alumnus; he does not have a twin, so he never gets any letters beginning ''Dear Alumni.'' Some schools refer to their graduates as ''alumni and alumnae'' (men and women) and preface their solicitation letters to couples on their lists as ''Dear Alumnus and Alumna'' (Mr. and Mrs.) **ALum** (accent on the second syllable) is the word of choice for some, but others find it confusing — see *alum*, (accent on the first syllable) below.

☞ *But not: adulate [adulari*, to flatter], praise excessively; *adulterate [adulterare*, to pollute, commit adultery], corrupt, spoil; *ailment* [AS *eglan*, to afflict], sickness; *alum [alumen]*, an astringent.

☞ *Combining forms: co-*, together.

☞ *Antonyms: adolescent* — full-grown, developed, tired, weary, ancient, knowledgeable, weathered, experienced, sophisticated; *adult* — unripe, green, tender, unfledged, inexperienced, callow, embryonic, inchoate; *coalesce* — divide, split, sever, cleave, fragment, separate, disintegrate; *coalition* — schism, split, severance, disagreement, enmity, antagonism.

ALLOS [Gk], other: ALLE

When Mrs. Malaprop says in Richard Sheridan's play *The Rivals*, ''She's as headstrong as an **ALLEgory** on the banks of the Nile,'' she means, of course, an alligator. The truth of the matter is that allegories, being fables or parables, are quite harmless and seldom sun themselves on the banks of any river. [When Mrs. M. said, ''Illiterate him. . . .'' she mean ''obliterate,'' and used ''delusions'' in place of ''allusions.'']

George Orwell's **ALLEgorical** novel *Animal Farm* is a satire about Russian communism: ''All animals are equal but some animals are more equal than others.'' As an **ALLEgorist**, Orwell created **parALLEls** between his animals and human beings: Napoleon, the head pig, represents Stalin; Snowball, his enemy, is Trotsky; and Boxer, the horse, stands for the ordinary person.

Dust, grass, and pollens are **ALLErgens**, common substances that can produce an **ALLErgy**, which, if seriously distressing, may have to be treated by an **ALLErgist**, a physician specializing in its diagnosis and treatment. However, some allergies do not respond to medical treatment; many people have strong aversions or dislikes toward certain activities or people. (Drabble claimed he was not **ALLErgic** to the work itself; it was the wood in the handle of the shovel.)

☞ *But not: allegation [legare*, to bind], assertion made without proof; *alleviate [levare*, to lighten], ease, mitigate.

☞ *Combining forms: -ergy*, work; *-gory*, speak in public; *para-*, beside.

☞ *Antonyms: allegory* — facts, history, true story; *parallel* — dissimilar, distinct, divergent, disparate, opposite, reverse, unlike.

An **AMAteur** is one who plays for the love of the game rather than for money; some consider it to be an endangered species. When something is said to be **AMAteurish**, however, it is considered not only unprofessional but inept, inexpert, and inadequate as well.

An **AMOrous** person is one who tends to fall in love; **AMOrous** or **AMAtory** literature is concerned with love. An **AMOur** is a love affair; to be **enAMOred** is to be inflamed with love. (We were enamored of the colorful countryside. An **AMOretto** is a cherub or cupid. An **inAMOrata** is a female lover; an **inAMOrato** is a male; if it is an illicit affair, he or she is a **parAMOur**.

But not: amorphous [Gk *a-*, without + *morphe*, form], vague, shapeless.

Combining forms: en-, in; *in-*, into; *para-*, with.

Antonyms: amateur — professional, expert, polished, skilled; *amorous* — indifferent.

AMARE, to love:
AMA, AMO

We all know that an **enemy** is not a friend; what we may not know is that the base of *enemy* means "friend" and that the French added the *en* prefix meaning "not." Among its synonyms are foe, opponent, adversary, antagonist, rival, and nemesis.

So it was with **inimical**, its literal meaning being "not friendly," hence harmful, unfavorable (Bea found the climate to be inimical to her lungs), as well as hostile, unfriendly (There was an inimical atmosphere about the castle, the source of which I could never pinpoint).

At the other end of the field are the friendly folk. An **AMIable** chap is genial, warm, kind, obliging, affable, sociable, cordial, just a real okay person. (Helen's such a wonderful neighbor, so amiable and gracious.)

AMIcable has the same general meaning, but some usage texts argue that it makes a better fit when used to describe actions, such as the relations between groups, parties, companies, governments, and countries, and its most common synonyms tend to reflect that: peaceable, harmonious, civil, benevolent. (The company and the union have reached an amicable settlement. Our two countries have enjoyed an amicable relationship for generations.) That is generally true of **AMIty** as well: cooperation, friendship, good will, cordiality, understanding, brotherhood. (The Secretary General said he hoped the accord between the two governments would result in lasting amity.)

Such books also make the claim that in Spanish only a male friend is an **AMIgo** and a female is an **AMIga**, but recent studies reveal that the vast majority of señoritas have no objection to being called an amigo. The same is rumored to be true in France, although the rules state that it's **AMI** for a male friend and **AMIe** for a female.

In court an **AMIcus** brief may be filed by a person or party not involved in the case who wants to offer relevant advice; it is called Friend of the Court or, officially *amicus curiae*, and, curiously enough, it works for both men and women.

AMICUS, friend:
AMI

☞ ***But not:*** *Amish* [G *amisch*, after Jokob Ammann, seventeenth-century Swiss Mennonite bishop], Mennonite religious groups primarily in Pennsylvania, Ohio, and Indiana.

☞ ***Combining forms:*** *curiae*, meeting place, court; *en-*, *in-*, not.

☞ ***Antonyms:*** *amiable* — hostile, ill-humored, sullen, disagreeable, surly, unfriendly, displeasing, unpleasant, cold, unapproachable; *amicable* — quarrelsome, antagonistic, belligerent, contentious, pugnacious, bellicose, nasty; *amity* — hostility, ill will, discord, enmity, animosity, contention, dissension, strife; *enemy* — ally, confederate, supporter, advocate, adherent, partisan; *inimical* — well-disposed, congenial, beneficial, salutary.

AMPLUS, large, wide: AMPL

An **AMPLifier**, a common household instrument, **AMPLifies** or increases sound at the twist of a knob. When listeners do not understand a statement made by a public official, they often ask the speaker to **AMPLify** or enlarge upon it. A synonym of **AMPLification** is enlargement. (The speaker's amplification did not satisfy the audience.) **AMPLitude** means size or scope. (The amplitude of the Milky Way is awesome.) Something that is **AMPLe** is sufficient. (We had ample room on the bus.) **AMPLy** is an adverb meaning sufficiently. (We were amply supplied with homework.)

☞ ***But not:*** *example* [*ex-*, out + *emere*, to buy], model, specimen.

☞ ***Combining forms:*** *-fic*, *-fy*, to make.

☞ ***Antonyms:*** *ample* — meager, scant; *amplitude* — limitation, circumscription.

ANGELUS [Gk], messenger: ANGEL

Someone who is truly **ANGELic** is supposed to be blessed with beauty, purity, and kindliness, but few parents or grandparents go by the rules. Chances are if Angelica is potty-trained by the time she's two, inverts her cereal bowl over her head only on Tuesdays, and has slept late on Sunday mornings at least twice in the last year, she's deemed to be angelic. The beauty, purity, and kindliness can be put off for at least a decade.

For some people an **ANGEL** is a messenger of God, a heavenly spirit, a celestial being, an **archANGEL**, or a cherub. Next door an angel is a dear, a dream, a saint, a doll, a jewel, a darling. Two blocks away an angel is a financial backer, a patron, a sponsor, a subsidizer, an underwriter, an investor. And for still at least one other — British author G.K. Chesterton — they have a rare, unique quality; said he, "Angels can fly because they take themselves lightly."

An **evANGELitst** is a preacher, one who may travel from revival to revival **evANGELizing** night after night. **TelevANGELists** stay closer to home, spreading their message electronically from their own **evANGELical** temples. The original **evANGELizers** were Matthew, Mark, Luke, and John of the New Testament. The **evANGEL** is the gospel; an evangel is also an evangelist.

An **ANGELeno** is a native or inhabitant of Los Angeles (City of Angels).

☞ ***But not:*** *evanescent* [*e-*, completely + *vanus*, empty], fleeting, fading away.

*Combining forms: arch-, chief; ev- (from eu-,), good.

*Antonyms: angelic — fiendish, diabolic, hellish, demonic, ugly, repulsive, impish, devilish, mischievous.

ANNUS, year:
ANNI, ANNU,
ENNI

An **ANNUal** event happens once a year, a **semiANNUal** twice a year, a **biENNIal** every second year, and a **perENNIal** is everlasting. A **biANNUal** event occurs twice a year (semiannual) or every two years (biennial), depending on who makes up the schedule; it's best to call before going. An **ANNIversary** is the annual return of the date of an event.

A cent is a 100th part of a dollar; hence a **centENNIal** is a 100th anniversary. Although a **semicentENNIal** is a 50th anniversary, a **bicentENNIal** occurs every two hundred years. The combining form "sesqui" means one and a half; therefore, a **sesquicentENNIal** is a 150th anniversary. The Columbus **quincentENNIal** was celebrated in 1992.

A mill is a 1,000th part of a dollar, so a **millENNIum** is a period of one thousand years, although the word is often used to mean any lengthy period of time. (Your long absence has seemed like a millennium to me.) An **ANNUity** is an annual payment, often made following one's retirement. **Annals** are yearly records kept by an **annalist** or historian. A.D. stands for **anno Domini**, meaning "in the year of our Lord" and referring to all years since the birth of Jesus Christ.

*But not: analyst [GK ana-, up + lyein, to loosen], psychoanalyst or shrink; annul [an-, to + nullus, none], to cancel or nullify.

*Combining forms: bi-, two; cent, 100; mill, 1,000; per-, through; quin-, five; semi-, half; sesqui-, one and a half; super-, above; -versary, to turn.

*Antonyms: annals — fantasy, novel, romance; perennial — ephemeral, sporadic, transient.

ANTIQUUS,
ancient: ANTIQU

"Want to have some fun?" the comedian Henny Youngman asked more than once. "Walk into an **ANTIQUe** shop and say, 'What's new?' "

And what would your answer be? As the shop owner, you could say, "Not much, good buddy, and yet" — and here you throw in a quote by Sir Thomas Browne (1605–1682) — " 'time, which **ANTIQUates ANTIQUities**, and hath an art to make dust of things, hath yet spared these minor monuments' — I have a very nice one-owner pterodactyl wing here."

Not all antiques are or eventually will be for sale. In "Ozymandias" Percy Bysshe Shelley says, "I met a traveller from an antique land." Matthew Arnold tells of a person "In hat of antique shape, and cloak of gray, / The same the Gipsies wore." And myriad teenagers feel thwarted by their parents' "antique" ideas.

To **ANTIQUate** something is to make it obsolete. (The camcorder has antiquated the home movie camera.) AN **ANTIQUity** is something ancient. (We found several tools of great antiquity.) "When my sonnet was rejected," wrote

Charles Lamb, an English writer and critic, in a letter, ''I exclaimed, 'Damn the age! I will write for Antiquity!' ''

From the Clouded Crystal Ball Division comes this misjudgment by a post–World War I British historian named George Peabody Gooch: ''We can now look forward with something like confidence to the time when war between civilized nations will be considered as **ANTIQUated** as a duel.''

An **ANTIQUary** is a dealer in antiques; an **ANTIQUer** may collect and deal, too, or possibly simulate the real thing; an **ANTIQUarian** is a collector, often specializing in rare books, but he or she may also be a person quite attached to the opinions and practices of ages past.

A very funny — and fun — book of parodies of American writers is entitled *The Antic Muse*. **Antic** as an adjective means funny and ludicrous; as a noun it is a playful trick, caper, stunt, prank, practical joke, or monkey business.

☛ *Antonyms: antic* — serious, solemn, dignified, sober, staid; *antiquated* — modern, current, recent, fresh, novel, up-to-date, modish, smart, stylish, fashionable; *antique* — fashionable, modern; *antiquity* — modernity, modern times, today.

APERIRE, to open; OPERIRE, to close: PER, VER

A **coVERt** action, message, or operation is one that is surreptitious, clandestine, and *sub rosa*; something that is done **coVERtly** is done secretly. (The president denied knowing anything about the covert negotiations.) **OVERt** negotiations would be open, public, manifest, and carried out **oVERtly**, openly, and publicly. (The candidate's overt racism was quickly seized upon by the reporters who **coVERed** the speech; his remarks received wide **coVERage**.) A **coVER** as a noun is a blanket, cloak, veil, shelter, asylum, camouflage, subterfuge, disguise, and more. (The girls took cover from the storm in an old barn.)

An **oVERture** is a prelude or prologue; it is the introductory part of a poem or opera. In other fields it is a proposal, a kind of feeling out or trying to **discoVER** what the situation is. (Sources demanding anonymity said today that they had made a revealing **discoVERy**: the university athletic director has made several **undercoVER** overtures to the Vultures' football coach.)

An **aPERient** is a food or medicine that acts as a mild laxative. A drink or food that has a stimulating effect on the appetite is **aPERitive**. From that came **aPERitif**, a wine or other alcoholic drink taken to stimulate the appetite before a meal.

The opening that regulates the amount of light that can enter a camera or telescope is called the **aPERture**. The word **PERt** once meant clever; now it means bolding forward in speech or behavior, impertinent, and saucy; stylish, chic, and natty; jaunty, lively, and in good health. All that packed into four little letters. A **malaPERt** person is considered impudent and saucy; it is labeled archaic or rare today, but one can stumble onto it while reading Shakespeare: ''Untutored lad, thou art too malapert.''

The exact origin of the name of our fourth month is unknown and may never be **uncoVERed**, but a Roman scholar named Varro (116–27 B.C.) said that *April* likely comes from *aperire* because that's the time of year when the buds of flowers and leaves begin to open. So let's vote to leave it at that before someone **recoVERs** it, that is, goes over it again.

But not: covetous [*cupere*, to desire], greedy; *introvert* [*intro-*, inwardly + *vert*, to turn], a shy person; *perturb* [*turbare*, to disturb], to agitate; *recover*]*recuperare*, to recover], get back, heal.

Combining forms: co-, with; *mal-*, bad.

Antonyms: cover — remove, unwrap, expose, reveal, show, unmask, omit, leave out, exclude; *pert* — respectful, demure, reserved, shy, bashful, meek, diffident, courteous, homely, shabby, indolent, lethargic, ill.

Arson is the malicious, criminal setting on fire of property; the perpetrator is an **arsonist**, and if anyone is killed in the fire, the charges will include murder. **Ardor** is warmth of varying degrees, ranging from animation to zeal, with eagerness, enthusiasm, excitement, fervor, intensity, passion, and vehemence in between. (Lil's ardor on behalf of the homeless fired up the rest of us.)

ARDERE, to burn

An **ardent** person's intensity ranges from burning to zealous. (Gil's an ardent pacifist, and he speaks **ardently** on the subject.) Such people are never apathetic, indifferent, lethargic, lukewarm, or sluggish in their attitudes toward their causes.

Once uPUN a time a fire marshal knocked on the door of a house where a young boy lived who had been seen near the site of a fire. "But officer," the boy's mother said, "it couldn't have been arson. He's been home all evening!"

But not: arduous [*arduus*, steep], strenuous.

If a matter is **ARGUable**, it is open to doubt, it is questionable, and it is susceptible to challenge or debate. (Whether the superintendent's plan was the most feasible that was presented was certainly arguable.) **ARGUably** seems to be an in word these days; it means possibly, conceivably. (Willie Mays is arguably the most exciting baseball player in the history of the game.) Score an extra point whenever you throw "arguably" into a discussion.

ARGUERE, to prove: ARGU

To **ARGUe** is to dispute, quarrel, bicker, debate, haggle, contend, wrangle; James Agate put the case cogently: "I don't know very much, but what I do know I know better than anybody, and I don't want to argue about it. . . . My mind is not a bed to be made and re-made."

As did James Whistler, the painter: "I am not **ARGUing** with you — I am telling you." British prime minister Margaret Thatcher took a less combative position: "I love argument. I love debate. I don't expect anyone just to sit there and agree with me, that's not their job."

An **ARGUment** is a subject matter or theme. (Henkfurth's central argument was a disaster, as holey as Swiss cheese and easy to refute.) It is a reason or statement for or against a point of view. (We had to admit that her argument was a strong point in favor of the amendment.) It is a quarrel, conflict, squabble, spat, altercation, or feud. (At parties Rander was invariably engaged in heated and noisy arguments that ruined many a gathering.) One can justifiably argue that Rander was an **ARGUmentative** person, disputatius, contentious, quarrelsome, cantankerous, and bullheaded. **ARGUmentations** can be discussions, but they can also unravel into spats, rhubarbs, imbroglios, tiffs, hubbubs, brouhahas, donnybrooks, set-tos, fallings-out, as well as brangles, jangles, and wrangles.

The only safe way for some people is to just flat-out quit **ARGUfying**.

☛ *Antonyms: arguable* — proven, obvious, indubitable, definite, unimpeachable; *argue* — agree, concede, assent, accept, grant, concur, dispute; *argument* — accord, concord, unanimity, refutation, rejoinder, response, rebuttal, retort; *argumentative* — amenable, conciliatory, compliant, tractable.

ARISTOS [Gk],
best

Aristocrats are members of the nobility in countries that still have noblemen and noblewomen; they are blue bloods, Brahmins, lords and ladies, and peers and peeresses. They do not often hobnob with such as peasants, commoners, plebeians, or just plain ordinary folks. They are or make an effort to be regal, courtly, lordly or ladylike, gentlemanly or gentlewomanly (being "of gentle blood"), and, above all, **aristocratic**. Those not of that particular blood type are members of the lower, middle, or working classes.

An **aristocracy** is a government or state ruled by the elite, the upper crust, the gentry, the *haut monde*; those they rule are the common people, the populace, the rabble, the hoi polloi, the canaille.

☛ *Combining forms: -crat,* ruler.

ARKHEIN [Gk],
to rule, begin:
ARCH

Shortly after noon on January 20, 1961, when Robert Frost, then eighty-six years old, tried to read a poem he had written for the inauguration of John F. Kennedy as president of the United States, the bright sunlight blinded him so that he had to give it up. Undaunted, he recited a poem he had written some years before entitled "The Gift Outright." "The land was ours before we were the land's" he began, ". . . but we were England's, still colonials, possessing what we still were unpossessed by. . . ."

England's ruler in the time of which he spoke was the **monARCH** George III. But there was to be no **monARCHy** or **autARCHy** here with a built-in autocratic, despotic ruler; no **oligARCHy**, a government controlled by a few; no **anARCHy**, a state without government or law. Those were, the Founding Fathers felt, **ARCHaic** forms, long out of date; we would become, instead, a representative democracy, an **ARCHetype**, a prototype, a model for the world to look up to.

Among the earliest social groups were those based upon families or clans or tribes. **PatriARCHies** were headed by the father or **patriARCH**, **matriARCHies** by the mother or **matriARCH**. Throughout the centuries that humankind has lived with social organizations, many positions of leadership have been so identified. The **hierARCH** or high priest is at the top of the

hierARCHy, the ladder of rank and importance. An **ARCHbishop** presides over an **ARCHbishopric** or **ARCHdiocese** and is followed by an **ARCHdeacon** and then an **ARCHpriest**. A chief angel is an **ARCHangel**, as is a Russian port city north of Moscow named long ago for the archangel Michael and known to the Russians as Arkhangelsk.

ARCHitects were originally thought of as the chief workers or builders or carpenters or artisans, none of which describes their tasks these days. An **ARCHipelago**, a group or chain of islands, got its name from the Aegean Sea, which was sometimes called "the Chief Sea." Important documents and records are kept in **ARCHives**, a word stemming from *archeion*, Greek for "public office"; the person in charge is an **ARCHivist**. **ARCHaeology** (also **ARCHeology**) is the study of antiquity, of times long since past.

In yesterday's world there were great numbers of **ARCHduchesses** and **ARCHdukes**, who were in charge of the **ARCHducal** matters of their **ARCH-duchies** or **ARCHdukedoms**. However, as some comedian once put it, if one wrote their history today, the most appropriate title might be, "The Case of the Fallen Arches."

An **ARCHconservative** is someone like Archie Bunker of TV's long-running, prize-winning *All in the Family*; it means "extreme," for he was so prejudiced and bigoted that he was against every racial, religious, and political group other than his own. *Arch* has the meaning of "principal" in **ARCHenemy** and **ARCH-rival**. An **ARCH** smile is one that is playfully mischievous or sly.

But not: *arch* [*arcus*, bowl], part of the foot.

Combining forms: *an-*, without; *-diocese*, district; *hier-*, sacred; *matri-*, mother; *mon-*, one; *olig-*, few; *patri-*, father, *-pelago*, sea; *-tect*, artisan.

Antonyms: *anarchy* — order, discipline, organization, control, regimentation; *archaic* — current, modern, modish, trendy.

ARS, art: ART

Dictionary definitions of **ART** list skill, craft, talent, dexterity, and knack as well as cunning, wile, deceit, contrivance, and duplicity. The novelist Willa Cather looked at it this way: "Religion and art spring from the same root and are close kin. Economics and art are strangers." But Andy Warhol, the artist, thought that "Being good in business is the most fascinating kind of art." And humorist Ogden Nash had his own, inimitable slant: "Any kiddie in school can love like a fool, / But hating, my boy, is an art." And Pablo Picasso wondered why "Everyone wants to understand art. Why not try to understand the song of a bird?"

An **ARTist** is one who is engaged in some type of fine art: a painter or sculptor; a writer or poet; a skilled public performer as in dance, mime, music, acting — one who has earned the accolade *virtuoso*. An **ARTisan**, one who also has superior skill and ability, is engaged in crafts or applied arts that usually have utilitarian applications. The **ARTistry** of both can reach **ARTistic** levels. An **ARTiste** is a skilled public performer, most often a dancer or singer and often a woman. **Ars poetica** is a treatise on the art of poetry, and **ART nouveau** (new art) is a style of painting that was current about one hundred years ago.

An **ARTy** person is a dabbler, a dilettante, one whose interest in art is primarily showy and pretentious. **ARTsy** and **ARTsy-craftsy** persons and objects fit into the same category as arty.

One who is **ARTful** is foxy, shrewd, scheming, and disingenuous; the character who made it a household word is the Artful Dodger, the youthful pickpocket and member of Fagin's gang in Charles Dickens' novel *Oliver Twist*. One who is **ARTless** is best described as being unsophisticated, innocent, ingenuous, natural, simple, homespun, clumsy, and inept, all of which the Artful Dodger was decidedly not.

An **ARTifact** is a human-made article, an invention, creation, or fabrication; it is often as small an object as the shard of pottery that is an archaeologist's reward. An **ARTificer** is a skilled maker of things, an inventor, an artisan. But an **ARTifice** is a trick or ruse or subterfuge or maneuver. (Janis never believed one promise that Biligote made; she always suspected that he was a master of artifice.) And something that is **ARTificial** is synthetic, contrived, simulated, counterfeit, fake, false, and phony.

☞ *But not: artery* [Gk *arteria*], blood vessel, main road, etc.; *artesian* [*Artois*, region of northern France], pertaining to water from the area where it was first drilled; *article* [*artus*, a joint, limb], item, written composition, part of speech.

☞ *Combining forms:* -fact, -fic, to make; *poetica*, poetry.

☞ *Antonyms: art* — science, junk, worthless objects; ineptitude, inability, incompetency; *artful* — sincere, candid, naive, ingenuous, natural, authentic, straightforward, dull, clumsy, maladroit, plodding; *artifice* — candor, sincerity, honesty, openness; *artificial* — genuine, real, bona fide, actual, true, unaffected, unstudied, down-to-earth; *artist* — tyro, novice, neophyte, amateur, apprentice; *artistic* — tasteless, vulgar, crude, unrefined, inelegant, unaesthetic; *artless* — worldly, sophisticated, polished, slick, fancy, insincere, self-conscious, suspicious, skillful, expert, adept, adroit, dexterous, artistic, aesthetic; *arty* — modest, humdrum, pedestrian.

ASTRON [Gk], star: ASTER, ASTRO

The setting is Rome in 44 B.C. The people have gathered to heap praise upon Julius Caesar, and Brutus and Cassius, standing nearby, according to Shakespeare, hear the shouts. "I do believe," Brutus says, "that these applauses are / For some new honours that are heap'd on Caesar." To which Cassius replies, "Men at some time are masters of their fates: / The fault, dear Brutus, is not in our stars, / But in ourselves, that we are underlings."

People who hold with **ASTROlogy** might not agree with Cassius, for it is their belief that the position of the stars and planets at the exact moment of one's birth has a powerful influence on one's life, today, tomorrow, and beyond. The words **disASTER** and **disASTROus** reflect the belief in the influence of heavenly bodies on our lives. Shakespeare commented on that, too, saying in *King Lear*, "We make guilty of our disasters the sun, the moon, and the stars." Instead of, as Cassius said, taking the rap ourselves.

Departments of science in many universities offer courses in **ASTROnomy**, some even have access to observatories where aspiring **ASTROnomers** can learn to track the stars and planets for scientific purposes.

Astral refers to something star-shaped. An **astral body** is both any heavenly body such as a comet, planet, or star and, in a far different field, an eternal substance that accompanies us while we're alive and survives us after we die. The flower we call an **ASTER** is shaped like a star, as is the **ASTERisk** (*). An **ASTERism** is a constellation or group of stars, and thousands of **ASTERoids**, minor planets, form a belt between Mars and Jupiter. An **ASTERoidean** is a starfish.

The Houston **ASTROs**, so named because of the city's Johnson Space Center, play on **ASTROturf** in the **ASTROdome**. **ASTROnautics** is the science of space travel, which is the occupation of American **ASTROnauts** and Russian cosmonauts. In the sixteenth century **ASTROnomical** came to mean extremely large, exceedingly great, enormous, and, today, humongous.

***But not:** astern* [Icel *stjorn*, helm], in a position behind a ship.

***Combining forms:** dis-*, in a pejorative or sinister sense; *-isk*, small; *-logy*, the study of; *-naut*, ship; *-nomy*, law; *-oid*, similar.

***Antonyms:** astronomical* — miniscule, Lilliputian, diminutive, minute, infinitesimal, microscopic, tiny, itty-bitty, teeny-weeny; *disastrous* — advantageous, providential, beneficial, favorable, propitious, heaven-sent.

If you thumbed through a few thesauruses (also, thesauri), you probably wouldn't be surprised to discover that the most common synonyms for **ATHLetic** are strong, husky, burly, brawny, and muscular (the antonyms are usually frail, weak, and puny). The world of **ATHLetics** is a wide one, however, and the attributes that benefit a weightlifter, shotputter, or football lineman would destroy the chances of a gymnast, polevaulter, swimmer, or soccer forward.

ATHLON [Gk], a prize: ATHL

An **ATHLete** competes for a prize. Some of the most demanding competitions are the **decATHLon**, a contest comprising ten track and field events; the modern **pentATHLon**, featuring swimming, running, horseback riding, fencing, and target shooting; and the **triATHLon**, the men's consisting of three consecutive races — swimming, bicycling, and running — the women's of a 100-meter run, the shotput, and the high jump. The **heptATHLon** consists of seven track and field events; it is for women only.

Not all decathlons, however, are competitions for an athletic title. The National Academic Decathlon is held each year for high school teams that have won their state contests. These **decATHLetes** must write essays and answer questions on ten subjects including economics, fine arts, literature and language, math, science, and social studies.

***Combining forms:** deca-*, ten; *hepta-*, seven; *penta-*, five; *tri-*, three.

AUGERE,
to increase:
AUG, AUT

When people "moonlight," they take a second job to **AUGment** their income; sometimes the **AUGmentation** enables them to buy their baby some new shoes. There is a similar sense to the word **auxiliary** in that it means additional, supplementary, reserve as an adjective (The hospital needs an auxiliary power system) and "a helper" as a noun (The ladies' auxiliary has finally been merged with the men's organization). A helping verb is also known as an auxiliary verb. (You wouldn't say, "I reading"; you would use an auxiliary verb: "I *am* reading".)

AUGury is the ancient practice of divination or prognostication, predicting the future. In Rome **AUGurs** were officials of the state who were charged with observing and interpreting omens, a practice vaguely related to the current one of keeping a close eye on the opinion polls. Thus the soothsayer's warning to the **AUGust** Julius Caesar to "Beware the ides of March" is similar to the latest poll that warns Caesar's current counterpart to "Beware the conservationists' (or veterans' or white-collar workers') vote." To **AUGur** is to foreshadow or predict. (This fat "F" on your report card does not augur well for your success in college, Meathead.)

If such powers of prediction were for real, they would certainly be helpful at **auctions**; if one could foretell who was going to bid and how high he or she would go before dropping out, both the bidder and the **auctioneer** would save a lot of energy and voice.

AUThoritarian or **AUThoritative**? Which to use when? If you are referring to someone who is a dogmatic, strict, rigid, inflexible, imperious, tyrannical, despotic dictator, autocrat, martinet, and disciplinarian, you choose authoritarian. (Dr. Beasley is such an authoritarian he makes a drill sergeant look like Private Milquetoast.) If you want a word that means authentic, trustworthy, impressive, imposing, scholarly, learned, sanctioned, official, and commanding, you want what's left, authoritative. (This is the most authoritative book on the movement that I know of; as one of the prime figures, she is a bona fide **AUThority**.)

The King James Version of the Bible is also known as the **AUThorized** Version. to **AUThorize** is to empower, license, permit. (Congress authorized an increase in the so-called sin tax. As of this day, Middley is **AUThorized** to sign purchase orders. This **AUThorization** is granted by M.R. Petterson, CEO.)

One does not have to write a book to be an **AUThor**. One can author a set of rules for a club, author a system for filing receipts, author a trend in fashions, or whatever. One should keep in mind, however, that purists do not approve of using the word as a verb, even though George Chapman used it as such in his translation of Homer in 1596. **AUThorship** refers to the origin of a written work. (Bart's teachers questioned the authorship of the term paper he said he wrote.)

☞   ***But not:*** *auger* [AS *nafogar*, a nave-piercer], the bit end of a bit and brace, drill; *August* [*Augustus*, the adopted son of Julius Caesar], eighth month; *authentic* [Gk *authentikos*, authoritative, genuine], genuine.

Antonyms: augment — decrease, diminish, shrink, deflate, reduce, curtail, abridge, subside; *august* — unimpressive, uninspiring, common, ignoble, paltry, humble, vulgar, ridiculous, comic; *authoritarian* — lenient, permissive, indulgent, tolerant, anarchic, heretical, flexible, nonconformist; *authoritative* — disputed, dubious, unreliable, questionable, facetious, frivolous, deceptive, subservient, apocryphal; *authorize* — prohibit, enjoin, forbid, proscribe, preclude, prevent, interdict, say no; *auxiliary* — main, principal, major, primary, chief, first-line, hindrance, drawback.

B

BASSUS, low, short: BASE, BASS

In Sergei Prokofiev's symphonic children's tale *Peter and the Wolf*, the characters are represented by musical instruments, the duck by an oboe, the bird by a flute, the cat by a ''clarinet in a low register,'' and Grandfather by a **BASSoon**, an instrument that is deep and low in sound. This is most appropriate, for it matches Grandfather's **BASS** voice, one so deep and low that as a singer he would be classified as a **BASSo profundo**. We know this when the narrator of the story takes on Grandfather's role and says to Peter, who has wandered off from the house, ''The meadow is a dangerous place. What if a wolf should come out of the forest. What would you do *then*?''

Something that is **BASE** is contemptible, sordid, vile, despicable, evil, sinister. (''If [man] be not of kin to God by his spirit, he is a base and ignoble creature,'' Francis Bacon.) It also has the meaning of menial, servile, inferior, lowly, wretched. (''I have always heard, Sancho, that doing good to base fellows is like throwing water into the sea,'' Miguel de Cervantes.)

The verb **aBASE** means to lower in esteem, prestige, office, or rank. Synonyms are humiliate, belittle, scorn, shame, demean. (''Whosoever exalteth himself shall be abased,'' Luke, 14:11.) A person who has been **aBASEd** has been humbled, brought down, degraded. An **aBASEment** is the act of being abased. (Every appearance before the Board was one more abasement for poor Rafael.) Although the definitions of abase and **deBASE** are quite similar in meaning — to lower in rank, dignity, or importance (Inflation is bound to debase the nation's currency) — synonyms of the latter have a sharper, harsher, and more drastic edge: to cheapen, adulterate, desecrate, bastardize, dishonor, disgrace (Dr. Bey spoke of the cruel debasing of human values by the Nazis).

A **BASSet** hound is low to the ground, a **bas-relief** is a form of sculpture in which the figures project only slightly from the background (it is also called ''low relief''), and **bouillabaisse** is a soup or stew made with several kinds of fish along with tomatoes and olive oil; cooking directions are contained in the word: boil and then lower the heat.)

☛ *Once uPUN a time* a musician who had been fishing for hours with no luck at all said, ''If I don't catch a bass soon, I'm going to junk my rod and reel.'' Whereupon he pulled in a large woodwind instrument of low range.

☛ *But not: base* [Gk *bainein*, to go], foundation, bottom, support; *bass* [ME *bas*], a fish.

☛ *Combining forms: a-*, to; *bouilla-*, to boil; *de-*, down; *profundo*, deep; *relief*, projection in a sculpture.

☛ *Antonyms: abase* — dignify, elevate, uplift, acclaim, extol, laud; *abased* — honored, enhanced, enriched, praised, strengthened; *base* — noble, exalted, worthy, important, superior; *debase* — consecrate, hallow, sanctify, enshrine, exalt.

The **BEATitudes** are the declarations made by Jesus in the Sermon on the Mount, such as ''Blessed are the peacemakers: for they shall be called the children of God'' (Matthew, 5:3–11). **BEATitude** is also a state of supreme blessedness, of perfect happiness. In the Roman Catholic church **BEATification** is the act by which a decreased person is said by the pope to be blessed and a proper subject for a mass. Hence to **BEATify** is to make blessedly happy, and a **BEATified** person, deceased, is entitled to special religious honors. The **BEATific** Vision is the sight of God at the moment of death; a beatific peace is one that is blissful and rapturous.

BEATrice is a feminine given name meaning ''one who brings joy.'' It is the name of the heroine of Shakespeare's *Much Ado About Nothing* and of the lady whom Dante first saw when she was eight years old who became his ideal of womanhood and guided him through Paradise in his *Divine Comedy*. The name of the queen of the Netherlands since 1980 is **BEATrix**.

But not: beatinest, most remarkable, [AS *beaten*, Southern U.S., R.H. Unabridged].

Antonyms: beatific — accursed, hellish, blighted, doomed, miserable.

One day during his long stretch (1934–45) as mayor of New York City, Fiorello LaGuardia acknowledged that he had been guilty of making an unwise appointment for a job in his administration by saying, ''When I make a mistake, it's a **BEAUt!**'' With that he assured himself of a place, however brief, in various books of famous quotations.

In 1836, when he was twenty-six years old, Edgar Allen Poe married his cousin, Virginia Clemm, a girl of thirteen. Virginia died in 1847, and two years later Poe wrote his famous poem ''Annabel Lee'' in memory of his wife. It is a moving profession of his love: ''For the moon never beams, without bringing me dreams / Of the **BEAUtiful** Annabel Lee; / And the stars never rise, but I feel the bright eyes / Of the beautiful Annabel Lee.'' Edgar was Virginia's **BEAU** (pl. **BEAUs, BEAUx**), and Virginia was Edgar's **BELLe**, his **BEAUteous** child-wife.

A **beldam** used to be a name for one's grandmother, but today it refers to an old woman, especially an ugly one, in short, a hag. **BELLadonna**, the name of a poisonous plant that is also known as ''deadly nightshade,'' literally means ''fair lady.'' It is so-called because in earlier times women chewed or ate just enough of its leaves to cause the pupils of their eyes to dilate and enhance their **BEAUty**. Today there seem to be **BEAUcoup** ways for ladies to **BEAUtify** or **emBELLish** themselves without taking such risks. **BEAUticians** and employees of fashion shops are **emBELLishment** specialists.

A **belvedere** is a summer house with a view, one no doubt at home to the **BEAUx-arts** (music and painting) and **BELLes-lettres** (literature) as well as those who make up the fashionable world known as **BEAU monde**.

But not: antebellum [*ante-* before + *bellum*, war], existing before the war; *bellicose* [*bellum*], belligerent; *bellwether* [AS the lead ram (wether) that wears a bell], a leader.

BEATUS, happy:
BEAT

BELLUS, pretty, handsome:
BEAU, BELL

☞ *Combining forms: -coup,* successful action; *-dam,* mother; *-donna,* lady; *em-,* in; *lettres,* literature; *monde,* world; *-vedere,* to see.

☞ *Antonyms: beautiful* — plain, unattractive, unsightly, misshapen, grotesque; *beautify* — mar, spoil, distort, uglify; *beauty* — eyesore, dog, hag, fright, homeliness, repulsiveness; *embellish* — divest, strip.

BENE, good, well; MALUS, bad, evil: BENE, BENI, MAL, MALE, MALI

BENEdictions and BENIsons are blessings (Reverend High will now give the benediction); MALEdictions and MALIsons are curses (In Shakespeare's *Romeo and Juliet,* Mercutio's ''A plague o' both your houses!'' is a curse).

A BENEfactor is one who gives aid; the deed is a BENEfaction. A MALEfactor is one who does ill or breaks the law; the act is a MALEfaction. It is interesting to note that while a lady benefactor is listed in the unabridged dictionaries as both a BENEfactress (pl. BENEfactresses) and BENEfactrix (pl. BENEfactrixes or BENEfactrices), the evil, criminal, wrongdoing lady malefactors are honored with only MALEfactress (pl. MALEfactresses). How sad. No ''trix,'' no treats!

BENEfic and BENEficent acts — they are BENEficences — are kindly ones, while MALEfic and MALEficent ones — they are MALEficences — are harmful.

BENEvolent people desire to do good to others. They are filled with good will, charitableness, and BENEvolence, and are amicable, compassionate, and merciful. But MALEvolent people wish evil or harm to others. They are filled with ill will, hatred, and MALEvolence and are spiteful, vicious, and pernicious.

A BENIgn climate is pleasant, a benign grandfather is kindhearted, and a benign tumor is harmless. A long siege of gloomy weather can have a MALIgn influence on people, giving them a malign disposition; but the word *malign* is more frequently used as a verb: to disparage, speak ill of, slander, vilify, bad mouth, or put down another. (The two candidates maligned each other through the entire campaign.) When tumors are toxic, cancerous, deadly, virulent, or inoperable, they are MALIgnant. Such abnormal growths and other evils are called MALIgnancies.

If you're keeping score, you probably have come to the conclusion that there's a pretty good balance between good and evil. Read on.

There are matching words here — BENIgnant and BENIgnancies — but they are not in common usage. And chalk these up as good words that have no matching mal counterparts: BENEfit, noun and verb. (The benefit brought in several hundred dollars. I trust you will benefit from our little talk.) BENEficial, helpful, profitable, propitious. (The new treaty will certainly be beneficial to our country.) BENEficiary, heir, legatee, inheritor. (We'll need to change the beneficiary on that insurance policy. Claxton County was the beneficiary of yesterday's soaking rain.)

Slim pickin's, however, compared to what follows:

MALadroit, gauche, clumsy, klutzy. (The lineman's maladroit move at the line of scrimmage resulted in an illegal-procedure flag.)

MALady, ailment, disease, affliction. (Not one doctor could diagnose Helmit's mysterious malady.)

MALaise, discomfort, lassitude, fatigue. (Her vague, general feeling of malaise led her to think she was on the brink of death.)

MALapert, saucy, impudent; hussy, minx. (No thumbs up for the acting of that thirteen-year-old malapert.)

MALapropism, the ridiculous misuse of words, from Mrs. Malaprop, a character in Richard Sheridan's play *The Rivals*; for an example, see *allos*, page 10.

MALapropos, inopportune, inappropriate, unsuitable. (Phignewt's remarks to the critically ill patient about his insurance policy were most malapropos.)

MALaria, disease caused by a mosquito bites. ("Oh, no, you don't give *me* malaria," she cried as she slapped the mosquito dead.)

MALcontent, a rebel, agitator, fomenter. (She was described as a malcontent by her very own sister.)

MALfeasance, wrongdoing, especially in public office. (The Attorney General was charged with malfeasance.)

MALice, spite, animosity, ill will. ("This," the judge said, "was done with malice aforethought.")

MALicious, spiteful, vicious, pernicious. (The principal stressed the malicious nature of the boys' actions.)

MALinger, to pretend illness in order to avoid work. (Beetle Bailey of the comics is often accused of malingering.)

MALodorous, foul-smelling, obnoxious, highly improper. (My opponent's malodorous public record is there for all to see!)

MALpractice, wrong, error, misconduct. (The costs of malpractice insurance are driving many doctors away from medical practice.)

MALversation, corrupt administration, turning away from honesty in public office. (The Dodge administration was accused of malversation.)

Petit MAL, grand MAL, literally, "little sickness, great sickness," forms of epilepsy. (Arlene was grateful that her seizures were the mild, "petit mal" kind.)

And **MAL de mer**, a French phrase meaning seasickness.

There are others, too, but their meanings are largely self-evident: **MALadapted, MALadjusted, MALformation, MALfunction, MALnutrition**, and **MALtreat**.

*Once uPUN a time in a vocabulary class the teacher asked a bright young student if she could use the words "malady," "malaria," and "malice" in one sentence. "I think so," the young lady replied. " 'No malady,' the butler said, 'I don't think you would enjoy the opera; I hear there is one very malaria, and I don't recommend that you go skating on account of the malice.' "

*But not: benefit [alteration of *Benedick*, a bachelor in Shakespeare's *Much Ado about Nothing*], a long-time bachelor who is newly married; *malamute* [Inupiaq *malimiut*, name for Indians who bred sled dogs], Alaskan sled dog; *malarky* [?], nonsense, bunkum; [*malleus*, hammer], adaptable.

☞ *Combining forms:* -adroit, clever; -ady, to have; -aise, ease; -apert, able; -apropos, to the point; -aria, air; -diction, to say; -factor, one who does; -feasance, to do; -fic, to do; -inger, thin; -versation, to turn; -volent, to wish.

☞ *Antonyms:* benediction — curse, execration, calumniation; beneficence — selfishness, stinginess; beneficial — hurtful, disadvantageous, baneful; benefit — disservice, detriment; undermine, impair, hamper; benevolence — animosity, malice, heartlessness; benevolent — cold, hostile, nasty, misanthropic; benign — mean, violent, unhealthy, stormy, inclement, tempestuous; maladroit — deft, nimble, skilled, elegant, suave; malaise — vigor, well-being; malapropos — suitable, proper, apt, becoming, befitting, seemly; malevolent — cordial, kind, compassionate; malignant — amicable, amiable, efficacious, salubrious.

BONUS, good:
BON, BOUNT

A **BONBON** is a piece of candy; it began as a nursery word, the equivalent of "good-good." A **BON ami** is a very good friend, perhaps a lover or sweetheart. If one chooses well, the friend might be de**BON**air, that is, charming and refined, dapper and carefree, as well as radiating **BON**homie, all the friendliness and geniality that the word suggests. The English humorist P.G. Wodehouse described a jovial university friend as a "**BON**homous young fellow." A **BON**ny being is pleasant, agreeable, healthy, and good. People with such qualities are likely to be **boon** companions.

BONjour means "good morning," **BON**soir "good evening." A **BON mar-che** is a bargain in the marketplace, and a **BON mot** is a witty remark. All from France.

A **BON**anza is a windfall, a gold mine. A **BON**us is something extra, a prize or reward, as is a **BOUNT**y. And if those extra somethings come in **BOUNT**eous, **BOUNT**iful amounts of cash, one should make sure that the money is **BON**a fide, that is, authentic and genuine. If it's a cruise that you won, well, **BON voyage**!

Pro BONo means "for the public good," free, done or donated without charge. (Supreme Court Justice Sandra Day O'Connor proposed that all law students be required to take on some pro bono legal work). *Pro bono publico* means "for the public good or welfare."

☞ *But not:* bonfire [ME banefyre, a fire for the burning of bones], a fire built in the open; boon [ON bon, prayer], a blessing.

☞ *Combining forms:* -aire, lineage; ami, friend; de-, of; fide, faith; -homie, man; jour, day; marche, market; mot, word; pro, for; soir, evening; voyage, journey.

☞ *Antonyms:* bonanza — disaster; bonhomie — cheerless, sour, somber, sober, dour, morose, gloomy, pensive, lugubrious; bona fide — counterfeit, spurious; bounteous, bountiful — miserly, small; debonair — gauche, rude, awkward, uncivil, serious, shy, self-conscious.

BOS, ox:
BEEF

The word **BEEF** came into the English language following the victory of the forces of William the Conqueror in 1066. While it is doubtful that the Normans brought any cattle with them, they did bring the Old French word *boef*, which before long became the Anglo-French *beof*, which between 1250 and 1300 became *beef*. Before all that, the Anglo-Saxons' Sunday dinners featured such delicacies as boiled bull, roast cow, and fried ox.

The famed **BEEFeater** guards at the Tower of London were fed beef to make them strong, and **BEEFy** is used to describe heavy, muscular, brawny people. When we **BEEF up** something, we reinforce or strengthen it. (Our coach says we'll have to beef up our line before next season if we hope to win a game.) A **BEEFalo** is a cross between a cow and a buffalo; which isn't too bad a name, considering that it might have come out cowfalo, bulfalo, steerfalo, or even buffabeef.

Farmers and ranchers have long called their calves and cows **boss** and **bossy**; the words stem from their Latin root and are not even second cousins to the boss who is an employer or the bossy person who is forever trying to order others around. (Those words derive from the Dutch *baas*, a foreman or master.)

As porcine is to swine (piggish or hoggish), vulpine is to fox (crafty or cunning), and ovine is to sheep (docile or meek), **bovine** is to cows, buffalo, and kudus (dull, lethargic, or stolid).

But not: *deboss* [F *boce*, a swelling, bump], to indent into a surface; *emboss* [*boce*], to raise a design or figure on a surface.

Antonyms: *beef up* — weaken, sap, drain, water down, enervate; *beefy* — feeble, frail, debilitated, emaciated.

C

CABALLUS,
horse: CAVAL

In the English Civil War that broke out in 1642, those who supported Charles I in his battle against Parliament chose to call themselves **CAVALiers** and their opponents Roundheads. (As it turned out, the head that was round enough to roll belonged to Charles; it was chopped off.) In a book entitled *1066 and All That*, authors W.C. Sellar and R.J. Yeatman call it "the utterly memorable Struggle between the Cavaliers (Wrong but Wromantic) and the Roundheads (Right but Repulsive)."

Today people who are cavalier are arrogant, haughty, curt, and lofty, just as if they were looking down from the horses their namesakes always rode. (No matter what you say, Smidgen'll **CAVALierly** tell you you're wrong.)

A **CAVALcade** used to be a ceremonial parade of horsemen, but today it's more likely to be a pageant of sorts, just as the **CAVALry** charge of old is now one of motor-powered armored vehicles.

☞ ***Antonyms:*** *cavalier* — courteous, attentive, obliging, considerate, conscientious, diligent, caring, sincere, thoughtful, humble.

CAEDERE,
to cut: CIDE,
CIS, CISE

Caedere gives us not only words for cutting instruments, such as **sCISsors, chisel**, and the eight **inCISors** in our jaws, but also words that reflect other kinds of cutting. For example, when we are confronted with a problem, we have to cut away those parts of it that we do not feel are necessary. In other words, we have to **deCIDE** what we want to keep or throw out. We end up making a **deCISion**. If we are quick about it, we are looked up to as being **deCISive** rather than **indeCISive, undeCIDEd**, irresolute, spineless, and wishy-washy. Having the strength to make a firm decision has **deCIDEd**, definite advantages.

A teacher who assigns a **preCIS** hopes to get a **conCISe** summary, that is, a paper with all the claptrap and gobbledygook **exCISEd**, completely cut out. Such a **preCISE** report — clear-cut, explicit, and unequivocal — will insure the student that no **inCISive** or cutting remarks will be forthcoming.

When operating, a surgeon makes an **inCISion**; when carving a linoleum block, an artist **inCISes** a pattern or design with a sharp, pointed instrument. In the Roman Catholic, Eastern, and Anglican churches **CircumCISion** is a feast held on January 1 in honor of the circumcision of Jesus.

The **CIDE** in **genoCIDE, homiCIDE**, and **suiCIDE** means "killing" or "the act of killing." When Cain killed his brother Abel, he committed **fratriCIDE**. When King Lear's daughter Goneril poisoned her sister Regan, she committed **soroCIDE**. When Macbeth murdered Duncan, the King of Scotland, it was **regiCIDE**, but when Oedipus did away with his king, he doubled up, for the king was also his father, and that's **patriCIDE**. And then in 1893 Lizzie Bordon allegedly "took an ax and gave her mother forty whacks, and when she saw what she had done, she gave her father forty-one." The jury found her not guilty. Some say it was her stepmother who got the ax, and, strictly speaking, that's not **matriCIDE**.

But not: excise [prob. *censere*, to assess], an indirect tax or duty; *exercise* [*arcere*, to restrain], work out; a ceremony.

Combining forms: con-, thorough; *de-*, down; *ex-*, out; *gen-*, race; *hom-*, man; *im-*, not; *in-*, not; *pre-*, before; *re-*, back; *sui-*, oneself; *un-*, not.

Antonyms: concise — discursive, verbose, wordy, long-winded, redundant, prolix; *decided* — dubious, ambiguous, vague, wavering, indefinite; *incisive* — bland, dull, superficial, innocuous, charitable; *precise* — implicit, nebulous, haphazard, equivocal, hazy, casual, informal.

CALVI, to deceive: CAL, CHAL

As Hamlet urges Ophelia to "get thee to a nunnery," he says, ". . . be thou as chaste as ice, as pure as snow, thou shalt not escape **CALumny**." For slander is difficult to escape. "**CALumnies**," Ben Jonson says in *Volpone*, "are answered best with silence," but it is not easy to keep one's cool when **CALumnious**, slanderous, malicious, libelous, disparaging barbs are being hurled your way. Mark Twain observed that it takes both your enemy and your friend to do you that harm, the enemy to **CALumniate**, injure, smear, and vilify you and the friend to bring you the news.

"The New Frontier of which I speak," John F. Kennedy said in his inaugural address, "is not a set of promises — it is a set of **CHALlenges**." Challenges are dares, spurs, stimuli, threats, provocations, and lures. Leaders must often be **CHALlengers**, prodding, goading, provoking, stimulating, and egging on. Being president is **CHALlenging**, but, said Bromide, a person given to trite remarks, so is life, you know, like intriguing, stirring, exciting, inspiring, and galvanic.

But not: calumet [*calamus*, a reed], a ceremonial peace pipe used by North American Indians; *chalupa* (Sp boat, launch], fried tortilla topped with meat, lettuce, tomato, hot sauce, etc.

Antonyms: caluminous — eulogistic, laudatory, commendatory, flattering; *calumny* — eulogy, praise, approval; extol, commend; *challenge* — accept, concede, agree with, acquiesce.

CANIS [L], KYON [Gk], dog: CAN, CYN

The history of some words is a surprisingly twisted path, and that of **CANary** is one of them. A scholar in ancient Rome recorded that a group of islands off the northwest coast of Africa was "Canaria, so-called from the multitude of dogs [*canes*] of great size." When later explorers found flocks of small finches there, they took them back to Europe to be sold as caged pets and named them after the islands that bore the Latin word for dogs.

A **CYNic** is a pessimist and faultfinder, one whose attitude toward the world is sneering, sarcastic, and distrustful, in short, **CYNical**. The words come to us from a group of Greek philosophers of twenty-four centuries ago who were called "the snarlers," in the manner of certain dogs of the time.

Quinsy is an inflammation of the tonsils; the word stems from a Greek word for a sore throat, which, in turn, apparently reminded someone of a dog choking. The wagging tail at the other end of the dog has given us the word **CYNosure**, meaning a center of attention, something that serves as a guide. Hence, the North Star is a cynosure for sailors and hikers.

Three other words come from *canis*: **chenille**, the name of a soft fabric often used in bedspreads, which apparently reminded someone of the soft coat of a dog; **kennel**, which got to us from *canile*; and **CANine**, which pertains to the family of dogs, foxes, and wolves, as well as to those long, sharp teeth we have on either side of our incisors.

☞ *But not: sinecure [sine-,* without + *cure,* care], a position that pays very well for very little work.

☞ *Combining forms: -sy,* choking; *-ure,* tail.

☞ *Antonyms: cynic* — humanitarian, optimist; *cynical* — hopeful, ingenuous, philanthropic.

CAPUT, head:
CAP, CHAP,
CHIEF, CIP

From *caput* come words that pertain to our heads: **CAP, CHAPeau, kerCHIEF** (and its offspring **handkerCHIEF**), and the kind of **CAPe** that wicked landlords who preyed on helpless widows in old-fashioned melodramas could hide their sneering faces in.

Capes were popular garments in olden times for other reasons, too. When one's cape was grasped during an attack, one could easily slip out of it and **esCAPe**. Thus was born **esCAPade**, a synonym of **CAPrice** and **misCHIEF** and their siblings, **CAPricious** (erratic, fickle) and **misCHIEvous** (playful, wicked).

Medieval knights dressed **CAP-a-pie** (head to foot) in armor would have had a surer defense against possible **deCAPitation**, but in a boat the extra weight would have made **CAPsizing** (headfirst) a safe bet.

It was a very special cape that gave us the words **CHAPel** and **CHAPlain**. Early in the Middle Ages the *cappella* or small cape of St. Martin was stored in a chest with other sacred relics; the place where it was kept came to be called a *chapelle* and its keeper the *chapelain*. The musical term **a CAPpella** means "in the manner of a chapel"; hence, it is music without instrumental accompaniment.

It should be noted here that other capes such as Massachusetts' Cod and Africa's Good Hope are also heads — of lands.

A **CAPtain** is a head, too, as is a **cadet** (tomorrow's general), a **CAPital** (the head city) and a **CAPitol** (the head building in the capital), a **CHAPeron** (also **CHAPerone**, an adult supervisor), a **chef**, a **CHIEF**, a **corporal**, and even **cattle**, for as personal property they were the leading source of wealth in ancient times. The literal meaning of **per CAPita** is "by heads." (Our town's per capita consumption of hot dogs is the largest in the state.)

An **achievement** is something accomplished or attained by extraordinary courage, skill, or industry. (Jonas Salk's remarkable achievements saved countless human beings from the ravages of polio.) To **achieve** is to accomplish, fulfill, attain, realize, reach, bring off, effectuate. ([Today's students] can put dope in their veins or hope in their brains. . . . If they can conceive it and believe it, they can achieve it,'' said Jesse Jackson.)

To **CAPitulate** is to surrender. Somehow the addition of a prefix gave **reCAPitulate** the meaning of summarize, restate, rephrase, or **reCAP**. Students are sometimes assigned **CHAPters** of textbooks to do that to.

A **preCIPice** is the almost straight-up-and-down (or **preCIPitous**) side of a cliff. To be on the edge is dangerous, as it is to be on the precipice or edge of war. To **preCIPitate** is to rush headlong into something or to hasten the occurrence of an event. (The act precipitated an international crisis.) As an adjective it means headlong, impetuous, rash. **PreCIPitation** means haste, recklessness, but most of us know it best from the declaration, ''Neither precipitation or heat nor gloom of night are **handiCAPS** enough to stop the postal carrier from delivering the mail.'' To fail the mission? Done for! Finished! **Kaput**!

The two-headed muscles on our arms and thighs are called **biceps**; the three-headed muscles on the back of our arms that allow us to straighten the elbow are called **triceps**.

*But not: caper [capra, goat], a trick, stunt, high jinks; to romp; capstan [capere, to take], a device for winding in ropes, cables; corporal [corpus, body], related to the body.

*Combining forms: a, to; bi-, two; de-, off; es-, out of; ker-, to cover; mis-, less; pie, foot; pre-, before; re-, again; tri-, three.

*Antonyms: capitulate — be victorious, defeat; capricious — consistent, resolute; mischievous — sedate, somber, well-mannered, wholesome; precipitate — deliberate, slow; delay; precipitous — gradual, sloping; recapitulate — embroider, expand.

''Take a perfect circle, **caress** it and you'll have a vicious circle.'' (Eugene Ionesco, 1950, *The Bald Soprano*). To caress is to cuddle, embrace, pat, hug, kiss, stroke.

''Let us . . . **CHERish**, therefore, the means of knowledge. Let us dare to read, think, speak, write'' (John Adams, 1765, *A Dissertation of the Canon and Feudal Law*). To cherish is to hold dear, care for, value, prize, appreciate.

''The scholar who **CHERIshes** the love of comfort is not fit to be deemed a scholar'' (Confucius, c. 500 B.C., *The Confucian Analects*). Cherishes means loves, dotes on, esteems, relishes, delights in.

''I pray that our heavenly Father may assuage the anguish of your bereavement, and leave you only the **CHERished** memory of the loved and lost'' (Abraham Lincoln, November 21, 1864, Letter to Mrs. Bixby following the death of her five sons on the field of battle). Cherished: treasured, revered, venerated, honored, idolized.

CARUS, dear: CHERI, CHARI

''From all blindness of heart, from pride, vainglory, and hypocrisy; from envy, hatred, and malice, and all **unCHARItableness**, Good Lord, deliver us'' *The Book of Common Prayer*, 1662). Uncharitableness: unkindness, harshness, censoriousness, mercilessness.

''You never saw my name on a **CHARIty** list [for making a donation] did you? . . . but I built whole blocks of buildings in Chicago when the working men there had to have employment'' (Hetty Green, financier, c. 1900). Charity is benevolence, brotherly love, humanity, good will, generosity, kindness.

''But how shall we expect charity towards others, when we are **unCHARItable** to ourselves?'' (Sir Thomas Browne, 1642, *Religio Medici*). Uncharitable is unkind, harsh, unforgiving, mean, not generous.

''The happiness of life is made up of minute fractions — the little soon forgotten **CHARIties** of a kiss or smile, a kind look, a heartfelt compliment. . . . (Samuel Taylor Coleridge, 1828, *The Friend. The Improvisatore*). Charities are kindnesses, favors, gifts.

''I bequeath my soul to God. . . . / For my name and memory, I leave it to men's **CHARItable** speeches . . .'' (Francis Bacon, from his will, 1626). Charitable: tolerant, liberal, unstinting, magnanimous, indulgent, eleemosynary.

☛ ***But not:*** *charisma* [GK *charizesthai*, to favor], magnetism; *cherub* [cherubim], innocent child.

☛ ***Combining form:*** *un-*, not.

☛ ***Antonyms:*** *charitable* — mean, stingy, miserly, penurious, niggardly, cruel, stern, malevolent.

CAVERE, beware, take care: CAU

A **caveat** is a legal notice in a court to stop a certain proceeding until a hearing is held. (The attorney filed a caveat to prevent the probating of Grandfather's will.) But it is not the sole property of the legal system; it is also a warning. (I did get to take the car to the prom, but not until after Dad read off a long list of caveats.) **Caveat emptor** is the best known of them all; it means let the buyer beware, be **CAUtious**. (If you don't get something in writing on that jalopy, forget it; old C.E. — that stands for caveat emptor — guarantees nothing!) An anonymous Roman sage once said (in Latin, of course), ''Whatever you do, do **CAUtiously** and look to the end,'' that is, do it warily, prudently, discreetly, carefully, charily.

CAUtion is care, wariness, prudence, and an admonition; it is to alert, to admonish, to tip off. It also used to be slang to describe a person who is unusual in an interesting or odd way. (You should have seen Aunt Sally going after those coins at the bottom of the fountain; she certainly is a caution!) A **CAUtionary** tale is one that contains a warning.

A **preCAUtion** is a safety measure taken in advance. (We take lots of vitamin C as a precaution against winter colds.) **PreCAUtionary** is suggesting or advising precaution. (Since noon the National Weather Service has been broadcasting precautionary warnings about the possibility of tornadoes in this area.)

But not: caustic [Gk *kaiein*, to burn], sarcastic; *cavernous* [*cavus*, hollow], like a cavern.

Combining forms: emptor, buyer; *pre-*, before.

Antonyms: caution — neglect, indiscretion, imprudence, daring, daredeviltry; *cautious* — rash, reckless, impetuous, venturous, heedless; *cautiously* — carelessly, hastily, impulsively, thoughtlessly.

When the **CENsus** was taken in ancient Rome, all citizens had to register themselves and their property for purposes of taxation. There are people these days who feel that the census takers seek more information than they think the government has a right to know about them. It is a battle that occurs every ten years.

CENsure is the blaming or criticizing of someone. In a legislative body it is an official reprimand. (There is a resolution on the floor to censure Rep. O'Wilix.) Outside those hallowed halls, however, we may censure anyone we wish to — or not. (Bull Feathers, our 0 and 9 football coach, is more to be pitied than censured.)

A **reCENsion** is the editing and revision of a literary work; it is also the product of that revising. An **excise** tax is an internal duty on certain commodities such as tobacco and alcoholic beverages within a country. (''Excise, a hateful tax levied upon commodities,'' said Samuel Johnson in his 1755 English dictionary.) **Excisable** articles are those subject to excise taxes.

CENsors are people who manage to delete or ban articles, books, movies, art works, or anything else they consider objectionable. They are folks who attempt to expurgate, suppress, bowdlerize, or bury whatever they do not approve of, and they often carry out their mission with **CENsorious** attitudes: abusive, carping, faultfinding, querulous, captious, condemnatory.

''**CENsorship**, like charity,'' said Clare Boothe Luce, ''should begin at home; but unlike charity, it should end there.''

But not: censer [*cendere*, to set on fire], container for burning incense; *excise* [*caedere*, to cut], to cut out; *recent* [*recens*, fresh], current.

Combining forms: ex-, to; *re-*, thoroughly.

Antonyms: censorious — endorsing, uncritical, flattering, praising, encouraging, laudatory; *censure* — approval, eulogy, encouragement, eulogize, laud, compliment.

An **anaCHRONism** occurs when a person or event is placed in the wrong time period. In Shakespeare's *Julius Caesar*, Cassius says, ''The clock has striken three.'' But striking clocks were some 1,400 years in the future. His *Antony*

*CENSERE,
to assess, judge:
CEN*

*CHRONOS [Gk],
time: CHRON*

and Cleopatra includes a reference to the game of billiards, but the two lovers died about 1,500 years before the game is believed to have originated in France. The legend about young George Washington throwing a silver dollar across the Potomac River is also **anaCHRONistic**; our first silver dollars were not issued until 1794, when he was sixty-two years old.

A **CHRONic** complainer is a person for whom complaining is continual, habitual, and persistent; it goes on all the time.

A **CHRONicler** of events has to list them in their proper **CHRONological** order; if the **CHRONicle** reports that the *Lusitania* was sunk by a German U-boat before the *Titanic* hit an iceberg, an error in **CHRONology** has been made. Just as it would if you listed two of the books of the Old Testament by placing **2 CHRONicles** before the first one.

SynCHRONOus events or movements occur simultaneously. Thus the members of a **synCHRONized** swimming team perform certain movements at the same time and in the same way. Officials who time sporting events have to make sure their watches — which are most likely highly accurate **CHRONometers** — are **synCHRONized**. They are then said to be in **sync** (or **synch**). When the lips of the movie actor do not move in harmony with the spoken words, the picture and the soundtrack are out of sync. (Rock stars Milli Vanilli were censured for **lip-syncing** the songs on their Grammy-winning recording.) Relationships between people can be in or out of sync, too: Dad and Mom were completely out of sync on where we should spend our vacation.

A **CHRONogram** is a complicated word game that involves hiding Roman numerals in a phrase or sentence and having them add up to a certain date. Upon the death of Queen Elizabeth I someone supposedly wrote, ''My Day Closed Is In Immortality.'' The initial letters of each word are, in order, MDCIII, which, translated, is 1603, the year she died. Beginners would be best advised to stick with simpler forms, however, such as XL which translates to forty and sounds like ''excel.''

When Harold Ickes, a member of President Franklin Roosevelt's cabinet, said, ''I am against government by **crony**,'' he was referring to the practice of **cronyism**, the appointing of one's close friends to important positions. Originally **chrony**, a slang word at Cambridge University, it meant a close and long-time companion.

☞ ***Combining forms:*** *ana-*, against; *-gram*, something written; *-meter*, a measuring device; *syn-*, together.

☞ ***Antonyms:*** *chronic* — fleeting, temporary; *crony* — foe, adversary, rival; *synchronous* — different, staggered.

**CIVIS, citizen:
CIT, CIV**

To **CIVilize** someone is to educate, cultivate, enlighten, refine that person. That may be what the Romans did to the barbarians way back when, and the barbarians may well have benefited from it. But Huckleberry Finn didn't want any of it. On the first page of Mark Twain's classic, Huck says, ''The Widow Douglas she took me for her son, and allowed she would sivilize me; but it was rough living in the house all the time, considering how dismal regular and decent the widow was in all her way; and so when I couldn't stand it no longer I lit out. I got into my old rags . . . and was free and satisfied.''

CIVilization was hardly Huck's cup of tea; for one thing, it tolerated slavery, and Huck's companion on the raft was Jim, the runaway. If Huck had been able to read, he would have taken to the sentiments of a Frenchman who wrote under the name of Voltaire: ''I know I am among **CIVilized** men because they are fighting so savagely.'' Note that he did not call his fellow men **unCIVil** or **unCIVilized**.

Huck was certainly **CIVil**; he said ''Mam'' and ''Sir'' and was always respectful to his elders. He most likely never came within a country mile of the word ''**inCIVility**,'' but the Widow Douglas made darn sure he knew what discourteous behaviour was even if she couldn't teach him how to spell it. One may not be able to envision him becoming **CITified**, owning a condo in the heart of a **CITy**, but despite his final words — ''I got to light out for the territory . . . because Aunt Sally she's going to adopt me and sivilize me, and I can't stand it. I been there before'' — somehow one knows that he will be a good **CITizen**, exchanging **CIVilities** with his neighbors, and doing his **CIVic** duty when called upon. One doesn't have to take a course in **CIVics** to appreciate the privileges, rights, and responsibilities of **CITizenship**. Had Mr. Twain written a sequel to this story of Huck's childhood, he might well have had Huck, at about forty years of age, find his way to the nearest **CITadel** or recruiting station where he would shuck his **CIVvies** and his **CIVilian** status in exchange for the blue uniform of the Union Army and a rifle.

*But not: citation [ciere, to move], award, summons.

*Combining forms: in-, not; un-, not.

*Antonyms: citified — countrified, rustic, rural, pastoral; *citizen* — alien, foreigner, transient, outlander, immigrant; *civil* — boorish, churlish, hostile, rude;   *civility* — insolence, rudeness, hostility; *civilization* — savagery, backwardness, barbarousness; wilderness; *civilized* — brutish, savage, provincial, unenlightened.

CLAUDERE, to shut, close: CLOSE, CLUDE, CLUS

Prefixes are the key to many of the words from *claudere*. Consider these six words in the *clude* group, all of which have a basic meaning of to close. To **conCLUDE** has the sense of bringing something together, as to an end. To **exCLUDE** is to shut something or someone out. When one **inCLUDEs** others, they are shut or closed in. To **ocCLUDE** is to close, shut, or stop up, as an opening or passage. (The crowd brought in cars to occlude access to the capitol.) To **preCLUDE** is to shut off something ahead of time. (My failure to get my degree **precluded** my getting the promotion.) To **seCLUDE** is to close something off by setting it apart.

Prefixes tell the story of these words, too — **disCLOSE, enCLOSE,** and **foreCLOSE** — just as they serve the following group of adjectives: **conCLUSive,** decisive, final (Her fingerprints on the vase turned out to be the conclusive evidence); **exCLUSive**, private, restricted (The Gloobers moved into a very exclusive neighborhood); sole, unshared (A *clause* in my contract guarantees me this town as my exclusive sales territory); **inCLUSive**, comprehensive (He worked here from 1981 to 1987 inclusive); **reCLUSive**, ascetic, **cloistered, seCLUDEd** (Because of his reclusive habits, he seems uncomfortable at our town meetings).

ConCLUSion, judgment, outcome, termination. (The two judges reached different conclusions.) **DisCLOSure**, announcement, leak, revelation. (The witness's disclosure that L.K. Hosperson had served time rocked the courtroom.) **EnCLOSure**, pen, yard, item enclosed. (The enclosure did not turn out to be the check we hoped for.) **ExCLUSion**, barring, prevention, rejection. (The country club's exclusion of women was taken to court.) **Seclusion**, hideaway, isolation, solitude (After the trial, the defendant went into seclusion.)

A **cloister** is a courtyard with open walkways, often in a religious institution; it can also be any quiet, secluded place. (The **closure** of the cloister took away our place for meditation.) A **claustrophobe** is a person who has an abnormal fear of enclosed places, such as a locked **closet**. **Cloture** is a method sometimes employed in Congress to close off debate and force an immediate vote.

☛ *But not: occult* [*occulere*, to hide], mysterious, secret.

☛ *Combining forms: con-*, together; *dis-*, not; *en-*, in; *ex-*, out; *fore-*, outside; *in-*, in; *oc-*, against; *phobe*, fear; *pre-*, before; *se-*, apart.

☛ *Antonyms: cloistered* — public, social; *conclusive* — doubtful, questionable; *exclusion* — acceptance, admittance; *exclusive* — open, shared, unrestricted; *inclusive* — apart, discrete; *reclusive* — clubbable, gregarious, sociable; *secluded* — open, public; *seclusion* — accessibility.

COLARE,
to strain

A **coulee** is a deep gulch, canyon, or gorge originally formed by running water. One of these on the Columbia River in central Washington is the site of the Grand Coulee Dam, begun in 1934 and finished eight years later.

To **percolate** a liquid is to pass it through a filter. When coffee is brewed in a percolator, the liquid is forced up a hollow tube and into a small, usually glass-topped, dome. It gets pretty lively as it **perks.** So it is with people when they say, ''I never begin to percolate until at least 9:00; some days I don't start perking until noon.''

A **colander** (also **cullender**) is a perforated kitchen utensil used to drain off water and juices from foods. (Just put the lettuce in the colander and let it drain into the sink.)

A **portcullis** is a heavy, protective gate seen mostly on medieval castles.

☛ *Once uPUN a time* there was a young man named Perk who often got to work at 8:01. Every time it happened, the boss would boil over and call him a drip and refuse to offer him a cup of coffee. ''Why?'' the young man would ask. ''On what grounds?'' And the boss would shake his head, and say, ''Perk, you late!''

*But not: culvert [?] a drain pipe under a road or embankment; perk [perquirere, to search everywhere for], short for perquisite, a fringe benefit, gratuity; perk [ME perken], to become lively.

*Combining forms: per-, through; port-, gate.

*Antonym: percolate — be lifeless.

For centuries **COPYists** recorded and preserved the world's histories and literary works by laboriously writing them all out by hand. In one tiny tick on eternity's clock, that task was eliminated. Today's copyist taps away at a word processor, and the **COPIer** of old has been supplanted by a wondrous machine that turns out one **COPY** or **COPIous** numbers of **COPIes** in seconds.

COPYrights have changed, too. From 1909 until 1978 an author had a legal right to his or her works for twenty-eight years plus a renewal of twenty-eight years. Now the artist's and author's protection lasts until fifty years after his or her death.

COPYboys and **COPYgirls** are still around, principally in black-and-white late-night movies in which reporters turn out their stories using two fingers on manual typewriters. **COPYcats** are still accused of plagiarism from time to time. **COPYeditors** still **COPYedit** manuscripts for publication, and **COPYwriters** continue to grind out advertisements and publicity releases in a supply that would more than fill up any **cornuCOPIa**, literally "horn of plenty" but generally used today to mean an abundant supply or as a symbol of abundance and often seen as a decoration during Thanksgiving.

*But not: copacetic [?], excellent, fine, first-rate, okay; coping [Gk kolaphos, a blow on the ear], facing, striving, struggling.

*Combining form: cornu-, horn of an animal.

*Antonyms: copious — few, meager, paltry, scant, skimpy, sparse, spare; copy — model, pattern, archetype, prototype, original; create, originate.

One day when Little Willie Wooliebrain was building a bird house, his sister Susu noticed that he was discarding about half the nails. "Why are you doing that?" she asked.

"Because they have the heads on the wrong end," Willie said.

"How silly," Susu said. "And here I thought you were **preCOCious**, you know, smart, bright, quick, mature, advanced, clever. Don't you realize that you can use those nails on the other side of the house?"

PreCOCity was not one of Susu's gifts, either.

The literal meaning of precocious is "early ripened, cooked beforehand." And that's how the **apriCOT** got its name; it was thought of as an early-ripening, sun-cooked peach. Like the German zwieback (twice-baked), originally a **biscuit** was twice-cooked, for it was a seaman's bread and had to be put on shipboard already cooked to reduce the chance of spoilage. Presumably,

COPIA, abundance, wealth: COPI, COPY

COQUERE, to cook: COC, COT

it was heated again before it made its way into the messroom along with other **culinary** (**kitchen**) con**COC**tions (**creations**) that the **cooky** (ship's **cook**) con-**COC**ted (dreamed up) in the ship's galley.

Many recipes in the Italian **cuisine** call for generous amounts of ri**COT**ta; similar to our cottage cheese, it is a **recooked** cheese used in sandwiches, salads, and desserts.

☞ *But not: cookie* [D *koekie*, cake], a small cake.

☞ *Combining forms: apri-*, beforehand; *bis-*, twice; *con-*, together; *pre-*, before; *ri-*, again.

☞ *Antonyms: precocious* — backward, dull, immature, undeveloped.

CORPUS, body:
CORP

A **leprechaun** is a mischievous little old man who lives in Ireland, is believed to be a cobbler or shoemaker by trade, and is rumored to be closely related to the banshee, brownie, dwarf, elf, fay, fairy, goblin, gnome, gremlin, hobgoblin, imp, kobold, nisse, pixie, puck, sprite, and troll. He has never been caught, but if you can catch him, he will reveal the location of a crock of gold.

He is not **CORP**ulent, for if he were fat or obese, he would have been caught long ago. No leprechaun has ever been known to be of such **CORP**ulence as to need a **corset** to hold in a fat tummy.

There is a sizable **CORP**us or body of literature about leprechauns, and many of the stories pay tribute to their **esprit de CORP**s, their unity, their camaraderie, their fellowship.

Of course, there are always doubters and skeptics. One day a dozen of such people met on the edge of a peat bog in the south of the Emerald Isle, as Ireland is sometimes called. "We believe," one of them said in a loud voice, "that you creatures who call yourselves leprechauns are not **CORP**oreal beings, that you are neither tangible, real, solid, palpable, or somatic."

"What?" cried a leprechaun spokesperson who had suddenly materialized. "Not real, you say? Just because we do not believe in **CORP**oral punishment, like spankings and whippings and paddlings, it surely does not follow that we are but ethereal, in**CORP**oreal creatures, mere products of overworked imaginations! We are made of flesh and blood, with both red and white **CORP**uscles!

"We were here in Erin," the spokesperson continued, "when St. Patrick, bless his soul, trapped the last snake in a box and threw it into the sea. That was in about A.D. 450 by your calendar. We leprechauns in**CORP**orated shortly after that, and our **CORP**oration, Leprechaun & Sons, Ltd., is alive and well today.

"You skeptics complain that you have never seen a leprechaun **CORP**se!" the spokesperson went on. "Oh, yes, wouldn't you like to stumble onto one **CORP**us delicti, so to speak, a body that would serve as evidence to prove that we live and we die. Tsk! We honor our dead, but that is our affair, our secret." He smiled, and then suddenly a dozen beautiful **corsages** materialized.

''One for each of you skeptics to take home to your wife,'' he said, and then was gone as mysteriously as he had come.

*But not: corporal [caput, head], a noncommissioned officer.

*Combining forms: delicti, offense; esprit, spirit, in-, in, not; le-, small.

*Antonyms: corporeal — spiritual, heavenly, religious, intellectual, mental; corpulence — thinness, slenderness; corpulent — gaunt, lanky, emaciated.

Interest earned on money in a savings account **accrues**; the amount that is earned is its **acCREtion** or accumulation. A club can have an accretion of rules and a person can have an accretion of pounds, but the more familiar **inCREase** and **inCREment** are usually preferable. On the other side of that coin are **deCREase** and **deCREment**.

A **CREscendo** is a steady increase in loudness or force; although it is primarily used in music, the sound of rain on the roof or a bad bearing in a car motor can become **inCREasingly** louder. The new moon has the shape of a thin **CREscent**, then grows (waxes) into its full shape. Hence crescent also means growing, increasing.

When an additional **crew** of soldiers or workers is called into action, it increases the power or force already there. A **recruit** in the service is expected to grow into a regular; so is a **rookie** on a baseball team, which is thought to come from ''recruit.'' Many teachers urge their students to use **conCREte** rather than abstract and general ideas and words. It literally means ''to grow together,'' which is what the ingredients in concrete do when they are mixed. Students' ideas and thoughts invariably become more cogent, comprehensible, and cohesive when they go with the explicit, tangible, and specific.

*But not: crease [creaste, a ridge], a fold; create [creare, to make], to bring about; credit [credere, to believe], trust.

*Combining forms: ac-, to; con-, together; de-, from, away; in-, on; re-, again.

*Antonyms: accrue — dissipate, spend; accretion — loss, reduction; concrete — abstract, theoretical, vague, indefinite, intangible; crescent — diminishing, subsiding; decrease — escalate, burgeon; growth; increase — abridge, condense, dwindle, decline.

*CRESCERE,
to grow: CRE*

When we hear the word **CULPrit**, we usually think of a person who has been charged with or is guilty of a crime and is about to go on trial. In an odd twist, the poet Emily Dickinson saw it this way: ''Surgeons must be very careful / When they take the knife! / Underneath their fine incisions / Stirs the culprit — Life!''

Persons who are **CULPable** are at fault, deserving of blame, guilty of wrongdoing. Their attorneys' task is to try to **exCULPate** them, to prove them innocent, to clear their names, to exonerate them. A timely piece of **exCULPatory**

*CULPA, blame,
guilt: CULP*

evidence would be most helpful. Where are Dr. Watson and Paul Drake when they're needed?

To **inCULPate** people is to blame or incriminate them, but if they are blameless, free from guilt, and innocent, they are **inCULPable**!

The guilt and blame do not always lie with others. This from *The Missal*, a Roman Catholic prayer book: in Latin, "*Mea CULPA, mea culpa, mea maxima culpa*"; in English, "Through my fault, through my fault, through my most grievous fault." (Captain Olingar's mea culpa saved the lives of a half-dozen enlisted men.)

☛ *But not:* sculpture [*sculpere*, to carve], statuary.

☛ *Combining forms: ex-*, out; *in-*, in, not; *mea*, my.

☛ *Antonyms: culpable* — blameless, innocent, guiltless, impeccable; *exculpate* — indict, accuse, incriminate, blame, convict, charge; *inculpable* — guilty, iniquitous, nefarious, disingenuous, sullied, malicious, wicked.

CURRERE, to run: COUR, CUR

Almost all the words that have come down to us from *currere* retain in one or more senses the idea of running. This is obvious with **corsair**, the name of both a pirate of old and his fast ship as well as the U.S. Navy's World War II fighter plane. A **COURier** is a messenger usually on the run with important papers. When the poet Shelley wrote, "My **COURsers** are fed with lightning, / They drink of the whirlwind's stream," he was using another word for swift horses. A **corridor** is a hallway or passageway that runs from one place to another.

People who operate computers or word processors frequently make their **CURsors** run up, down, and sideways, and a student's **CURsory** stab at a homework assignment is hurried, hasty, and superficial and will be lucky to net a D-. When as children we step from printing our names with separate letters to **CURsive** writing, we learn to make our letters run or flow together.

There is a sense of "run" in **CURrency**, too, both as money (Where in the world did my paycheck go so fast?) and in its meaning of vogue, popularity, acceptance (We never believed his story despite the great currency it enjoyed at the time). As an adjective **CURrent** means present (We discuss current events on Fridays) and popular (It's the current rage), but as a noun it rings of "run." (The glider soared upward on the strong air current. The river's strong current ran the boy's canoe off its **COURse**.) An **underCURrent** is a suggestion, an atmosphere, a hint, a drift. (An undercurrent of unrest swept through the factory.)

The course that the boys were attempting to follow in their canoe was a path or channel or route; and so it is in Shakespeare's *A Midsummer Night's Dream* when Lysander says to Hermia, the woman he loves, "The course of true love never did run smooth."

A course is also a progression, an advancement, a way. (In the course of our conversation we learned that we were cousins.) In school it is a subject or a part of a **CURriculum** or course of study. It is a method, a mode, a procedure. Courses or activities that are not required in schools are called **extraCURricular**. (Your best course of action is to take on some extracurricular activities; that will look good on your record.) And in the wide world of sports it's the place where one plays golf and the oval on which racehorses run.

As a verb, course means to run, hurry, race, hasten, or sprint. (The blood of his seafaring ancestors coursed through his veins. The swift waters of the trout stream coursed over the huge boulders.)

Our word **coarse**, meaning rough, unrefined, vulgar, foul-mouthed, gross and the latter's slang counterpart, grody, came to us from the phrase **in course**. (I had hoped to graduate with honors, but I got my degree in course.) Hence, something taken or done in course is ordinary and, by extension, rough, unrefined, and, *violà*: coarse. To **coarsen** something is to make it rough. (You'll need to coarsen both surfaces before you attempt to glue them together.)

Prefixes play a major role in the rest of the words from *currere*. A **conCOURse** is many things: It is a meeting, a gathering, an assemblage, a confluence, a crowd, a throng. (A concourse of drivers rubbernecking an accident slowed the freeway traffic to a crawl.) It is the place where large crowds tend to gather. (Thousands of holiday travelers jammed into the concourse as they awaited their flights.) In some areas it is a driveway or boulevard or a place where racing or athletic events are held.

To **conCUR** is to be in agreement or accord, to coincide, correspond, go along with. (How convenient that his and her birthdays concur. Members of both groups concurred.) A **conCURrence** is an agreement, concord, unanimity, or meeting of the minds. (The two parties hoped to reach concurrence by the end of the day.) It also means a simultaneous incident, a happening of two or more things at the same time. (The concurrence of the carnival and the parade created a dilemma.) The adjective **conCURrent** has the same general meanings: harmonious, agreeing, and simultaneous, coexisting (The two movie reviews were concurrent. The concurrent concerts created a massive traffic jam.)

A **disCOURse** is a conversation, talk, colloquy, intercourse, or chat. (It was a good meeting; we enjoyed an intelligent and informative discourse.) It can also be a more formal lecture, speech, address, sermon, or even a harangue or diatribe; in writing it is an essay, dissertation, or treatise. (The article was a boring discourse on a subject none of us cared a hoot about.) **DisCURsive** and **exCURsive** have similar meanings: digressive, rambling, wandering, longwinded, maundering, prolix, circuitous, and fustian. (I don't care if she won the Nobel Prize! Her discursive/excursive style is too hard to follow!) So with **disCURsion** and **exCURsus**: they both mean digression. An **exCURsion**, however, is a wandering of a different kind; it is an expedition, tour, outing, cruise, trip, junket, or voyage.

InCUR means to bring on, to acquire, to fall into, to arouse, to incite. (I'll never understand how I incurred so many debts. The obstreperous child incurred the teacher's wrath.) An **inCURsion** is an invasion, attack, foray, raid, assault. (The rebellious troops made two incursions over the border.) **Inter-**

COURse is a discourse, conversation, exchange, colloquy, as well as copulation and fornication. (The coup d'état brought a halt to the intercourse between the two governments. Pregnancy is a result of sexual intercourse.)

When something **ocCURs**, it happens, takes place, comes about. (An eclipse will occur shortly after midnight.) It appears, turns up, develops. (Shortness of breath is likely to occur when one runs.) It suggests itself, enters one's mind. (Did it ever occur to you that I don't like that kind of music?) An **ocCURrence** is a happening, event, incident, experience, situation. (There was a strange occurrence that night that I will never forget.)

PreCURsors are forerunners, heralds, harbingers, predecessors, pioneers, warnings. (Checking out the lawnmower is Franks' precursor of spring.) Introductory and preliminary remarks are **preCURsory**.

Synonyms for **reCOURse** are resort, option, choice, means, remedy, and access. (We were thankful we had recourse to the courts.) When something **reCURs** it happens again, persists, returns. (If this kind of behavior recurs, you will be on report.) It also means to return to mind, to flash across one's memory. (Those bad old days frequently recur to me; their **reCURrence** is not very pleasant). If one has a **reCURrent** dream, it is one that is periodic, intermittent, cyclical, episodic, repetitive.

Succor is both a noun and a verb. It is help, relief, comfort, support, aid, a helping hand. (The paramedic gave succor to the accident victim.) It is to assist, help, relieve, sustain, minister to, nurse, protect, befriend. (The pastor was always there to succor people in need.)

☛ ***But not:*** *courage* [*cor*, heart], bravery; *court* [*cohors*, farmyard], judicial assembly; *currant* [ME raisins from Corinth, the name of the Greek port from which they came], small fruit; *curry* [OF *conreder*, to make ready], to groom, as a horse; *curry* [Tamil *kari*, sauce], a mixture of certain spices.

☛ ***Combining forms:*** *con-*, together; *dis-*, apart; *ex-*, out; *extra-*, beyond; *in-*, in; *inter-*, between; *oc-*, toward; *pre-*, before; *re-*, again; *suc-*, up.

☛ ***Antonyms:*** *coarse* — polite, suave, finished, polished, elegant; *concur* — object, differ, diverge, contend; *concurrent* — antithetical, contrasting, counter, contradictory; *course* — delay, slow; *current* — previous, past, former, outmoded, unfashionable, outré; *cursory* — detailed, thorough, painstaking, diligent; *discursive* — straightforward, focused, unambiguous; *excursive* — direct, to-the-point; *precursor* — follower, imitator, disciple, heir, successor; *recurrent* — singular, rare, unusual; *succor* — hinder, obstruct, harm, impede, thwart, frustrate.

D

DEXTerity is agility, aptitude, adroitness, skill, as opposed to maladroitness, ineptitude, and awkwardness. And so a **DEXTerous** (also **dextrous**) person is clever, agile, resourceful, and gifted rather than inept, bumbling, and gauche.

Gauche? It is a French word meaning left, as in left-handed; a gaucherie, then, is an awkward movement, a tactless remark. A sinister act is an evil one, and the Latin *sinister* means to the left hand or side, hence it also means unlucky, unfavorable, disastrous. A person who is **DEXTrosinistral** is left-handed (sinistral) but has trained the right hand for writing. Consider the bumper sticker: ''Lefties have rights, too!''

An **ambiDEXTrous** baseball pitcher, of which there are few, can throw with either hand. (We know you're ambidextrous, Jenny, but please, just one hand when eating.) **DEXTrose** (from a chemical term meaning ''turning clockwise'') is used in foods and beverages, in making caramel, and in intravenous feeding; it is also called corn sugar and grape sugar.

Combining form: ambi- both.

A **DIary** is the record of one's day. **Per DIem** means ''by the day,'' which is how some employees are paid. In earlier times a **DIet** was an assembly or court that had to be within a day's journey of its people. Today the national legislatures of Denmark, Germany, Japan, and Paraguay are called diets. **Quoti-DIan** means everyday and, from there, ordinary.

The **meriDIan** of one's career is its high point, just as the sun's meridian is at midday. A.M. and P.M. stand for *ante* and *post* **meriDIem**, the ''before'' and ''after'' of the sun's — and the day's — midpoint. The position of the sun's shadow may have been people's first indicator or **DIal** of the time of day. Originaly it took an evil omen to turn one's day into a **DIsmal** one; today it's more likely to be something like a history test that we just plain forgot to study for.

Some people are nocturnal creatures, but most of humankind operates on a **DIurnal** or daytime schedule. It is that word that somewhere along the family line changed into the form that gives us **adJOURN** (quit for the day), **JOURNal** (a daily record), **JOURNey** (as far as one could go in one day), **soJOURN** (a temporary stay), and a steaming bowl of clam chowder, the soup **du jour** (of the day). A **JOURNeyman** is a person who has served an apprenticeship, and **JOURNeywork** denotes routine tasks. Newspapers (many of which go by the name *Journal* for obvious reasons) are staffed by **JOURNalists** who were lectured in **JOURNalism** school about the pitfalls of employing the cliché-packed writing style that is called **JOURNalese. Bonjour!**

But not: day [AS *daeg*]; *diet* [Gk *diaita*, way of living], food and drink.

*DEXTER,
on the right,
skillful; DEXT*

*DIES, day:
DI, JOURN*

☛   *Combining forms: ad-*, to; *ante-*, before; *-mal*, bad, evil; *meri-*, mid; *post-*, after; *quot-*, how many; *so-*, under.

☛   *Antonyms: dismal* — cheerful, pleasing; *diurnal* — nightly; *meridian* — depths, nadir, the pits.

DIGNITAS,
worth: **DIGN**

One gloomy day (in May, they say) a **DIGNitary** in our little town became very angry as a result of an incident that none of us was witness to. This usually **DIGNified** person was **inDIGNant**, irate, provoked, and incensed. It might be said that he reeked of **inDIGNation**, disgust, rage, and ire. We did not know if it was an intentional **inDIGNity**, insult, outrage, or affront, but on purpose or not, an acquaintance had caused him to act in a most **unDIGNified**, crass, vulgar, and lowly manner. When we finally approached him and tried to get the two antagonists to end their quarreling, he turned on us and said, ''I will never **deign** to speak to that [expletive deleted] again! Never stoop! Never condescend! Never consent! Never see fit! So there!

''I have nothing but **disdain** — scorn, contempt, abhorrence, and disrespect for a man like that! He caused me to lose my **DIGNity**, my very self-possession, my station, my demeanor, my self-respect, and I shall never **DIGNify** nor honor nor raise nor elevate him by so much as a glance in his direction again, so help me God!'' With that, he took a **dainty** little handkerchief from the breast pocket of his suitcoat and wiped at his eyes. His fellow townsfolk sentenced him to be silent for one entire week. Even he accepted this punishment as being quite **conDIGN**. ''It is appropriate, fitting, suitable, and deserved,'' were his last words.

☛   *But not: indigent*, [*indu*, in + *egere*, to need], poor.

☛   *Combining forms: con-*, thoroughly; *dis-*, away; *-fy*, to make; *in-*, not; *un-*, not.

☛   *Antonyms: dignified* — humble, unimposing, informal; *dignify* — humiliate, demean, degrade, abase; *dignitary* — nobody, common person, cipher, nonentity, unperson; *dignity* — disrepute, ignobility, self-abasement, self-disgust; *disdain* — respect, admire, like; admiration, reverence, regard; *indignant* — calm, tranquil, composed, pleased, delighted.

DROMEIN
[Gk], to run:
DROME

If during World War I you had been an English Royal Air Force pilot revving up a Sopworth Camel to engage a German Fokker Eindecker in aerial combat (Charlie Brown's dog Snoopy flies a Sopworth on occasion), chances are it would have been at an **aeroDROME**, the British version of our **airDROME**, a word that has been largely superseded by ''landing field'' and, later, ''airport.''

There were a few **hippoDROMES** in various places today, usually arenas where horse shows are held. In ancient Greece and Rome those were the structures such as the Colosseum, where chariot and other forms of horse racing were held. A race track in Athens or thereabouts was called a *dromos*. The one-humped camel, native to Arabia and northern Africa and known as a

DROMEdary, was once bred for riding and racing. (There is also a double-humped camel, the Asian Bactrian, but it is an endangered species today.)

ProDROME comes to us from medicine and means a sign or symptom of an oncoming disease; a **synDROME** is a group of symptoms that are characteristic of a specific disease or disorder. Meanings of that word, however, have spread out like ripples on a pond until today we have a whole passel of them, such as the ''retirement syndrome'' of golf and bridge games, the ''empty-nest syndrome'' that writer Barbara Ehrenreich says may occur when one's children have left home, and the ''middle-age syndrome'' that is not uncommon to men and women who suffer from anxiety when they suddenly come to feel that their youth has slipped away from them.

The **palinDROME** — a word, phrase, or sentence that reads the same forward and backward — dates back some four hundred years, which is a pretty long run for a word game, although the anagram (rearrange the letters in ''post'' and you get ''opts,'' ''pots,'' ''tops,'' ''spot,'' and ''stop'') has an even longer history. ''Did,'' ''mam,'' and ''noon'' are **palindromic** starters, a step below ''live-evil,'' ''Madam, I'm Adam,'' and ''Poor Dan is in a droop.'' Napoleon's lament regarding his exile to the island of Elba is the subject of this one: ''Able was I ere I saw Elba,'' and the last is in tribute to G.W. Goethals, the engineer of the Panama Canal: ''A man, a plan, a canal — Panama.''

Willard Espy, America's premier wordsmith, offers the ''semordnilap'' (''palindromes'' spelled backward), meaning a word that spells a different word when shifted into reverse, such as ''warts'' (straw), ''repaid'' (diaper), and ''spot'' (tops). In the meantime, over in England, Gyles Brandreth presents what he calls **pseudoDROMEs**, sentences in which the words rather than the letters read the same forward and backward: ''So patient a doctor to doctor a patient so,'' and ''Girl, bathing on Bikini, eyeing boy, finds boy eyeing bikini on bathing girl.''

But not: drone [AS *dran*, a non-working bee], to speak in a dull, monotonous tone; a lazy person.

Combining forms: hippo-, horse; *palin-*, again; *pro-*, before; *pseudo-*, false; *syn-*, together.

EDERE, to eat

Comestible, edible, and **esculent** are synonyms meaning fit to be eaten and derive from *edere*. **Escarole** is a broad-leaved salad green that is twin to endive, which is, in turn, the alter ego of Belgian endive, French endive, and witloof [Dutch, *wit*, white + *loof*, leaf]. It should not be mistaken for **escargot**, an edible snail flavored with seasoned butter and baked in its shell.

A person with an **edacious** appetite, which is about the same thing as having a ravenous, gluttonous, voracious, hoggish, and crapulous one, is likely to put on excess weight if the rest of his or her energy supply isn't channeled into physical activities. Becoming **obese** is synonymous with becoming corpulent, porky, rotund, fleshy, or fat. **Obesity** is a condition that apparently doesn't faze everyone, not Bill Cosby's Fat Albert, and certainly not two French kings of an earlier era: Charles II the Fat and Louis VI the Fat. History does not record whether they also developed blackheads or **comedos**, a word stemming from a Latin form of **edere** meaning glutton.

☞ ***But not:*** *comedy* [Gk *komoidos*, comedian + *aoidos*, singer]; *succulent* [*succus*, juice], juicy.

☞ ***Combining forms:*** *com-*, thoroughly; *ob-*, completely.

☞ ***Antonyms:*** *edible* — dangerous, indigestible, poisonous, inedible; *obese* — gaunt, underweight, lean, emaciated, scrawny, angular, spare.

EIKON [Gk],
image, likeness:
ICON

An **ICON** (also **ikon**) is an image, often of a Christian saint, Jesus, or Mary. An **ICONoclast** was originally one who literally broke up such images or statues, but today the word refers to anyone who attacks cherished beliefs or attitudes with words. (The instructor's **ICONoclastic** article attacking the basic philosophy of this college is the talk of the campus.) **ICONoclasm** is the action or the spirit of those who attack traditions or beliefs that they think are based on error or superstition. (''Rough work, iconoclasm — but the only way to get at truth,'' Oliver Wendell Holmes, Sr.)

ICONolatry is the worship of icons, and **ICONology** is the study and analysis of icons, images, and symbols.

☞ ***Combining forms:*** *-clast*, to break; *-olatry*, worship; *-ology*, body of knowledge.

EUS [Gk],
good, well: EU

EUphemisms are words that ''sound'' better, not to the ear, but to one's sensibilities. Because we are sometimes embarrassed by references to body parts, we put a ''drumstick'' on Sissy's plate and some ''white meat'' on Grandma's. Ladies excuse themselves to go to the powder room, men look for ''Gentlemen'' on the door, and when traveling with the kids, we are ever alert for signs reading ''Rest Stop,'' ''Restrooms,'' or ''Comfort Station.'' Taxes have become revenue enhancements, a place where one learns to cut and style hair and give manicures has been upgraded to a College of Cosmetology, and a few decades ago "unmentionables" was used as a cover, so to speak, for those undergarments that nice people don't mention.

EUphoria is a feeling of relaxation and well-being, or, as Robert Browning put it in "Pippa Passes," "God's in his heaven, / All's right with the world." **EU**phonious sounds are sweet and mellow, like church bells in the distance and the cooing of a mourning dove. Hence a **EU**phonia is a small tanager with yellow and black feathers and a pleasing song, and a **EU**phonium is a musical instrument similar to the tuba but with a more mellow tone. **EU**phony means agreeable sound, but when one hears it as "You phony!" the impact is quite different.

EUlogies are standard fare at funerals, ceremonies at which we can indulge in high praise without being contradicted or questioned. To **EU**logize someone on less solemn occasions often seems awkward. Language that is **EU**phuistic is affected and ornate and no longer read by anyone.

EUgenics is the controversial science of improving the health and strength of human begins through heredity and breeding; Adolf Hitler, the dictator of Nazi Germany, considered it his mission to help perpetuate a "master race" through eugenics and selective breeding. **EU**thenics is the science of bettering the human condition through the improvement of the environment.

The **EU**charist is the sacrament of Holy Communion in the Christian church. **EU**thanasia refers to mercy killing, painless death, but it is often pronounced as though it referred to the young people of the largest continent. **EU**nice, a girl's name, means good victory, and **EU**gene, a boy's name, means wellborn.

*But not: eunuch [Gk *eune*, bed + *echein*, to guard], castrated man; *eureka* [Gk *heureka*, "I have found (it)!"], expression of triumph at a discovery; *utopia* [Gk *ou-* not + *top(os)*, a place], the perfect place, from Sir Thomas More's book.

*Combining forms: -charist, to show favor; *-genics*, born; *-log*, to speak; *-phemism*, to speak; *-phony*, sound; *-phoria*, to bear; *-phuism*, grown; *-thanasia*, death; *-thenics*, to thrive.

*Antonyms: eulogize — criticize, condemn, disparage, censure; *eulogy* — condemnation, rebuke, denunciation, disapproval, vilification, aspersion; *euphonious* — cacophonous, raucous, grating, harsh, jarring, hoarse; *euphony* — cacophony.

F

FACERE,
to make, do:
FAC, FACE

A line in T.S. Eliot's "The Love Song of J. Alfred Prufrock" illustrates more than one meaning of **FACE**: "There will be time to / Prepare a face to meet the faces that you meet." It is one's visage or countenance; it is also a look or **FACial** expression that we design and fashion to suit the occasion. When we attempt to save face, we try to protect our reputation or self-respect.

In the following example it means to confront: "When I backed Mother's new car into the gate, I didn't have the nerve to face her. I wanted to disappear into a **FACEless** crowd." Something **ineffFACEable** is indelible. (The man's ineffaceable liability is his dishonesty.)

To **deFACE** the **surFACE** of an object is to disfigure or mar it. To **efFACE** an unhappy memory is to eradicate or obliterate it.

An ombudsman in government, a corporation, or a university serves as an intermediary or **interFACE**. (Troutsen will attempt to interface between the students and certain members of the **FACulty**. Faculty also means skill, capacity, knack, talent, penchant, flair. (Natalie has a faculty for putting folks at ease.) It refers to one's functions and powers. (The accident destroyed her faculty of speech. We were pleased that at her advanced age the landlady was still in possession of her **FACulties**.)

A **FACade** is a front or a mask. (Jeremy always puts up a facade of innocence.) **FACing** is decorative trim on such things as clothing or walls. A **FACsimile** is something "made similar," such as a copy, reproduction, xerox, photostat, duplicate, replica, or likeness. From facsimile comes **fax**, a way of transmitting copies of documents electronically.

Someone who is **FACile** might be skillful or fluent or superficial. Or, possibly, all three: "The artisan, extremely facile with his hands, spoke facile English, but because of his facile defense of his outrageously high prices, we walked away."

The **FACets** of a diamond are the small cut surfaces. A facet of one's character (or personality or conduct or argument or philosophy) might be a part (or phase or side or aspect or angle or perspective). (Ann's upbeat attitude is one of the finer facets of her personality.)

FACility is a word that has a wide range of meanings: dexterity and proficiency (Tonya speaks German with enough facility to get around); ease and effortlessness (These machines will provide us with far greater facility in our packaging procedure; in fact, they will **FACilitate** our entire mailing operation); buildings and conveniences (Their new house has every modern facility imaginable). And lest we forget: restrooms. (We drove for more than a hundred miles before we happened upon public facilities.)

☛ ***But not:*** *facetious* [*facetia,* humorous, witty], humorous; *preface* [*pre-,* before + *fari,* to speak], introductory statement.

*Combining forms: de-, undoing; ef-, out; inter-, between; -simile, similar; sur-, above.

*Antonyms: face — back off, avoid; facile — arduous, complex, difficult, clumsy, plodding; facilitate — complicate, hinder; facility — ineptness, rigidity, difficulty, hardship; facsimile — original; faculty — inability, incapacity.

A **FACT** is reality, truth, deed, occurrence, happening, verity. And that's a fact. **FACT**ual accounts are authentic, matter-of-fact, actual, scrupulous, and unembroidered. A **FACT**itious action or object is the opposite: artificial, contrived, spurious, synthetic, unnatural. (Mr. Blasingame's factitious sympathy annoyed us. Jean detests factitious floral decorations; for one thing, she says they cheat her **olFACT**ory senses, being without fragrance.) A **FACT**oid is a false or made-up statement presented as a fact, often to gain publicity. (The press agent's factoids didn't fool the newspaper reporters.)

A **FACT**ion is a group, a sect, a bloc, often one that splinters or breaks off from the larger body, sometimes in conflict and disagreement. Those who break away are charged with being **FACT**ious, divisive, contentious, and rebellious and promoting **FACT**ionalism and selfish interests. The noun form of the verb satisfy, to please, fulfill, convince, is satis**FACT**ion. (Note: -fy is also from facere; see page 54.)

A **FACT**or is a consideration or an element. (Many factors led to Janine's leaving home.) In math it is a divisor. In business it may be a person who acts for another as an agent. (Uncle Bert is a factor for a company that manu**FACT**ures lawn mowers; he is their leading agent and yet has never visited the **FACT**ory. He recently dropped his line of coffee mugs, key chains, and other such arti**FACT**s.)

Lawn mowers and coffee mugs are manufactured; excuses and apologies and explanations and alibis also may be fabricated, invented, concocted, and cooked up. The factory in such cases is an often fertile — but sometimes untruthful — brain.

Bene**FACT**ors and male**FACT**ors are opposites. The former is a helper, a patron, a donor, a supporter, or an angel, that is, a person who provides financial backing. The latter is an offender, a lawbreaker, a felon, a hoodlum, a scoundrel. **FACT**otums are most likely neither; most often they are solid, conscientious folk who as jacks-of-all-trades go about the business of tending to their many responsibilities.

An ex post **FACT**o law is one in which a person is punished for having done something that was not punishable by law when it was done. (My cousin was charged ex post facto with having smuggled a certain tropical plant into the country; she was finally able to prove that it happened before the plant was banned.)

*Combining forms: arti-, art; bene-, good, well; male-, bad, evil; manu-, hand; ol(ere)-, to smell.

FACERE, to make, do: FACT

☛ *Antonyms: fact* — fiction, invention, fancy, delusion, opinion, supposition; *factious* — neutral, independent, objective, uncommitted; *factitious* — natural, genuine, artless, real; *factual* — illusory, false, fictitious, fanciful, whimsical, imaginary, speculative; *manufacture* — demolish, destroy.

FACERE,
to make, do:
FEAS, FEAT

One's **FEATures** are one's qualities (Sharon has the delightful feature of being a good listener) or the elements of one's face (The huge brim on her hat obscured her fine features). A feature story in a magazine or newspaper is one that is given a prominent position; the feature film is the main one on a movie program; and the feature act at the circus is the main item, the special attraction, the drawing card, the highlight. As a verb, feature means to display prominently (The next act features Zelda Zoe) and to envision, to imagine. To **disFEATure** something is to deface or mar it.

In law **FEASance** means the performing of one's duty. **DeFEASance** is the voiding of a contract or deed. **MisFEASance** occurs when a lawful act is carried out in an unlawful manner. (The judge ruled that the officer's arrest for speeding of the man with whom he had hitchhiked a ride was misfeasance.) **MalFEASance** is malpractice, misbehavior, or misconduct, especially by a public official. A **FEASible** idea is one that is workable, practicable, and suitable.

Ignatz K. Sflick is a **deFEATist**, that is, a pessimist, sourpuss, wet blanket, Calamity Jane, gloomy Gus, quitter. All this because life has been one **deFEAT** after another for him. Checkmated, thwarted, frustrated, vanquished, and **deFEATed** have become the name of the game for him.

☛ *But not: feast* [*festus*, joyous], elaborate meal; *feather* [OE *fether*], type, kind, as in "two birds of a feather."

☛ *Combining forms: de-*, not; *dis-*, away; *mal-*, bad, evil; *mis-*, wrong.

☛ *Antonyms: defeat* — victory, triumph; *defeated* — triumphant, successful; *defeatist* — optimist, Pollyanna; *feasible* — impractical, unachievable.

FACERE,
to make, do:
FECT

AfFECT is a verb with several different meanings. To change (Is the rain going to affect our plans?), to move (His sad plight affected all of us), to fake or feign (Two days in London and Martha affects a British accent! Now that's an **afFECTation**!).

EfFECT is both a noun and a verb. As a noun it means outcome, result (The town felt the effect of the flood for months); force, cloud (My pleading to use the car had no effect on Mom); operation, action (The new rules go into effect immediately); possessions (The court ordered all his personal effects confiscated). As a verb it means to bring about. (Her rabbi's lecture effected a complete change in Kathi's attitude.)

The adjective **afFECTed** means touched (Eve was deeply affected by her friends' generosity); conceited, phony (They're so affected you can't even talk to them). An **unafFECTed** person is sincere, genuine, and without **afFECTations**. **AfFECTing** means heartrending, poignant. (It was a surprisingly affecting movie; four out of five on the Kleenex scale.) An **afFECTionate** person is filled with love or **afFECTion**; oddly enough, the latter also means sickness, disease. (The heavy smoker suffered from a pulmonary affection.) Its plural form means feelings. (She was simply toying with his affections.)

To **disafFECT** others is to alienate them. (The new office manager lost no time in disaffecting all of us.) The **disafFECTed** are alienated, discontented. (There was no way the governor would get the support of that large bloc of disaffected voters.)

The **deFECT** group suffers from the same malady. One who defects is a **deFECTor**, a deserter from the ranks, and **deFECTions** are not usually taken lightly. A defect is a fault, blemish, failing, peccadillo, and **deFECTive** products are not reliable or worth one's while. Who'd ever read a mystery story entitled "Filbert Flaw, Defective Detective"?

EfFECTive and **efFECTual** are generally interchangeable, both meaning "adequate, useful, forceful," ("Learning, I knew, would be the most effective weapon against the coming years," Gordon Parks, *A Choice of Weapons*). Both become negatives when the prefix "*in-*" is affixed. **EfFECTuate** means "to bring about," (We "strove to effectuate a settlement not by force but by reason," Franklin D. Roosevelt.)

InFECT, inFECTion, and **inFECTious** are relatively negative terms. The flu bug contaminates its prey, as our bad moods or angry words tend to infect or leave a mark on those around us. Infections and infectious ailments are bad news; we try to avoid them. There is, however, a glimmer of light here: laughter can be infectious, too, as it catches others in its net.

PerFECTion may be the ideal state, but that does not mean it is always easy to live with. In the movie *The Odd Couple* there was a **perFECT** contrast between roommates Felix, the **perFECTionist**, and Oscar, the **perFECTly** dreadful slob who would sooner flick the ashes from his **perFECTo** onto the rug than into a handy ashtray. Eventually they split; Oscar was totally **imperFECTible**, and his **imperFECTions** were far too numerous for Felix to bear. Oscar the Oaf and Felix the Finicky made for an **imperFECT** union.

In English grammar the past perfect tense of a verb is also called the **pluperFECT** tense; it is the "had" in "She had left by the time I got home." But it also has a broader meaning: "more than perfect." Columnist Mary McGrory, in describing a scene in an airplane: "The man in seat 66 has been a pluperfect jerk, giving the stewardess a hard time from takeoff to landing."

A **conFECTion** is a sweet preserve or candy sold by a **conFECTioner** in a tidy little **conFECTionery** in a corner of the mall.

The dining hall in some colleges and monasteries is called a **reFECTory**. It is a place where **reFECTions** are served; they are usually light refreshments, with perhaps a confection for dessert.

If the refectory is in a Jesuit college, the dean or **preFECT** might be at the table, and if the college is in France, a chief civil officer of that **preFECTure** or district might be there, too. In this country some private secondary schools refer to their student leaders as prefects.

☛ *Combining forms: af-, to; con-, together; de-, not; dis-, away; ef-, out; im-, not; in-, in, not; pre-, thoroughly; plu-, plus; pre-, before; re-, again; un-, not.

☛ *Antonyms: affectation — sincerity, the real thing, spontaneity; affected — natural, sincere; affection — coolness, antipathy; affectionate — uncaring, distant; defection — loyalty, fealty, allegiance; defective — intact, functional, whole, normal; disaffected — compliant, cooperative; effective — weak, impotent, negligible, inconsequential; imperfect — flawless, ideal; ineffective — capable, effectual; perfect — flawed, inept, inaccurate.

FACERE,
to make, do:
FEIT, FIT

A **comFIT** is a confection, but to **discomFIT** others is to embarrass or upset or frustrate them; they thus suffer the pangs of **discomFITure**.

To **proFIT** from something is to gain from it, be it greenbacks or experience. A profit is a gain, but when that amount becomes excessive, a **surFEIT** results, and charges of "**ProFITeer!**" can be heard. The moral of our story is that people do not always **beneFIT** from **proFITable** financial transactions. Sometimes the one whose schemes create outrageous paybacks is forced to **forFEIT** not only the excess $$$, but perhaps a few years of freedom as well. Today's **counterFEITers**, when caught, suffer that fate, making it a most **unproFITable** venture. There was a time in the distant past when a counterfeit was a close likeness or portrait of someone. (Lady Nell is having her counterfeit painted by Von Sist.)

Organizations engaged in civic or charitable endeavors are usually classified as **nonproFIT**, but because the word is often used facetiously ("Of course, I'm running a nonprofit business here," Phig Knewton said. "I haven't made a nickel since I first opened the doors!"), many people prefer the term "not for profit." It's more joke-proof.

☛ *But not: fit [AS fitt, struggle], spasm, tantrum; fit [ME fitten], appropriate, healthy.

☛ *Combining forms: bene-, good, well; com-, together; counter-, against; dis-, apart, away; for-, outside; non-, not; pro-, forward; sur-, above.

☛ *Antonyms: benefit — loss, detriment; hinder, undermine; counterfeit — genuine, authentic, bona fide, honest, open; discomfit — support, expedite, encourage; profit — drawback, disadvantage; retard, handicap; surfeit — dearth, fast.

FACERE,
to make, do:
FIC, FICE

An enthusiastic fan of bullfighting in Spanish-speaking countries is called an **aFICionado** [a-, to]; its use has broadened over the years, and it now means any enthusiast. (James is an aficionado of murder mysteries.) **DeFICient** means lacking something [de-, away]. (I'll prove I'm not deficient in stamina!) A **deFICiency** is a flaw or inadequacy. (Medication controls iron deficiency anemia.) A **deFICit** is a shortage. (My allowance is a deficit). A **difFICult** reading assignment can be arduous, demanding, and tough sledding; a difficult math problem can be perplexing, enigmatic, and intricate; a difficult new kid on the block can be ill-behaved, intractable, and obstinate, [*dif-*, not]. A **difFICulty** is a problem, obstacle, tribulation, hardship, pitfall, contretemps); in the 6th century B.C. the Chinese philosopher Lao-tzu said, "He who accounts all things easy will have many difficulties."

An **efFICient** person is capable. (Vinny's a very efficient office manager.) An **efFICiency** is a small apartment (They lived in an efficiency before their baby was born); it is also a measure of the effectiveness of an operation (The plan proceeded with great speed and efficiency). Something that is **efFICacious** can be efficient, productive, or useful. (I doubt that the new law will prove to be very efficacious). A **proFICient** business person is adept, expert and skillful, one who displays **proFICiency**, competence, and expertise. A **sufFICient** amount of food is enough; not enough is an **insufFICiency**. To **sufFICe** means to satisfy, to fill the bill. (Just a simple "thank you" will suffice.)

An **artiFICE** is a trick or deception. **ArtiFICial** objects are human-made, synthetic, or spurious, and an artificial smile is insincere, forced, or feigned. A **beneFICiary** is one who receives something, such as money from a will or trust fund. An **ediFICE** is a building, a place where one might find **ofFICEs, ofFICErs, ofFICials**, and, alas, a few **ofFICious** fellow workers, the nosy, obtrusive, meddlesome kind. An **oriFICE** is an opening, aperture, vent, pore, mouth, hole, lacuna, fistula.

An **honoriFIC** is a title that is given to one out of appreciation. ("Doc" Sherman never went beyond high school; that's an **unofFICial** honorific we gave him years ago. I guess it was because he's such a **feliciFIC** fellow, always bringing about happiness in others.)

A **superFICial** person is one who is shallow, frivolous, myopic; a superficial cut is one that is only skin-deep. **ProliFIC** means fertile, productive, fruitful. (Rabbits are prolific breeders. Georges Simenon was a prolific writer of detective novels: he wrote over three hundred.)

A teacher who **pontiFICates**, always lecturing and sermonizing, is often **pontiFICal**, talking down to young people and droning on in such a **soporiFIC** tone and manner that almost everyone goes to sleep. Sometimes even the speaker.

But not: *fictitious* [*fingere*, to touch], imaginary, fanciful; *traffic* [*trans-*, across + *figere*, to fasten], commerce, trade, movement of vehicles.

Combining forms: *a-*, to; *arti-*, art; *bene-*, good, well; *de-*, away; *dif-*, not; *edi-*, building; *ef-*, out; *felici-*, happy; *honori-*, honor; *in-*, not; *of-*, work; *ori-*, mouth; *ponti-*, bridge; *pro-*, forward; *proli-*, offspring; *sopori-*, sleep; *suf-*, under; *super-*, over; *un-*, not.

Antonyms: *artifice* — honesty, candor; *deficient* — enough, plentiful; normal; *deficiency* — excess, glut, plethora; *deficit* — surplus; *difficult* — docile, obvious, tractable; *difficulty* — ease; *efficacious* — impotent, useless; *efficiency* — incompetency; *efficient* — unproductive, slipshod; *insufficient* — ample, adequate;

officious — aloof, indifferent, reticent; *proficient* — clumsy, inept; *prolific* — barren, sterile, jejune; *soporific* — exciting, stimulating; *suffice* — disappoint, fall short; *sufficient* — meager, scanty; *superficial* — complex, internal, authentic, thoughtful.

FACERE,
to make, do:
FICATION, FY

-Fication is a combining form of nouns ending in the suffix *-fy*. The following is a partial list:

ampliFY [*amplus*, wide], enlarge, increase: **ampliFICATION**
beatiFY [*beatus*, happy], make blissfully happy: **beautiFICATION**
beautiFY [*bellus*, beautiful], adorn, bedeck, decorate: **beautiFICATION**
certiFY [*certus*, certain], vouch for, guarantee: **certiFICATION**
clariFY [*clarus*, clear], explain, elucidate, explicate: **clariFICATION**
classiFY [*classis*, class], arrange, group: **classiFICATION**
deiFY [*deus*, a god], worship, idealize, glorify: **deiFICATION**
diversiFY [*vertere*, to turn], branch out, variegate: **diversiFICATION**
ediFY [*aedes*, a building], educate, enlighten, instruct: **ediFICATION**
electriFY [*electrum*, amber], amaze, excite, astound: **electriFICATION**
exempliFY [*emere*, to buy], illustrate, epitomize: **exempliFICATION**
fructiFY [*fructus*, fruit], become fruitful, fertilize: **fructiFICATION**
gloriFY [*gloria*, glory], praise, bless, deify: **gloriFICATION**
gratiFY [*gratus*, pleasing], please, coddle, gladden: **gratiFICATION**
identiFY [*idem*, the same], recognize, specify: **identiFICATION**
intensiFY [*tendere*, to stretch], emphasize, exacerbate: **intensiFICATION**
justiFY [*justus*, just], clear, excuse, warrant: **justiFICATION**
liqueFY [*liquere*, to become liquid], melt, thaw: **liqueFICATION**
magniFY [*magnus*, great], expand, exaggerate, embellish: **magniFICATION**
modiFY [*modus*, measure], alter, change, revise: **modiFICATION**
molliFY [*mollis*, soft], calm, appease, mitigate: **molliFICATION**
mortiFY [*mors*, death], humiliate, embarrass, chagrin: **mortiFICATION**
mystiFY [*mysterium*, mystery], perplex, confuse, nonplus: **mystiFICATION**
notiFY [*notus*, known], inform, tell: **notiFICATION**
mulliFY [*nullus*, none], cancel, annul, abrogate: **nulliFICATION**
ossiFY [*os*, bone], turn into bone, become rigid in habits: **ossiFICATION**
paciFY [*pax*, peace], appease, mollify, assuage: **paciFICATION**
personiFY [*persona*, mask], imitate, exemplify, typify: **personiFICATION**
petriFY [*petra*, a rock], daze, stun, dumbfound: **petriFICATION**
qualiFY [*qualis*, of what], prepare, moderate, name: **qualiFICATION**
ratiFY [*ratus*, fixed], approve, uphold, certify: **ratiFICATION**
rectiFY [*regere*, to lead], correct, amend, remedy: **rectiFICATION**
sanctiFY [*sanctus*, holy], exalt, glorify, deify: **santiFICATION**
simpliFY [*simplex*, simple], streamline, unscramble: **simpliFICATION**
stultiFY [*stultus*, foolish], frustrate, hinder, stifle: **stultiFICATION**
uniFY [*unus*, one], fuse, consolidate, coalesce: **uniFICATION**
veriFY [*verus*, true], confirm, check out, examine: **veriFICATION**

viliFY [*vilis*, cheap], libel, slander, calumniate: **viliFICATION**
viviFY [*vivre*, to live], animate, enliven, quicken: **viviFICATION**

*Once aPUN a time on a camping trip the scoutmaster said as he looked at the darkening sky, "Tonight everyone's sleeping *intensify* am reading those clouds correctly." As they sat in the main tent, one of the scouts said, "Math is one course I'm going to *pacify* have to take an apple to the teacher everyday." Another said, "Well, I'm going to be on time for English *classify* have to run in the halls." "Last week," the third scout said, "I was going to sneak out of school, but heck, I knew I'd be *mystify* did, and that would be trouble."

*But not: *crucify* [*cruci-*, cross + *figere*, to fix, fasten], persecute, torment; *salsify* [It *sassefrica*], vegetable sometimes called oyster plant; *sniffy, snuffy,* and *stuffy,* plus other words that add only a "y" such as *beefy, goofy,* and *leafy.*

*Antonyms: *beautify* — mar, distort, uglify; *clarify* — obscure, obfuscate; *deify* — profane, condemn, desecrate, execrate; *glorify* — mock, revile, blaspheme; *intensify* — diminish, weaken, lessen, abate; *liquefy* — harden, solidify, congeal; *magnify* — minimize, minify, reduce, belittle; *mortify* — extol, praise, uplift, laud; *mystify* — clarify, illuminate, edify, enlighten; *nullify* — validate, uphold, enforce; *ossify* — relax, be at ease; *pacify* — arouse, agitate, ruffle, perturb; *qualify* — disable, incapacitate, modify; *ratify* — veto, oppose, repudiate; *stultify* — expedite, foster, promote; *unify* — separate, divide, alienate; *vilify* — commend, eulogize, acclaim; *vivify* — dampen, dull, depress.

**FACERE,
to make, do**

The following document was reportedly discovered some years ago in a tomb that was unearthed in a remote English cemetery; on the tombstone were only these words "The Last Facere." The ink was badly faded, but this much could be made out: "My final group of words not only has no common base form, but all attempts to find a single letter common to all twelve words have been **feckless**. Rather than a group, they are like so many pieces of **confetti**! What a sorry **affair**! It sorely **chafes** me, for I like to get a handle on words. It's impossible to **fashion** any kind of system with these. When I journeyed from our most **unfashionable** hovel up to the magnificent **hacienda** in which my tutor, Lord Makedo and his elegantly **fashionable** Lady Audrey reside, all he said was, 'My lad, trying to put all one's vocabulary **affairs** into a tidy bundle is admirable, and, as you are no doubt aware, we favor a **laissez faire** atmosphere here at Pembrokeshire, meaning we let our people do as they choose, but one mustn't make a **fetish** of learning.' I wanted to tell him that it was not an obsession, but as a lowly commoner I knew I must keep my place. Perhaps I shall chance a call upon the local **pontiff**, as we are wont to call the bishop of our cathedral. But then again. . . ." The rest was, sad to say, illegible.

*But not: *chap* [ME *chappen*], to crack the skin; *fair* [AS *faeger*], pleasing, just; *fair* [*feria*, holiday], exhibition; *fettle* [ME *fetle*, to shape], shape.

☛ *Combining forms: -able, be capable of; af-, to; cha-, warm; con-, together; -less, without; laissez, let; pon-, bridge.

☛ *Antonyms: chafe — calm, placate, soothe; fashionable — passé, tacky, dowdy, obsolete; feckless — feasible, doable, viable, workable; laissez faire — interference, intervention, regimen, enforcement, regulated activity; unfashionable — smart, stylish, chic, modish.

FAMA, report:
FAM

"Yesterday, December 7, 1941," President Franklin Roosevelt said in a speech to Congress, "— a date that will live in **inFAMy** — the United States of America was suddenly and deliberately attacked by naval and air forces of the Empire of Japan." While the President chose infamy, he could have used any of these words instead: dishonor, disgrace, shame, villainy, evil, abomination, or opprobrium.

Had the president wanted an adjective to express his indignation and anger, he had **inFAMous** at his disposal as well as such synonyms as outrageous, dishonorable, disgraceful, ignoble, ignominious, perfidious, villainous, scandalous, abominable, and treacherous. Notorious would seem to have a place on that list, but if you consult a book of synonyms, you are likely to discover that the word has two opposite meanings, as in Webster's Collegiate Thesaurus: 1. "**FAMous**, popular"; 2. "infamous, **ill-FAMed**." So, when someone says, "Old Jake was a really notorious man," you might as well flip a coin, heads he was bad, tails he was good. Or vice versa.

Fortunately, none of the other words in this group leave any doubt about their meanings. A person who has achieved **FAMe** has gained popularity, public esteem, and celebrity. When one person **deFAMes** another, he libels, slanders, vilifies, traduces, and calumniates him. He may do this by making **deFAMatory** remarks, ones that are disparaging, denigrating, and derogatory. There is often the possibility of the victim threatening to sue for **deFAMation** of character.

☛ *But not: family [familia, a household], clan; famine [fames, hunger], starvation.

☛ *Combining forms: de-, undoing; in-, not.

☛ *Antonyms: defamatory — flattering, eulogistic; defame — compliment, applaud; fame — anonymity, obscurity; famous — obscure, humble; infamous — honorable; infamy — virtue, integrity.

FAMILIA,
a household:
FAMIL

In much of western Europe the word for **FAMILy** is easily recognized despite the language differences: in France. it's **FAMILle**; in Germany, **FAMILie**; in Italy, **famiglia**; in Spain, **FAMILia**; and in Sweden, **FAMILj**. They come in assorted sizes and types, from one's immediate family of adults and children to families of languages, nations, plants, animals, manufactured products, musical instruments, and what have you.

Some groups have close **FAMILial** ties and common traits, attributes, idiosyncrasies, diseases, and even atmospheres. (That small boarding school prides itself on its familial ambiance.)

Family members are usually **FAMILiar** with one another's pluses and minuses (if any). They develop a sense of **FAMILiarity**, sharing knowledge, experience, and know-how that help them deal with problems that arise. They **FAMILiarize** themselves with each other's habits and routines. (Before Lulu was ready for kindergarten, she had familiarized herself with her elders' nocturnal habits and knew exactly when she could raid the cookie jar.) Outsiders who are **unFAMILiar** with the in-jokes, peculiarities, and shtick of a family two doors away often concoct some very weird ideas about them.

*But not: famished [*fames*, hunger], extremely hungry.

*Combining forms: un-, not.

*Antonyms: familiar — distant, detached, aloof, indifferent, unversed, uninformed, new, unusual, infrequent, rare; *familiarity* — ignorance, inexperience, distance, reserve, formality, propriety, decorum, respect; *unfamiliar* — old, aware, usual, conversant, knowledgeable, run-of-the-mill, commonplace.

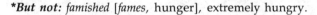

FARI, to speak:
FAB, FAN, FAT

The literal meaning of **inFANt** is "one not able to speak" [*in-*, not + *fant*, to speak]. One's **inFANcy** does not last long, however, and once some of us learn to talk, we never stop. A person who acts in a babyish manner is said to be **inFANtile**. An **inFANtryman** is a foot-soldier who, throughout history, has been young and inexperienced. **InFANticide** is the killing of babies, something that has happened often during humankind's many wars. When this occurs, people say it is **inefFABle**, that is, unspeakable, indescribable, awful beyond words.

A **FABle** is a myth, a legend, a yarn. Eons ago something that was **FABulous** was beyond description, almost impossible to be believed, but the word has lost much of its punch from overuse. "Gee," someone says today, "that's that most fabulous movie I've seen since last Tuesday." A **FABulist** is a maker-upper of fables; it is a polite synonym for a liar and a wise one to substitute when the person you are referring to is not truly **afFABable**, that is, friendly, easy-going, and amiable. When a sports reporter refers to the **FABled** Jim Thorpe or Jesse Owens, he means legendary and famous.

A **preface** is a piece of writing found at the beginning of a book; **preFATory** remarks are, therefore, similar to an introduction.

FATe is one's lot in life, one's destiny, outcome, kismet. It is sometimes referred to as "the fickle finger of fate." Who knows what will happen and when? "On the **FATeful** evening when Horrendyce K. Whitherfork noticed that the night was dark and stormy, he realized that he was **FATed** to be struck by lightning as he stood and watched an **ill-FATed** and blinding flash hit the steel rod he was holding over his head."

☛   *Once uPUN a time* a young farmer said to his neighbor, "I'd like to buy one of your bulls, Mr. Granger, but I've only got $200. What can I get for that much?" To which Mr. G. replied, "Affable."

☛   *But not:* fabricate [fabrica, craft], to make; fantasy [Gk phantasia, idea, image], dream, reverie; fatuous [fatuus, absurd], asinine, stupid.

☛   *Combining forms: af-*, to; *ef-*, out; *ill-*, bad, adverse; *in-*, not; *pre-*, before.

☛   *Antonyms: affable* — standoffish, cold, forbidding; *fabled* — ordinary, average, mediocre; *fabulous* — actual, factual, real, true; *infancy* — conclusion, termination, finish; *infantile* — developed, mature, adult; *preface* — epilogue, supplement, appendix, postscript; summarize, wind up; *prefatory* — concluding, terminating.

FERRE, to bear, bring, carry: FER

A is for **aquiFER**, an underground rock formation that supplies wells, springs, and other sources of our tap water.

C is for **conFER**, to bestow, consult, grant, advise, confabulate. (Not tonight, Cheslea; we'll confer in the morning.) A **conFERee** is one who attends a **conFERence** or on whom honors have been conferred. (Mother Teresa of Calcutta was the conferee of the Nobel Peace Prize in 1979). A **coniFERous** tree is cone-bearing; a deciduous tree bears leaves. (All the leaves from that oak will fall within the **circumFERence** of our yard!)

D is for **deFER**, to delay, put off, yield, acquiesce. (I'm sure little Eddie will defer to your judgment, Governor. He's not only a very considerate, **deFERential** youngster, but, too, out of **deFERence** for the fact that you're his father, you know.) A **deFERment** is a postponement.

D is also for **difFER** (to disagree) and **difFERence** (disagreement, distinction) and **difFERent** (extraordinary, dissimilar, *sui generis*). To be **indifFERent** is to be impartial, uninterested, mediocre, and insignificant, but, let us hope, not all at once; to **difFERentiate** is to understand the differences among those adjectives. The **difFERential** gear in a car enables one wheel to turn at a different rate than another. The difference between the cost of two comparable products is the differential. (I don't buy that brand; the price differential between it and this house brand is too great).

F is for **FERtile**, creative, productive, abundant. (Years of abuse had turned the once-fertile valley into a wasteland. Connat's fertile mind will come up with a new idea before long.) **FERtility** is fruitfulness. (Our constant composting of kitchen wastes and shredded leaves helps us maintain our garden's fertility. Without such **FERtilizing**, we'd end up with **inFERtile** and barren soil.)

I is for **inFER**, to deduce, conclude, suppose; obviously, an **inFERence** is a deduction, a conclusion, a supposition. Infer is often confused with *imply*. When Filfig says, "Hey, I saw you look over at my test paper," he is quite likely implying, insinuating, and hinting that you were cheating. The key point here is that we *imply* when *we* speak (or write); we *infer* from what *someone else* says (or writes or does). So, you now say, "Are you, perhance, implying

that I was trying to cop some answers off that sorry test paper you have up-
side down on your desk? If so, I can only infer that you are more of an idiot
than I thought.''

O is for **ofFER**. As a noun it is a proposal or bid; as a verb it is to put forward, tender, suggest, volunteer. (We made an offer for the car. I offered to
help at the library's book sale.) An **ofFERtory** is a collection at a religious service. **OfFERing** has that meaning, too, but it is also a contribution, donation,
or gift.

P is for **preFER**, to select, like, opt for, single out. The doggy in the window
that the little kid likes best is **preFERable** to the others; it is his **preFERence**
and will no doubt be given **preFERential** treatment until it chews up his baseball
glove.

P is also for **proliFERate**, to multiply, increase, overproduce. (Those who
introduced the rabbit into Australia apparently had no idea how rapidly they
would proliferate. The **proliFERation** of small businesses near the new stadium
shouldn't surprise anyone.)

R is for **reFER**, to turn to, pass on, associate with, attribute, cite. (Kindly
refer to my last letter. Dr. Key referred me to several books in the **reFERence**
room.) A **reFERent** is that which is referred to. (When she said, ''I love him,''
her referent, unfortunately, was Sliggly, not me.) A **reFERral** is an instance
of referring as well as a word for a person who has been recommended for
something. (Jon's referral as a transfer patient has finally been approved. Ninety
percent of the referrals to this office have found employment.) A **reFERen-
dum** is a popular vote on a measure such as a state lottery; if the results are
so close that they are disputed, a **reFERee** may have to be brought in to make
the call.

S is for **sufFER** as in ''Suffer the little children to come unto me,'' that is,
permit, let. It is also to ache and despair, to put up with and endure. Situa-
tions that are **sufFERable** are tolerable, bearable, and endurable. But those that
are not, as with certain salespersons, political candidates, and the neighbors'
children, are **insufFERable**. Oh, the **sufFERing** that they bring on, the pain, the
anguish, the woe! Note how in this passage from Shakespeare's *Measure for
Measure* one can substitute ''endurance'' for **sufFERance** without any great
loss: ''The poor beetle, that we tread upon, / In corporal sufferance finds a
pang as great / As when a giant dies.''

T is for **transFER**, to sign over, to consign, to deed, as well as the word for
a ticket used in changing from one public vehicle to another. (The folks hope
to transfer the title to the new owners tomorrow. This **transFERence** process
is usually one pain in the neck.)

V is for **vociFERate**. Only a noisy and boisterous person could rightly be
called **vociFERous**; only such a person would ever **vociferate**.

***But not:** ferocious [*ferox*, fierce], savage; *fervor* [*fervere*, to boil], zeal.

***Combining forms:** aqui-*, water; *circum-*, around; *con-*, together; *coni-*, cone;
de-, away; *dif-*, apart; *in-*, in, not; *of-*, to; *pre-*, before; *proli-*, offspring; *re-*, back;
suf-, up from under; *trans-*, across; *voci-*, voice.

☛ *Antonyms: defer* — advance, expedite, speed up; *deference* — impertinence, rudeness; *deferential* — insolent, boorish, uncouth; *differ* — correspond, cooperate; *difference* — similarity, accord, peace; *different* — unvaried, uniform; *differentiate* — homogenize, mix; *fertile* — sterile, impoverished; *indifferent* — concerned, avid, partisan, exceptional; *offer* — refusal; refuse; *prefer* — reject, demote, dislike; *preferable* — inferior, undesirable; *preference* — impartiality, fairness, evenhandedness; *suffer* — repudiate, eliminate, banish, oppose; *sufferance* — intolerance; *vociferous* — muted, silent, taciturn.

FIGERE,
to fasten: FIX

FIX is a word of many uses. Who's fixing dinner? Flats fixed here. Let's fix on a time to meet. How are we fixed for cash? I'm fixing to call them right now. This traffic ticket will fix his wagon.

We have light **FIXtures** in our houses, and at times even live people are looked upon as being kind of permanent. (Fred and Ginger Koss are regular fixtures at our high school games.) The seating at our assemblies is in a **FIXed** order; it never changes. **FIXings** (or *fixin's*) are the ingredients or extra dishes at mealtime. (Grandma'll have turkey and all the fixings.) A **FIXative** or **FIXer** is a substance or chemical used in the development of photographs and in preserving certain materials for study under a microscope. **FIX-it** shops are usually run by people who are good **FIXer-uppers**.

As a verb, **afFIX** means to attach, append. (The current inspection sticker has now been affixed to my windshield.) As a noun it means something attached or joined; hence a **preFIX** (*un*kind, *re*tire) is an affix placed before the base word and a **sufFIX** is one at the end (kind*ly*, retir*ing*). Titles such as Sergeant, Professor, and Mayor are also prefixes. To **inFIX** is to implant or fix something in the mind. (The coaches try to infix the concept of fair play in the athletes' minds.)

When we are **transFIXed**, we are frozen with amazement or awe. (We were transfixed by the daring spectacle of the tightrope walker.) A hunter using a bow and arrow, on the other hand, hopes to transfix his prey, that is, spike, skewer, or impale it. A **FIXation** is an idea that gets fixed in one's mind. Many people refer to it as a "fixed idea," but those who find foreign languages more impressive often prefer the French **idée FIXe**. Obsession, neurosis, complex, quirk, fetish, and even "thing" will also fit comfortably in place of "fixation" in the following sentence: "I'm afraid Auntie will never get over this *fixation* she's got about snakes.

A **cruciFIX** is a cross, with or without the figure of Jesus on it; it is also a gymnastics stunt. The **CruciFIXion** refers to that of Jesus or a picture of it; without the capital "C" it means persecution. The literal meaning of **crucify** is "to put to death on a cross." Its more general meaning (thankfully) is to persecute or torment, or just annoy, tease, or harass someone. (I hear Rex got crucified for blowing the whistle on the kids who cheated.)

☛ *Combining forms: af-*, to; *cruci-*, cross; *in-*, in; *pre-*, before; *suf-*, under; *trans-*, through.

Antonyms: affix — detach, remove, unfasten; *crucify* — soothe, console, assuage; *fix* — loosen, undo, break, damage; *fixed* — mobile, wavering, pliant, varying; *transfix* — bore, weary.

"Help Wanted: **ReFLECTive** [thoughtful] young person to join small group of **FLEXible** [versatile, responsive] pioneers in the founding of an innovative organization that will **reFLECT** [mirror] the vibrant spirit of our community. Must be able to **deFLECT** [turn aside, ward off] the negative objections that will come from the **inFLEXible** [hidebound, obstinate] naysayers who insist on standing in the way of progress. Because of such opposition, applicant must have the **FLEXibility** [resilience, buoyancy] to spring back from attacks. Include your **reFLECTions** [thoughts, reactions] about our program with your résumé. Box 99, *Press-Herald*."

A **reFLEX** is a reaction, an impulse, an involuntary response. (Holding my hands in front of my face was just a natural reflex.) A **reFLEXive** pronoun is one in which the action is directed back at the subject. (Iris saw *herself* in the mirror.) When one bends at the knee, as in worship, one **genuFLECTs** (All the congregants genuflected before they sat down); it also means to act in a servile fashion, to kowtow.

A **FLEXuous** path is one filled with curves and bends. To **FLEX** is to bend or tense. (The weightlifter flexed his muscles before beginning to lift the barbells.)

But not: fleck [ME *flekked*, spotted], a speck.

Combining forms: de-, away; genu-, the knee; in-, in, not; re-, back.

Antonyms: flex — relax, unbend, straighten; *flexible* — rigid, stiff, brittle, adamantine, stubborn, obdurate, resolute, intransigent; *flexibility* — stiffness, rigidity, unresponsiveness; *inflexible* — elastic, resilient, pliant, variable, supple, plastic; *inflexibility* — docility, elasticity, pliancy, tractability; *reflective* — impulsive, rash, thoughtless, spontaneous.

AfFLUent people have wealth; it flows to (*af-*) them; **afFLUence** is wealth, whether it be money, property, or other material goods.

The **conFLUence** of the two longest rivers in the United States, the Mississippi and the Missouri, is just north of St. Louis at the point where they flow together (*con-*). A confluence of people is a throng, crowd, or gathering.

EfFLUents such as the sewage and other liquid waste that flow out (*ef-*) of industrial plants and from heavily fertilized farm lands have poisoned the waters of many of the world's great rivers. At the same time the air we breathe is often polluted by the barely visible gases and vapors that we call **efFLUvia**.

The literal meaning of **inFLUence** is "a flowing in"; its noun synonyms are power, importance, control, domination, prestige, magnetism, charisma, clout, pull; as a verb it means sway, bend, induce, compel, affect, motivate, prompt, persuade. A common belief of ancient times was that the power of influence

**FLECTERE,
to bend:
FLECT, FLEX**

**FLUERE,
to flow: FLU**

that controlled our destinies flowed in from the stars above. Today most of us realize that we are more capable of being **inFLUential** in worldly affairs than are those distant points of light. The word **inFLUenza**, the name of a disease that killed nearly twenty-two million people in 1918, came from influence, for when it first struck the people of Italy ages ago, they assumed that the heavenly bodies were responsible for a sickness that is also called the *grip, grippe,* or **FLU.**

Any sound that is **melliFLUous** is sweet (*melli-*), musical, euphonious, melodious, harmonious, and mellow, such as the sounds of honeyed voices, velvety musical instruments, and those pleasant calls of nature, among which is the singing of the birds.

Something that is considered **superFLUous** is extra, excessive, redundant, needless, inessential, useless, and, well, more than enough (*super-*). If we were to add more synonyms to the above list, we would have a **superFLUity** or two.

FLUorescent lamps are commonplace in our lives, as are the fluorescent colors that make some children's toys glow so vividly. **FLUoridation** is the addition of sodium **FLUoride** to drinking water to prevent tooth decay. A **FLUoroscope** is a device used to view the internal structure of certain objects. (Ted's father said that when he was a child, the shoe stores used to have fluoroscopes so customers could see how their feet fit into the shoes they were trying on.)

A recent notice from the *Daily Times:* ''A large **inFLUx** of visitors is expected next month for the Track and Field Meet of the Americas. Applicants who desire to work at the meet must be **FLUent** in English, Portuguese, and Spanish. Due to unsettled political conditions, until recently the number of participants has been in a state of **FLUx, FLUctuating** from a mere handful to more than six hundred. It has now stabilized. Fans can expect to see the **FLUid** stride of such outstanding runners as Jackie Joiner-Kersey and a host of other smooth-running athletes.''

A **FLUsh**, as most card players know, is a poker hand with all cards of one suit. A player with only four cards of one suit has a **four FLUsh**. If that person tries to bluff the others, he or she **four-FLUshes**. In poker that's all part of the game, but in the world outside, a **four-FLUsher**, a person who deceives or tries to deceive others, is not treated so kindly.

☛ ***But not:*** *flumadiddle* [*flum*(mery), nonsense + *diddle*, to waste time], utter nonsense; *flurry* [blend of *flutter* and *hurry*], brief bit of activity or excitement, a light snowfall, to confuse; *flush* [ME *flusshen*], to drive birds from cover.

☛ ***Combining forms:*** *af-*, to; *con-*, together; *ef-*, out; *in-*, in; *melli-*, honey; *re-*, back; *-scope*, instrument for viewing; *super-*, over.

☛ ***Antonyms:*** *affluence* — need, poverty, insolvency, penury; *affluent* — down-and-out, indigent, insolvent; *fluent* — halting, constrained, hesitant, tongue-tied; *fluid* — solid, congealed, inflexible, fixed, stumbling, faltering; *influence* — ineffectiveness, debility; dissuade, impede; *influential* — unimportant, weak, powerless; *mellifluous* — harsh, rough; *superfluity* — dearth, lack, shortage; *superfluous* — essential, vital, indispensable.

FORTuna was the ancient Roman goddess of **FORTune**, that aspect of life that we have little or no control over, although there are those who claim that "Fortune favors the brave." For those of us not **FORTunate** enough to score high on the bravery scale, it still adds up to chance, luck, destiny, and fate. A fortune is also wealth, riches, capital, income, and circumstances. ("There certainly are not so many men of large fortune in the world, as there are pretty women to deserve them," Jane Austen, *Mansfield Park*.)

FORTuitous meetings or events are accidental, unintentional, unexpected, and unforeseen. (My running into Uncle Rich after all these years was entirely fortuitous.) A **FORTuity** is an accidental occurrence, but it is most often one on which Lady Luck or Dame Fortune has smiled.

The other side of the coin is that **misFORTune** (not Miss Fortune, **unFORTunately**) is sorrow and trouble and adversity often resulting from an injury or accident or calamity. The victims then join the ranks of the **unFORTunate**.

FORTUNA, luck: FORT

*Once uPUN a time as a fisherman started out to sea, a landlubber asked him what he was going out after.

"For tuna," said the fisherman.

"Good fortune," said the landlubber.

*But not: forte [*fortis*, strong], one's strong point; *fortnight* [ME *fourtene* niht], two weeks.

*Combining forms: mis-, bad; un-, not.

*Antonyms: fortuitous — planned, deliberate, expected; *fortunate* — cursed, hapless, ill-fated; *fortune* — poverty, indigence, destitution, purpose, intent, design; *misfortune* — prosperity, godsend; *unfortunate* — affluent, blessed, lucky, proper, commendable, praiseworthy.

ReFRACtion is the bending of light and other rays as they pass from one medium into another, for example, the light from a star as it enters the earth's atmosphere. This is a matter of great importance to astronomers and ophthalmologists and other people who work with lenses. Some metals are said to be **reFRACtory** because they are difficult to fuse or work, and that may be why and how the word came to mean unruly, stubbornly disobedient. ("Calvin has been extraordinarily refractory recently," Miss Hobbes wrote on his report.) As if it wasn't bad enough that she had previously called him **FRACtious**, which means quarrelsome, ill-tempered, irascible, petulant, rebellious, perverse, recalcitrant, unmanageable, and, of all things, "shirty."

When teachers suspect that a **FRACas** (or scuffle, brawl, hubbub, rhubarb, donnybrook, melee, brouhaha, foofaraw) is about to break out in the schoolyard, they are likely to look for the children who have the most rule **inFRACtions** on their records. There are rules in schools and elsewhere that

FRANGERE, to break: FRAC, FRAG, FRANG

are considered **inFRANGible**, that cannot be broken. An example of this is an **efFRACtion**, the forcible entry into a building. Neither breaking into nor breaking out of school is looked kindly upon.

Schools are for learning about **FRACtions** and **FRACtional** numbers in math, **FRACtures** in health, **FRAGmented** political parties in civics, and sentence **FRAGments** in English. Serious students will not be content with information that is **FRAGmentary**; they will want to know the whole story whenever possible, just as they will look upon a serious class disruption as **infringing** (or being an **infringement**) upon their right to learn. **FRAGmentation** means collapse, breakdown, disintegration. (The absence of discipline brought about the fragmentation of the school system.)

Rules and toys that are **FRANGible** are easily broken. **FRAGile** and **frail** have similar meanings; all three are usually interchangeable, but when referring to someone's poor health, the latter two are preferable. Because all three words mean breakable, delicate, vulnerable, perishable, the authors of this passage from the 1979 edition of *The Book of Common Prayer* could take their pick; this is what they chose: "At your command all things came to be: the . . . galaxies, suns, the planets in their courses, and this fragile earth, our island home."

When Hamlet muses about the murder of his father, the king of Denmark, he cannot understand why his mother, within the short time of a month, would marry Claudius, the king's brother and killer. "**Frailty**, thy name is woman!" he says, accusing her of moral weakness, weakness of character, fault, sin, vice, fallibility, and foible.

☞ **But now: fragrant [fragrare, to smell sweet], pleasant, sweet-smelling; fringe [fimbria, border], border, margin.*

☞ **Combining forms: -cas, to shake; ef-, open; in-, in, not.*

☞ **Antonyms: fraction — sum, all, whole; fractious — docile, amiable, obliging, agreeable; fragile, frail — robust, sturdy, durable; fragment — entirety, whole, everything; fragmentary — intact, complete, unified, entire, connected; frailty — virtue, strength; frangible — sturdy, stout, vigorous; infringe — respect, honor, protect, observe, recognize; refractory — amiable, complaisant, genial, good-natured.*

FRATER, brother: FRAT

When the Angles and the Saxons first populated the island off the northwest coast of the European continent, the word for one's male sibling was *brothor*; it took only a few centuries to evolve into *brother*. Across the English Channel its equivalents are varied. In Bordeaux it's **frere** and in Naples **FRATello**, in Amsterdam it's *broeder*, in Stockholm and Copenhagen *broder*, in Munich *Bruder*, and in St. Petersburg and Warsaw *brat*, a distantly related look-alike to our word for an especially nasty child.

While the English *brother* has not spawned many other words — *brotherhood*, *brotherly*, *brother-in-law*, and *brethren*, a word in limited use today — there are

are numerous offspring of the Latin root. In 1789 the battle cry of the French Revolution was ''Liberty! Equality! **FRATernity!**'' The fraternity houses that rim many of our college and university campuses today are usually called **FRATs**, and **FRATers** live in them. **Confreres** are fellow members of a fraternity or profession, colleagues, cohorts, associates, collaborators, compeers. (We all had great respect for our confreres in the legal profession.)

FRATernal orders or societies or clubs, largely of male membership, are devoted to charitable, professional, religious, or social activities. Fraternal twins often do not resemble each other, and they are not always of the same sex. A **conFRATernity** is a brotherhood devoted to charitable or religious benevolence. To **FRATernize** is to associate in a social or fraternal way.

A **friar** is a member of a religious order of the Roman Catholic church. In the Prologue to *The Canterbury Tales* Chaucer describes one: ''A Frere ther was, a wantowne and a merye.'' Friar Tuck was a member of Robin Hood's band. Friars Laurence and John are players in *Romeo and Juliet*. **Fra** is a friar's title, and many of them live in a monastery called a **friary**; years ago the refectory or dining hall of that building was called a **FRATer**.

Brothers are sometimes pals, and pals are sometimes as close as brothers. The word *pal* comes from Romany, the language of the Gypsies, and can be traced to the Sanskrit *bhratr*, ''brother,'' where it all began in the first place.

*Once uPUN a time, as an ancient story has it, a man in search of a carry-out order of fish and chips stumbled onto a monastery. ''Oh, I'm so sorry,'' said the man who answered his knock, ''but I'm afraid I could furnish you with only half your order. You see, I *am* the chip monk, but the fish friar is out for the evening.''

*But not: friable [*friare*, to crumble], easily crumbled.

*Combining form: con-, together.

*Antonyms: fraternize — stand aloof, snub, high-hat, avoid; *pal* — rival, adversary, foe, enemy, opponent.

When we think of a **FUGitive**, our first thought may be of someone on the lam, fleeing from the law, but the poet speaks of the fugitive clouds, the student is frustrated by the fugitive concept that he or she has difficulty grasping, and we look back wistfully on those fugitive vacation days, the ones that went by so fast. They were fleeting, transitory, ephemeral, and **FUGacious**.

A **reFUGe** is a place of shelter. (I took refuge under the eave of the old house when the storm came up.) It is a haven, an asylum, a sanctuary. (America has been the refuge for ''huddled masses yearning to breathe free,'' for **reFUGees** from every part of the earth). It is sometimes an escape, a way out. (''The patriotism [I believe in is] opposed to the kind that is the last refuge of a scoundrel,'' Erica Jong.)

A flight from reality is called a **FUGue** by psychologists; a fugue is also a musical composition.

FUGERE,
to flee: FUG

The word **feverfew**, an herb that our ancestors employed to treat fever and headaches, comes to us from **febriFUGia**, meaning literally, "to drive fever away." A **subterFUGe** is a trick or dodge or device someone uses to get around a rule or to hide something. (Whenever I got called on in class and wasn't prepared, I had this neat subterfuge of faking a coughing attack.) **CentriFUGal** force is evident in the spin-dry cycle of the washing machine, all the clothes fleeing away from the center; the opposite is centripetal, which means "center-seeking." (The centripetal force for a strong central government contrasted with the centrifugal force that wanted the power spread out to the states.) Both of these words were coined by Sir Isaac Newton, the English philosopher and mathematician; whether he was sitting under an apple tree at the time is not known.

☛ *But not: fugu*, a fish eaten as a delicacy in Japan but not until the skin and certain organs that contain a deadly poison have been removed.

☛ *Combining forms: centri-*, center; *fever-*, fever; *re-*, back; *subter-*, below.

☛ *Antonyms: fugitive, fugacious* — enduring, settled, permanent; *subterfuge* — openness, honesty.

FUNGI, to perform: FUNCT, FUNG

A **FUNCTion** is a gathering that may range from an informal get-together to a ceremonial reception, gala, fete, or bash. (A number of social functions are planned for the conventioneers.) It is an assigned duty. (I made it clear that one of my functions is *not* making coffee.) It is a specific role. (I talked with the reporters in my function as secretary to the mayor.) It is a purpose. (Athletics fills its function when it provides physical conditioning.)

Something that is **FUNCTional** is practical, utilitarian, useful, serviceable, pragmatic, efficient. (Functional furniture need not be unattractive. Will our car ever be functional again?) A **FUNCTionary** is an official, leader, office holder, bureaucrat, wheel, brass, big-shot. (When we saw all the functionaries at the gathering, we wondered just who was tending the store.)

When a public entertainer, whether an actor, musician, athlete, or speaker, puts forth a **perFUNCTory** performance, it can also be described as being routine, mechanical, superficial, as well as listless, halfhearted, lukewarm, lackadaisical, and blasé. (After shelling out $30 for seats, we expected more than a perfunctory performance.) Even a smile or a hello can be uninterested, offhand, indifferent, and cursory. (After that perfunctory greeting, I guess we know where we stand.)

Anything that is **deFUNCT** is dead, obsolete, nonexistent, extinct, or kaput. (That factory has been defunct since the end of the Cold War.)

The Latin *fungi* is said to have either come from or been influenced by the Greek *spongos*, "sponge"; hence it also gives us **FUNGus** and its plural **FUNGi**, the name of a biological group that includes mushrooms, toadstools, molds, yeasts, mildews, and rusts. A **FUNGicide** is a dust or spray used to destroy fungi, **FUNGivorous** insects feed on fungi, and something that has the shape of a mushroom is said to be **FUNGiform**.

   FUNGible means interchangeable. Goods that are traded and are exchangeable are fungible; hence a debt of a pound of sugar is repayable by a pound of sugar, no more, no less. (When you borrowed $5.00 from me, I expected $5.00 in return, not $4.99 or an excuse; after all, money is a fungible commodity.)

***But not:** fungo* [?], in baseball, a practice fly ball hit to a fielder; *funicular* [*funiculus*, rope], mountainside cable railway.

__Combining forms:__ -cide, to fill; *de-*, not; *-form*, shape; *per-*, thoroughly; *-vorous*, eating.

__Antonyms:__ defunct — active, living, in force, functioning; *functional* — unworkable, unsuitable, inoperable, useless; *perfunctory* — earnest, thoughtful, intent, wholehearted, interested, attentive, spirited, dedicated, absorbed.

G

GIGNOSKEIN,
[Gk], to know:
GNOS

GNOSis means secret knowledge of spiritual matters. In the second to sixth centuries **GNOSticism** was a religious system of heretical Christians who called themselves **GNOStics** and held that matter is evil, spirit is good, and salvation comes from the acquisition of secret, esoteric knowledge, or gnosis.

In 1869 the British biologist T.H. Huxley coined the word **aGNOSticism**, the prefix *a-* meaning "not," thus "not knowing." Over a half century later, in Dayton, Tennessee, attorney Clarence Darrow said in a speech at the world-famous "monkey" trial of John Thomas Scopes, "I do not consider it an insult, but rather a compliment to be called an **aGNOStic**. I do not pretend to know where many ignorant men are sure — that is all that agnosticism means."

A medical doctor's **proGNOSis** is the prediction of the course and outcome of a disease, a sports reporter's of an athletic contest, an economist's of a boom or bust, a political analyst's of an upcoming election. Skeptics are convinced that many alleged **proGNOStic** powers depend on which side of the flipped coin lands face up. For those who find longer words more impressive, **proGNOSticate** and **proGNOSticator** are the words of choice, although they would find several to choose from among these synonyms respectively: adumbrate, augur, forecast, foretell, portend, predict, prophesy, soothsay, and vaticinate, and auspex, forecaster, foreseer, foreteller, haruspex, Nostradamus, predictor, prophesier, seer, and sybil.

One's **physiognomy** is one's face. Even though one of Shakespeare's characters long ago proclaimed that there is no way one can read another's mind or character by checking out his or her expressions (says King Duncan about the treasonous Thane of Cawdor: "There's no art / To find the mind's construction in the face. / He was a gentleman on whom I built / An absolute trust"), the habit lives on: "You sure can tell ol' Slim's got no character. Look at that weak chin of his. Know what I mean?"

To **diaGNOSe** or **diaGNOSticate** or analyze a situation, whether one is a medical or automotive **diaGNOStician**, requires knowledge and skill in the practice of **diaGNOStics**, and the resulting **diaGNOSis** will usually reflect that. **DiaGNOStic** past masters thrive in all of humankind's activities.

☞ ***But not:*** *cognomen* [*nocere*, to learn], one's surname; any name; *diagonal* [Gk *diagonios*, from angle to angle], having an oblique direction; *no-stick* [brand of polytetrafluorethylene], a Teflon kind of surface.

☞ ***Combining forms:*** *a-*, not; *dia-*, between; *physio-*, nature; *pro-*, before.

GLOSSA *[Gk]*,
tongue: GLOSS

The **GLOSSary** that we often find at the back of a professional or scientific text is a collection of **GLOSSes**, which are explanatory notes regarding an unusual or difficult word or expression; a gloss can often be called an annotation, footnote, note, commentary, addendum, or interpretation. Sometimes a gloss is placed in the margin of the page or in between the lines of print. As a verb, **GLOSS** means to explain away something, such as a difficult or

sticky problem. (The manufacturer's representative tried to gloss away the erroneous and dangerously misleading instructions in the owner's manual.)

A **polyglot** is a person who is multilingual, an **isoGLOSS** is a boundary line
made on a map to mark the areas where certain dialects are spoken, and
GLOSSolalia is unintelligible speech, sometimes the product of one's inven-
tiveness, as with a child, sometimes the involuntary "speaking in tongues"
that a person in a religious trance or state of ecstasy exhibits. **GLOSSal** pertains to the tongue; the **glottis** is the opening between the vocal cords at the
upper part of the larynx.

But not: gloss, glossy [Scand], sheen, luster; this word also has a verb form
with a meaning similar to the Latin derivative above: to give a better appearance
to something.

Combining forms: iso-, equal; *-lalia*, babble; *poly-*, many.

COGNitive experiences are those of learning, of gaining knowledge. (Elinor's
parents made the effort to oversee her cognitive as well as her emotional
development.) In doing so, Elinor's parents took **COGNizance** of the many
forces that influence a child's growth and maturation.

PreCOGNition is foreknowledge, clairvoyance, prescience, and telepathy;
preCOGNitive powers, then, are clairvoyant, prescient, and telepathic.

To **reCOGNize** someone or something is to identify, perceive, or
acknowledge. (The chair recognized the delegate from Elkton.) To be **COGNizant** is to be aware. (I suspect we were all cognizant of the danger we were
in.) **ReCOGNition** is a synonym of recollection, remembrance, attention, and
appreciation. (Kim was given an alarm clock in recognition of her chronic un-
punctuality.) A personal **reCOGNizance** bond in a legal proceeding binds a
person to a particular act, such as appearing in court. (Don was released early
this morning on a P.R. bond, according to court records.) A **COGNoscente**
is a person who has or claims to have top-drawer knowledge in a field, especially in literature, the fine arts, or fashion; if there are two or more of them, it's
COGNoscenti. They also like to be called **connoisseurs**, experts, authorities,
and, when dining, epicures or gourmets.

On a negative note, we have **IGNORance, IGNORant**, and **IGNORamous**,
all of which are best to **iGNORe**. A **noble** act is praiseworthy, excellent, and
admirable; add the prefix and we get **ignoble** and its coterie of contemptible,
despicable, mean, degraded, and vulgar. **Notoriety** qualifies for membership
in this company, too; check out these synonyms: infamy, dishonor, shame,
disrepute, and ignominy.

Ditto **notorious**: infamous, dishonored, shameless, disreputable, and ignominious. As has been discussed earlier in this book (see **fama**, page 56),
some editors have let notorious take on the sense of popular. It has long meant
outstanding, well-known, and it may be that they assumed — incorrectly —
that something with those attributes must also be well liked. This raises a question: of these two well-known figures in American history, John Wilkes Boothe

*GNOSCERE,
to get to know:
COGN, GNOR,
NOTI*

and Abraham Lincoln, which one deserves to be called "famous" and which one "notorious"? Our advice: Stick with the long tradition among writers that notorious has a pejorative connotation, that is, one that is unpleasant, negative, disparaging, and derogatory.

An **acquaintance** is a person one knows but who is not a close friend. To have an acquaintance with a subject, however, means to have knowledge, experience, familiarity with it. (Since you have a good acquaintance with this area, can you show me the best route?) To **acquaint** is to make familiar, thus to familiarize, enlighten, inform, reveal. (Let me try to acquaint you with how this plan works; as a long-time employee, I am well **acquainted** with it.)

Something that is **quaint** is charming, picturesque, old-fashioned. (That village is filled with quaint old houses.) It also has the meaning of strange, peculiar, bizarre, unusual, and singular. ("Yes; quaint and curious war is! / You shoot a fellow down / You'd treat if met where any bar is, / Or help to half-a-crown," Thomas Hardy.)

When Bill and Jill receive an invitation to a costume party, the message is "Come incog." They will, therefore, wear masks to hide their identity. They will both consider themselves to be **inCOGNito**, although, strictly speaking, Jill will be **inCOGNita**. An **incogitant** act or remark is a thoughtless or inconsiderate one. An **inCOGNizant** person is unaware or lacking in knowledge.

NOTIce as a noun means heed, observation, attention, perception, glance, cognizance (Sallie's new book is certainly worthy of notice); mention, information, knowledge (We never got a notice regarding the auction); warning, **NOTIfication**, forewarning (You know Al — he suddenly gave notice and was gone), review, critique, rating (Not that movie; the notices are awful). As a verb: see, observe, eye, catch sight of, recognize (Did you notice Betty's engagement ring?); mention, comment on, call attention to, describe, allude to ("You never even noticed my engagement ring," Betty said). To **NOTIfy** is to inform, advise, serve notice, tell, apprise. (I was never **NOTIfied** that the bill was past due.)

When something is **NOTIceable**, it is clear, plain, distinct, manifest, palpable, and perceptible. (The therapy has resulted in a noticeable improvement in Brother's disposition.) A **NOTIon** is a thought, opinion, idea, impression, concept, suspicion. (Writer José Ortega y Gasset offered this advice to novelists: "Better beware of notions like genius and inspiration; they are a magic wand and should be used sparingly by anybody who wants to see things clearly.") It is also a whim, fancy, inclination, hankering, bent, penchant. (When Tracy takes a notion to do something like that, she just does it.)

To **reconnoiter** is primarily a military term meaning to inspect or survey an area; today this is done with **reconnaissance** satellites. Many such missions would not be necessary if one were well acquainted with the target layout.

☛ ***But not:*** *ignominious* [*nomen*, name], disgraceful; *nota bene* [L], mark well.

☛ ***Combining forms:*** *ac-*, to; *co-*, together; *-fy*, to make; *i-*, not; *in-*, not; *pre-*, before; *re-*, again.

Antonyms: acquaint — conceal, hide, withhold, retain, keep secret; *acquaintance* — stranger, bosom buddy, intimate, boon companion; unfamiliarity; *connoisseur* — ignoramus, greenhorn, duffer, novice, tyro, amateur, dabbler, dilettante; *ignorance* — knowledge, wisdom, education, erudition, perception, insight, empathy; *ignorant* — wise, lettered, literate, cultured, aware, conscious, informed, astute, sagacious; *ignore* — notice, regard, acknowledge, heed, mark; *incognito* — well-known, identified, undisguised; *notice* — oversight, slight, omission; neglect, overlook, disregard; *quaint* — modern, current, everyday, novel, standard; fashionable, newfangled; *recognize* — miss, skip, pass over, cut, snub, disdain.

In New York City in 1841 a man named Phineas T. Barnum opened a museum that he stocked with hundreds of curiosities, dead and alive, real and phony. It was a great success and during the next twenty-five years more than eighty million customers crowded into the building, so many at times that hundreds had to wait outside.

One day when he saw that all those outside were growing impatient to be inside, Barnum racked his brain for a way to get the ins out and the outs in. What he did was simple: he posted a large sign that was similar to the ones that pointed to other exhibits. TO THE EGRESS was all it said.

When the insiders rushed to see the new "exhibit," they found themselves outside with the door locked behind them. An **eGRESS**, they suddenly learned, is an exit. The insiders were **eGRESSed** and the outsiders **inGRESSed**. Had the inside-outers known that the prefix *e-* means "out," and that *gress* means "to go, step, walk," they would not have been fooled.

And as it is with egress, it is with a number of other words that stem from *gradi*:

As a verb, **conGRESS** means to step together, but we use it primarily as a noun meaning an assembly or legislative body. (When May ran for Congress, she promised to work together harmoniously with her new **conGRESSional colleagues.**)

To diGRESS is to go away, around. ("Let me digress for a moment," the candidate said, "to relate this story." The **diGRESSion** went on for fifteen minutes. It was crammed full of pointless, **diGRESSive** remarks.)

To **inGRESS** means to go in. It is also a noun. (We were denied ingress to the bank.)

To **proGRESS** is to go forward. (His academic progress is satisfactory, but he is not **proGRESSing** in other areas. The chart outlined the company's yearly **proGRESSion**. She ran for reelection on her **proGRESSive** record.)

To **reGRESS** and **retroGRESS** mean to go back or backward. (His health has regressed over the past few months. The foreign ship was given ingress and regress rights.) **ReGRESSion** and **reGRESSive** have similar meanings.

To **transGRESS** is to step over or across. (Their conduct **transGRESSed** every code including that of common sense. We asked for forgiveness for our **transGRESSions**.)

GRADI, to go, step, walk: GRAD, GRESS

GRESSorial means adapted for walking, as with the feet of some birds.

The prefix *ag-* means to, toward, hence **agGRESSion** is assault, offense, encroachment, hostility (The rebels' aggression has to be stopped); **agGRESSive**, hostile, belligerent, forceful, competitive (We need more aggressive salespeople in this firm); **agGRESSor**, assailant, attacker, challenger (It was obvious who the aggressor was).

A **GRADe** is a mark or rank. (My grade in the course was third from the top.) It is also an incline or slope. (Count me out; that's too steep a grade for me to climb.) As a verb it means to rank or classify. (Jan said grading papers was just about like grading eggs.) A **GRADuate** is a person who receives a diploma or a **degree**, and it is a beaker in a chem lab. To graduate is to finish school; it is also to measure out, as **ingredients** when cooking, as you check the **GRADations** or degrees on the cup. If this is done **GRADually**, it may well be more accurate. A **GRADient** is a slope, rise, tilt, or incline that may be **GRADual**, steep, or in between (I wouldn't attempt that gradient without four-wheel drive). **GRADualism** is the policy of moving very slowly or **GRADually** toward a goal. Nearly a century after the Civil War United States Supreme Court Justice Thurgood Marshall, replying to the suggestion that African-Americans be patient, said, "I'm the world's original **GRADualist**. I just think ninety-odd years is gradual enough."

A corporal who becomes a private has been **deGRADed**, lowered in rank. A person who has been degraded has been shamed, dishonored, and humbled. When one suffers from **deGRADation**, humiliation, and disgrace, it can be a **deGRADing** experience.

DeGRADable materials can be broken down by chemicals; those that are **biodeGRADable** can be broken down or decayed by living organisms. (It is said that disposable diapers are biodegradable — in about one hundred years.)

☞ *But not: pedigree* [F *pie de grue*, crane's foot], an ancestral line.

☞ *Combining forms: ag-*, to; *bio-*, life; *con-*, together; *de-*, down; *di-*, away; *e-*, out; *in-*, in; *pro-*, forward; *re-*, back; *retro-*, back, backward; *trans-*, across.

☞ *Antonyms: aggressive* — peaceful, apathetic, timid, lethargic; *degrading* — dignified, worthy, uplifting; *digressive* — organized, straightforward, focused; *gradual* — sudden, hasty, intermittent, precipitate; *progress* — retreat, loss, decline; *progression* — regression; *progressive* — declining, conservative; stand-patter.

GRANUM,
seed, grain:
GRAN

The words of an old English folksong go like this, "Some talk of Alexander, and some of Hercules, of Hector and Lysander, and such great names as these; but of all the world's great heroes there's none that can compare, with . . . the British **Grenadiers**." About four hundred years ago, they were soldiers who, as it says in the second verse, threw "hand **grenades** . . . about the enemies' ears." A grenade is filled with explosives much as a **pomeGRANate** is with seeds; hence the name comes to us through the Spanish **GRANado**, "full of seeds" and the French **grenade**, "a **pomeGRANet**, a ball of wild-fire." The **garnet**, a gem used in jewelry, got its name from its resemblance to the color of the pomegranate seeds, and **grenadine** is a syrup made from the fruit.

Meanwhile, back at the farm or **GRANge**, as it is sometimes called, the **grain** is ready to be harvested. The **GRANger** and his family will be out in the field **garnering** it so they can store it in the **GRANary** until the time comes to take it to the mill to be ground into flour. If a coarsely ground product is desired, it will be **GRANulated**, resulting in a **GRANular** texture. Some of the **GRANules** will be put aside to be used in the making of whole or cracked grain breads or rolled to be put in **GRANola** or other cereals.

Gravy sometimes has grains in it, and **GRANite**, a rock used in building and road paving, is coarse-grained or **grainy**. An idea or attitude that is **ingrained** is deep-seated and fixed. (Pat has an ingrained fear of heights.)

But not: aggrandize [*ag-*, to + *grandir*, grow larger], enlarge, exaggerate; *gangrene* [Gk *gangraina*, a gnawing sore], death and decay of body tissue, moral decay; *grant* [*credere*, to trust], to consider, give.

Combining forms: in-, in; *pome-*, apple.

Antonyms: garner — broadcast, distribute, strew, disperse; *grainy* — creamy, unctuous; *granular* — smooth, homogenized; *ingrained* — superficial, external, surface, learned.

A **GREGarious** person is affable, convivial, genial, outgoing, sociable, and loves to be with people. (Good-time Charley says he's not really the gregarious type, he just likes the free eats he gets at parties.) Animals that **conGREGate** in flocks or herds are also gregarious. **ConGREGants** are members of **conGREGations**, which are usually assemblies of religious worshippers. The Pilgrims who sailed the *Mayflower* and landed at Plymouth Colony in 1620 were **ConGREGationalists**.

To **seGREGate** a group means to separate it from the flock. (In an experiment the teacher segregated the brown-eyed children from the others.) **SeGREGation** is the process of isolating a group, whether it is books in a library, children in a school, or violent criminals in a prison. On May 17, 1954, the United States Supreme Court unanimously declared in Brown *v.* Board of Education of Topeka that **seGREGated** schools were unconstitutional. One year later the court ordered the **deseGREGation** of public schools.

An **agGREGation** is a collection or gathering of people or things. (An aggregation of rare animals toured the small towns.) As an adjective **agGREGate** means amassed, combined, cumulative (The aggregate amount raised in the fund drive was disappointing); as a noun, sum, total (The aggregate of all his debts was overwhelming.); and as a verb, to bring together, to amount to, to gather into one mass (All the crowds on the tour aggregated nearly a million people).

Many years ago when someone was referred to as **eGREGious**, it was a com-

*GREGARE,
to herd: GREG*

pliment; it meant that that person was distinguished, eminent, illustrious, and outstanding. Today it still means outstanding, but now it means outstandingly bad, monstrous, gross, and glaring, such as an egregious error, fault, or mistake. (Getting the speaker's name wrong was an egregious mistake that I will never live down.) Where the word took a turn for the worse is not recorded.

☞   *But not: integrate [integrare, make complete], to unify.

☞   *Combining forms: ag-, to; con-, together; e-, out; se-, apart.

☞   *Antonyms: aggregate — individual, separate, discrete; congregate — disperse, scatter; egregious — minor, unnoticeable, moderate, tolerable; gregarious — standoffish, reclusive, introverted; segregate — unify, integrate.

H

How did we get the word **periOD** from *hodos*? It took just two steps. The prefix *peri-*, "around," was added to the root to result in *perihodos*. Then at some point along its journey a three-letter operation was performed, like so: perihodos.

No matter how it got to us, the word certainly covers a lot of ground. There's the dot that marks, as the British put it, the "full stop" at the end of a sentence. There are the **periODicals** we subscribe to that are published **periODically**. A period is also an interval of time, ranging from an age, eon, epoch, and era through the hour or so that a student spends in and between classes, to the stopwatch-measured minutes and seconds that a game may be divided into. It can also refer to a particular or special spell or stage in one's life. (It was during that difficult period that I decided I had to go back to school.)

A **periODic** sentence is one that creates a certain amount of suspense by leaving the completion of the main clause until the end. (Yesterday, just as I was leaving the classroom at the end of what I think must have been third period — no, come to think of it, it was second period — I fainted.) Note: move the final two words to the beginning of the sentence, and it changes from a "periodic" to a "loose" sentence.

An **episODe** is an incident, a happening; a TV soap opera is **episODic**. (Neither Margie's business activities nor the episodic format of "As the World Turns" kept her from knowing who had done what to whom.)

A **methOD** is a system, a procedure, a process, a plan, a design. A person who is **methODic** or **methODical** is one of those well-organized, businesslike, systematic, deliberate human beings that we disorganized slobs say we can't stand. **MethODology** is a system of methods and rules in, for example, schools of education. (Lil said she had four years of educational methodology, all about the how-to but hardly anything about the subject matter she was supposed to teach.)

The **MethODist** church was founded by John and Charles Wesley, who lived "by rule and method" while students at England's Oxford University in 1729. A **synOD** is a council of churches or church officials. "**ExODus**" is the second book of the Bible and means the departure of a large group of people.

A car's **ODometer** records the number of miles one drives, and our daily lives are filled with mysterious electronic thingamabobs called **anODes** and **diODes** and **cathODes**, the meanings and functions of which are not for those of us who still don't understand how the telephone works.

But not: modus, manner, measure, method, usually with *operandi*, method of operating or working, or *vivendi*, manner of living; *OD*, overdose, esp. a fatal one; officer of the day, Old Dutch, olive drab, overdrawn; *ode* [Gk *aeidein*, to sing], long lyric poem.

**HODOS [Gk],
way, journey:
OD**

☞   *Combining forms: an-, up; cath-, down; di-, through; epis-, into; ex-, out; met-, after; -meter, measure; peri-, around; syn-, together.

**HOSPES,
host, guest,
stranger:
HOSP, HOST**

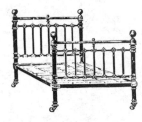

Hotels, HOSTels, HOSPices, and HOSPitals have at least one thing in common — beds. A hotel is for everyone who can afford it, a hostel is generally open to the young who are hiking or traveling, a hospice was originally a house of rest for pilgrims and strangers and was kept by a religious order but today is often a health-care facility for the terminally ill, and a hospital is for the sick and injured.

In France a *hôtel de ville* is a city hall ("mansion of the city"), and the tomb of Napoleon is in the *Hôtel des Invalides* in Paris, a building begun in the seventeenth century as a military hospital. When Americans are HOSPitalized, they go or are taken to *the* hospital. But not the British; they go to hospital. As you can see, it's shorter. In the United States, lots of cash or proof of medical or HOSPitalization insurance is needed.

Keepers of inns are generally known as innkeepers, but hotelkeepers frequently prefer to be called **hoteliers**. A hostel is kept by a HOSTeler, and the man who takes care of any horses that might show up is a HOSTler. Wherever one goes, one expects the HOST to be HOSPitable, genial, warm, cordial, and friendly. HOSPitality is, after all, the name of the game, no matter how obstreperous, demanding, and haughty the guest might be.

People who are inHOSPitable by nature or upbringing, being boorish, rude, impolite, and uncivil, do not rise high in the hotel world, nor are they the kind of folks one wants to open a discussion with, for they would not be considered hospitable, that is, open-minded, receptive, acccessible, tolerant, and amenable. (I do hope the incoming administrators are hospitable to new ideas.)

☞   *Combining form: in-, not.

☞   *Antonyms: hospitable* — antisocial, aloof, close-minded, inflexible, adamant; *inhospitable* — amicable, gracious, convivial, sociable, neighborly.

**HOSTIS,
enemy, stranger:
HOSTIL**

In a letter written in 1800 to Dr. Benjamin Rush, a fellow signer of the *Declaration of Independence*, Thomas Jefferson said, "I have sworn upon the altar of God, eternal HOSTILity against every form of tyranny over the mind of man." He was swearing, as well, animus, animosity, enmity, ill will, antagonism, bitterness, hatred, and venom.

Elizabeth Bowen, an Anglo-Irish novelist and short story writer, observed how "some people are moulded by their admirations, others by their HOSTILities." Although as she used the word, it is a plural of enmity and hatred, it is often used to mean conflict or fighting, ranging from a scuffle or fracas to an act or state of war. (Hostilities between France and Germany broke out on September 3, 1939.)

John Haynes Holmes, in his book entitled *The Sensible Man's View of the Universe*, wrote, "The universe is not HOSTILe, nor yet is it friendly. It is simply indifferent,'' that is, neither angry, unfriendly, contentious, malicious, malignant, nor cantankerous.

One afternoon in 1807 the British poet William Wordsworth ''wandered lonely as a cloud [when] all at once [he] saw a crowd, / A **host**, of golden daffodils.'' It soon began to rain, and he hurried on home, where, the story goes, he sat down and wrote the poem that was to become world-famous.

But not: host [*hospes*, guest], one who extends hospitality.

Antonyms: host — sprinkling, handful, scattering, few, remnant; *hostile* — friendly, amiable, peaceable, benevolent, irenic, kindly, congenial; *hostilities* — peace, truce, alliance, friendship; *hospitality* — agreement, amity, sympathy, love, affability, good will.

I

INSULA, island:
SOLA, SULA

As we look at the words *islet*, *isle*, *island*, our assumption is that they came from the same root. But only the first two did; the latter is from the Middle English word *iland*. Somehow over the years, no doubt because of its similarity to *isle*, the "s" found its way into the word. The relationship of the three is somewhat similar to that of the three bears, tiny, medium, and large. An **islet** is a very small tract of land surrounded by water, an **isle** is a larger piece of land, such as the Isle of Man (221 square miles) and an island can be as big as Greenland (840,000 square miles) but smaller than Australia, a continent of approximately 3,000,000 square miles.

A **peninSULA** is a land mass that is almost completely surrounded by water. Which is exactly what the parts of the word add up to: *pen-*, almost + *insula*, island.

Insula also gives us several words that have to do with a different kind of separation. Just as an island is separated from land, so we **inSULAte** our buildings to separate the inside from the heat or cold that is outside. **InSULAtion** is wrapped around electrical wires to spare us from the current that goes through them, and the insulation in cars is intended to filter the loudest of the road noises.

When a German doctor named Paul Langerhans discovered some islets of cells in the pancreas, a gland located near our stomachs, the hormone that they produce was given the name **insulin**. The cells are called the islet (or island) of Langerhans.

A person who lives on an island is said to be **iSOLAted**, standing alone, **inSULAr**. The word has also come to mean narrow-minded, provincial, petty, intolerant, bigoted, limited.

An **iSOLAto** is a person who is out of sync with the rest of the society he or she lives in. If the person has also removed himself or herself to a physical distance, the words "hermit" and "recluse" would likely be appropriate.

An **iSOLAtion** ward in a hospital is used to separate patients with contagious or infectious diseases from others. **ISOLAtionism** is the policy of refusing to have alliances or agreements with other nations.

☛ *But not:* insolate [*in-*, in + *sol*, sun], to dry or bleach in the sun; *insulting* [*in-*, in + *salire*, to jump], offensive.

☛ *Antonyms: insular* — urbane, tolerant, worldly, experienced, catholic, cosmopolitan; *isolate* — join, combine, mix, unite, blend.

J

Often on cold winter mornings we can trace the **traJECTory** of a **JET** by its contrail, that white skein of vapor etched against the blue sky. The passengers inside the plane probably boarded by walking through a movable tunnel called a **JETway** that connects it to the terminal; it is a trademark word, like cars called Ford and soap called Ivory. Meanwhile, down below, clusters of flotsam and **JETsam**, unwanted cargo **JETtisoned** by a ship far out at sea, **disEASed** sea creature, and a waterlogged house **joist** that the tide was returning to the land all bob up and down in the **EASy** undulations of the water along the huge rocks of a **JETty**.

In an **adJACent** area a falconer, a seldom-seen hunter who uses hawks as his weapon, holds his bird with his **jess**, the strap that holds the falcon on a short leash. Viewers who have gathered nearby **conJECture** that either the hawk will fly off, or that it is an electronic toy that is being controlled from the ground. Few of them seem to understand the **obJECT** of the hunt. Some seem to find it **obJECTionable**, assuming that the bird is being mistreated.

Gulls hover over an incoming fishing trawler, their **obJECTive** (or goal, target, aim) being the **reJECTs** that the crew throw into the water. The **EASe** of the birds' flight awes the tourists in a passing pleasure boat.

A statement that is objective is impartial, candid, open-minded, just, and impersonal; one that is **subJECTive** is personal, private, individual, selfish, and prejudiced. In an introduction to his novel *Native Son*, Richard Wright puzzles over an author's nearly impossible challenge of converting his subjective and private emotions and experiences into objective forms, ones that can be understood by the reader.

There are several words here that have to do with our language and its grammar. The **subJECT** and object of a sentence are two. For many cultured speakers of English, a subjective or hypothetical statement calls for a verb change: for example, I wish I *were* at the ballgame. If I *were* you, I wouldn't do that. They are statements contrary to fact, and the verbs are in the subjunctive mood. **AdJECTives** are our primary modifying words, and an **interJECTion** is a word or phrase that expresses emotion: Hey! Good grief! Holy cow! Ouch! Goldarn! Such expressions are often **interJECTed** into a conversation.

In a previous era authors such as Horatio Alger, Jr., were not content to use such simple speaker attributions as ''he said'' and ''she replied.'' These examples are from Alger's book *Andy Grant's Luck*: '''What a fool I was!' soliloquized the head salesman'' and (in reply to a friend's announcement that he has found a job) '''You have!' **eJACulated** John, in surprise.'' No writer except a satirist would use such verbs in that way today.

Prefixes provide the key to many of the *jacere* words. *Ab-*, ''down,'' hence **abJECT**, miserable, hopeless (They came from abject poverty) and contemptible, despicable (The braggart turned out to be an abject coward). *De-* also means down, hence **deJECT**, depress (The news from the front always dejects him),

JACERE, to lie, throw: EAS, JAC, JECT, JET

and, especially, **deJECTed**, depressed, disheartened, forlorn, sad, blue (Their dejected looks told us the story of the game). *E-*, ''out,'' gives us **eJECT**, to throw out; **eJECTa**, matter thrown out, as from an erupting volcano; **eJECTion**, a throwing out; and **eJECTor**, the person or thing that does the throwing out.

Pro-, ''forward,'' coupled with ''ject,'' gives us a verb meaning throw forward. (You must try to **proJECT** your voice to that back row.) As a noun it is a plan, scheme, undertaking, venture. (Our next project is to clean out the garage.) A **proJECTile** is a missile or bullet or arrow. A **proJECTion** is a prediction, estimate, extrapolation, or computation. (Their projection is that this town will double in size in the next decade.) It is also an overhang, ledge, protrusion, or protuberance. (How the actor kept from falling off that narrow projection baffled us.) A **proJECTor** is one who schemes or plans, as well as an apparatus for throwing an image on a screen.

Re-, ''back,'' accounts for **reJECT**, turn down, veto, expel, cast off, as a verb (The administration rejected only one of our suggestions) and waste, junk, castoff, pariah, loser, as a noun (This new machine actually spits out all the rejects). A **reJECTion** is a refusal, dismissal, or rebuff. (The voters' expected rejection of his candidacy caused him to withdraw from the race.)

Something **interJACent** lies between or among other objects, just as one lying below is **subJACent** and above, **superJACent**. Add **disEASe** and **malaise** and that pretty much covers the *jacere* territory. Or, one might say, that's the **gist** of it, you know, the essence, the core, the heart of the matter.

☞ *But not:* easel [D *ezel*, ass, easel], display stand; *jet* [Gk *gagates*, from *Gagai*, a mining town], a black coal used in making jewelry; *subjunctive* [*jungere*, to join], verb mood.

☞ *Combining forms:* *ab-*, from; *ad-*, to; *con-*, together; *de-*, down; *dis-*, away; *e-*, out; *inter-*, between; *mal-*, ill; *ob-*, against; *pro-*, forward; *re-*, back; *sub-*, below; *tra-*, across.

☞ *Antonyms:* *adjacent* — distant, remote, removed; *conjecture* — fact, truth, knowledge, certainty; *dejected* — cheerful, lighthearted, carefree; *dejection* — confidence, optimism, enthusiasm; *disease* — well-being, vitality, vigor, strength; *easy* — difficult, harsh, stern; *malaise* — complacency, contentment, serenity, vim; *object* — approve, advocate, support, espouse; shadow, vacuum, void, illusion; *objection* — agreement, accord, endorsement, affirmation; *objectionable* — pleasing, welcome, agreeable, acceptable; *objective* — mental, subjective, intellectual, internal, biased, prejudiced; *reject* — keep, accept, save, retain, embrace, endorse, grant; *subject* — privileged, immune, exempt, independent, unrelated, invulnerable, superior; ruler; *subjective* — impartial, objective, impersonal, disinterested, factual, verifiable, concrete, tangible.

JUGUM,
yoke: JUG

The **conJUGation** of a verb is the listing of its forms in a particular tense; for example, the present tense of the verb *be*: I am, you are, it/he/she is, we are, you are, they are. To **conJUGate** also means to join together, especially as a couple in marriage.

To **subJUGate** a people is to conquer, control, enslave, or overpower them. (The German forces under Hitler subjugated the citizens of six countries.) One can also attempt to subjugate or control one's own emotions, or an unruly student, or a wild horse. The famed orator and statesman Daniel Webster spoke of how the colonies "raised their flag against a power, to which, for purposes of foreign conquest and **subJUGation**, Rome, in the height of her glory, is not to be compared."

In anatomy **JUGular** pertains to the throat or neck, but the word takes on additional meanings in the phrase "Go for the jugular." (The candidate went right for the jugular in his attempt to destroy his opponent's credibility.)

But not: conjugal [*jungere*, to join], pertaining to marriage; *jug* [from *Jug*, pet form of *Joan* or *Judith*], tall, rounded container for liquids; *juggernaut* [Skt *Jaganatha*, "Lord of the world"], an overwhelming force; *juggle* [*joculare*, to joke], manipulate.

Combining forms: con-, together; *sub-*, under.

Antonyms: subjugate — free, liberate, release.

To **abJURe** is to recant, renounce, repudiate, or retract. (In 1616 Galileo was called to Rome and forced to abjure the Copernican doctrine that the earth revolves around the sun.)

To **adJURe** is to beg or entreat, to charge or solemnly command as if under oath or penalty. (Time after time the lawyer adjured the young girl to tell the truth about the witch that had allegedly put a curse upon her.)

To **conJURe** is to make appear, call forth, command, invoke (Goody Salem seemed to have conjured up the image she claimed she'd seen) and to bewitch, cast a spell, charm, hex, jinx, and practice magic (Oh, I've seen her conjure up a rabbit right out of a hat and then make that rabbit believe it was a chicken!) A **conJURer** is a magician, wizard, juggler, sleight-of-hand artist, or one who practices voodoo. A **conJURation** is an incantation, spell, mumbo jumbo, abracadabra, hocus-pocus, legerdemain.

To **inJURe** is to damage, hurt, offend, harm, impair, wound, do wrong. (My dear sir, I assure you I in no way intended to injure your reputation.) An **inJURy** is a hurt or wound or a violation of another's rights under the law. Something **inJURious** is abusive, defamatory, insulting, offensive. (Panfly gave serious thought to filing suit against Britt for his injurious personal attacks.) It can also be detrimental, deleterious, pernicious, and abusive. (Do you really believe that the tobacco you chew is not injurious to your health?)

To **obJURgate** is to renounce or rebuke or upbraid someone harshly, sharply, and vehemently. (The nominee objurgated his opponent for injecting racism into the campaign.)

JURARE,
to swear:
JUR, JUS

To **preJURe** is to lie under oath. (Mamie perjured herself when she denied ever meeting with Bradler.) **PerJURy** is the willful giving of false (or **perJURed**) testimony.

JURidical pertains to the administration of justice, to law or **JURisprudence**, the philosophy of law. (The quandary of whether this or that system was juridical or legal was one of the factors that led Thorpe to his study of jurisprudence.)

JURisdiction is the right to interpret and apply the law as well as the territory of such right. (Attley strongly objected to the judge's ruling that the local police had jurisdiction over the two soldiers.)

A **JURist** is a person versed in the law, as a judge or lawyer or scholar. (Prof. Ferrer called Chief Justice Warren the most outstanding jurist of our times.) A **JURor** is a member of a **JURy**, a word that came into English as *juree* and then *jurie* before settling into its present form. But perhaps not its present position of respect; here is Samuel Johnson's question, as recorded by James Boswell, his biographer: "Consider, Sir, how should you like, though conscious of your innocence, to be tried before a jury for a capital crime, once a week?"

To be **JUSt** is to be virtuous, decent, impartial, equitable, correct, and precise. (They tried to teach their children to be just. The court handed down what was generally regarded as a just ruling.) As an adverb it means precisely, perfectly, only, merely, very, positively. (That is just what we've been looking for. His honor was just an average student. The girls were just radiant.) **JUStly** is an adverb meaning fairly, honestly. (There's a passage in the Bible that asks, "What does the Lord require of thee, but to do justly, and to love mercy, and to walk humbly with thy God?") An **unJUSt** act is wrongful, inequitable, partial, iniquitous, unmerited, and **unJUStified**.

To **JUStify** one's actions is to legitimize them, as well as to vindicate, verify, authorize, approve, excuse, exculpate, and exonerate them. (The man asked, "Do you believe the end justifies the means?" To which the Soviet dictator Joseph Stalin answered, "Absolutely.") The **JUStification** of an action is a reason or fact or circumstance or explanation that defends or justifies it. (When asked what justification Betsy had for hitting Midge, she said, "Well, she hit me first.") Something that is **JUStifiable** is defensible, tenable, legitimate, right, proper, and fitting. (The court ruled that it was justifiable homicide.) An **unJUStifiable** act is inexcusable, unpardonable, unforgivable, unacceptable, intolerable, and outrageous. (Two senators today called the court's ruling completely unjustifiable.)

Living the satisfactory life is often a matter of **adJUSting, readJUSting**, correcting, and compromising. In his poem "The Star-Splitter," Robert Frost speaks of the man who burned his farmhouse down to get enough money to buy — of all things — a telescope. His neighbors got a bit riled up about it, but soon they realized that if they cut off everyone who had sinned, there wouldn't be anyone left they could jaw with over a cup of coffee. "For to be social is to be forgiving," the poet concluded. There you have it: **adJUStments** and **readJUStments**.

In a letter from Birmingham Jail in 1963 Martin Luther King, Jr., wrote, "**In-JUStice** anywhere is a threat to **JUStice** everywhere." Injustice is inequity, partiality, unfairness, bias, grievance, and prejudice; justice is integrity, virtue, probity, truth, legitimacy, honesty.

Jus is a legal term meaning a right or law as a system.

Once uPUN a time a farmer and his wife discussed the buying of a bull so their cow could, in time, have a calf.

"That's reason enough to justifiable, isn't it?" he asked.

"I guess so," she said. "But justify can have all the money we save on our meat bill."

"Veal talk about it later," he said. "Need anything from town?"

"Justice for our tea," she said.

But not: jury-rig [?], to improvise a repair; *jus* [F], juice, gravy, usu. *au jus*, served with its own juices.

Combining forms: ab-, away; *ad-*, to; *con-*, together; *-diction*, to say; *-fi, -fic, -fy*, to make, do; *-gate*, to drive, do; *in-*, not; *ob-*, against; *per-*, thoroughly; *-prudence*, knowledge; *un-*, not.

Antonyms: abjure — uphold, embrace, cling to, maintain, swear by; *injure* — soothe, heal, pacify, assist, benefit, help; *injurious* — advantageous, salutary, beneficial, healing, salubrious; *injury* — blessing, favor, benefit, boon; *injustice* — equity, fairness, right, impartiality, rectitude, lawfulness, evenhandedness; *just* — bad, base, dishonest, crooked, devious, corrupt, prejudiced, unreasonable, inequitable, inappropriate, unfit, undeserved, false, illegitimate; *justice* — favoritism, inequity, untruth, wrong, impropriety, invalidity, illegality, bias, perfidy; *justifiable* — unwarranted, implausible, unsound, indefensible; *objurgate* — approve, extol, eulogize, applaud, praise; *perjury* — verity, truth, fact, veracity, gospel.

JUVENIS, young: JUV

A **JUVenal** in Shakespeare's time was a youth: "The juvenal, the prince, whose chin is not yet fledged," *Henry IV, Part II.* A young bird's first feathers or plumage is called juvenal. This is not to be confused with Juvenal, A.D. c. 60–c. 140, a Roman poet and satirist who was born Decimus Junius Juvenalis, and who left us with gems like these: "Honesty is praised and left to shiver." "Travel light and you can sing in the robber's face." "It is not easy for men to rise whose qualities are thwarted by poverty."

Pity our poor **JUVeniles**, for their adjectives are most unflattering: pubescent, immature, childlike, puerile, callow, infantile, undeveloped, and sophomoric. Oh, that sophomore year [Gk *sophos*, wise + *moros*, dull, foolish, stupid]!

So on to the **junior** year: second-string, subordinate, lesser, minor, inferior, secondary, lower. Good grief! Oh, to be a senior, hence mature, advanced, superior.

But then, years later, comes the yearning for **reJUVenation**, to return to those years long past that one could hardly wait to grow out of, and dreaming of **JUVenescence**, of being youthful in appearance. But alas, the reality is that one's youth is gone, and it can be captured again only by reading one's **JUVenilia**, the writings of those years long past.

☞   *Combining form:* re-, again, back.

K

A **CAUstic** substance is capable of burning, corroding, or destroying living tissue; a caustic remark is capable of mortifying, outraging, and antagonizing a living being. To **CAUterize** a wound is to sear any abnormal or infected tissue.

A **holoCAUst** is any mass slaughter or destruction of life or any total devastation, especially by fire. (All the town's books and documents were destroyed when the holocaust wiped out the square). The Holocaust was the attempt by Nazi Germany before and during World War II to destroy the Jewish people. By the end of the war six million of the eight million Jews in the countries occupied by the Nazis had been murdered.

Calm comes to us from *kaiein* by way of the Latin *cauma*, heat of the day. Hence it meant a rest or resting place in the heat of the day, a place, preferably, that is placid and peaceful, cool and collected, sedate and serene. The verb **becalm** means that the sailor will have no wind to fill the sails and move the boat. (The girls were late for their appointment when their sailboat was becalmed for more than three hours.) A **calmative** is a sedative or a tranquilizer.

But not: cause (*causa*, reason], motive; *cautious* [*cavere*, to heed], wary.

Combining forms: be-, verb forming; *holo-*, whole, entire.

KAIEIN, [Gk], to burn: CAU

In Shakespeare's time a *cumrade* was a **CHAMber-fellow**, a person with whom one shared a room, barracks, lodging, usually in the military. Today it is **comrade** in English, **CAMarade** in French, **Kamerad** in German, **CAMarada** in Spanish, and is an associate, companion, friend, partner, colleague, ally, or coworker in any field of endeavor. According to Samuel Johnson's 1755 dictionary, a **chum** is ''a chamber-fellow, a term used in the universities.'' **CAMaraderie**, a word that means comradeship and good fellowship, also comes to us from that sharing of quarters.

A legislative hall is known as a chamber, as is the legislature itself. (Both chambers passed the resolution unanimously.) **CAMeral** pertains to a judicial or legislative chamber. (We learned that Nebraska is the only state with a **uniCAMeral** legislature, all the other states are **biCAMeral**.)

The **CAMera** that we take pictures with was originally a dark chamber or box invented in the sixteenth century by Giambattista dell Porta and called the *camera obscura*, meaning ''dark box.'' That name persisted until L.J.M. Daguerre developed the first photographic camera. The **CAMcorder** is a television camera with an incorporated VCR [cam(era) + (re)corder]. **On camera** refers to being filmed. (Please refrain from scratching when on camera.)

A judge's private office is called a camera, hence the phrase **in camera**, privately, in the privacy of a judge's **CHAMbers**. (The judge called the attorneys to a meeting in camera.)

Restaurants and cafes that offer music, a dance floor, and entertainment are often called **cabarets**. The literal meaning of the word is ''small chamber.''

KAMARA [Gk], vault: CAM, CHAM

A **CHAMberlain** used to be the manager of a royal household; today he is more likely to be a receiver of rents and revenues in a municipal government, a treasurer. **CHAMbermaids** were employed to keep those enormous households neat and tidy.

☞ *Combining forms: bi-,* two; *uni-,* one.

KRINEIN [Gk], to distinguish, separate: CRIT

William Hazlitt, a nineteenth-century English writer, said that "the only vice that cannot be forgiven is **hypocrisy**," which is another word for fakery, deceit, sham, insincerity, duplicity, and pretense. The culprit who rates such low praise is a **hypoCRITe**, one who pretends to be what he is not, a fake, imposter, charlatan, deceiver, Pecksniff, and pharisee, all of which add up to one who is insincere, false, two-faced, dissembling, and phony. In short, **hypoCRITical**.

A **crisis** is an emergency, crucial point, dilemma, predicament, and quandary. (Like, hey, I've got a real crisis in my life; I finally got a date with Cha Cha and I'm flat broke.) If you have two of these, you have **crises** but never crisises, mainly because no one could ever pronounce it.

A **CRITerion** means the same thing as "yardstick" when it is used in the sense of a standard, guideline, measure, parameter, touchstone, or model by which to judge something. (The criterion Professor Sills uses in her writing class is this book of essays by E.B. White.) No "s" here to form a plural either. (What are the **CRITeria** for judging the outstanding photographs at the exhibit?)

A **CRITic** is a judge, reviewer, expert, authority, or arbiter; in the words of writer Carolyn Wells, "A critic is a necessary evil." To which she added, "and **CRITicism** is an evil necessity." Exactly how evil might depend upon which of its three faces criticism shows. It is often negative, that is, sarcastic, panning, and censuring. (Your poem has no redeeming features; I suggest you take up another occupation.) When it is constructive, it is a horse of a different feather. (While I think your theme is rather badly organized, you have some cogent points here, and if you will follow my suggestions, you can turn this into a fine paper.) Often it is neutral, such as in a factual, objective review of a book or play. (This is a factual account of the rise and fall of a family business.) It is also known as an evaluation, review, comment, analysis, or **CRITique**.

Synonyms of **CRITicize** are generally divided into two camps: 1. judge, evaluate, survey, appraise, review, analyze, and examine; and 2. condemn, ridicule, blame, denounce, fault, slam, censure, oppugn, animadvert, and excoriate.

A person who is **CRITical** of another may be faultfinding, carping, captious, picky, disparaging, and derogatory. If a speaker claims that this is a critical time in our lives, it is grave, serious, crucial, important, risky, perilous, precarious, hairy, and touch-and-go. If a hospitalized patient's vital signs are abnormal and unstable, his or her condition is grave, serious, and critical. A critical measurement must be exact, precise, and true.

The shortened form of critic, criticism, and critique is **CRIT**.

But not: critter [var. of *creature*], animal, bug, or little kid.

Combining form: hypo-, under.

Antonyms: critic — advocate, supporter; *critical* — supportive, helpful, approving, safe, sound, sure, loose, lax; *criticism* — approval, acclaim, praise, accolade; *criticize* — laud, extol, commend, applaud; *hypocrisy* — sincerity, honesty, fairness, integrity, candor; *hypocritical* — genuine, heartfelt, true, faithful.

L

LACERE,
to allure, entice:
DELE, DELI

"Good afternoon, ladies and gentlemen," the master of ceremonies said. "I'm **DELIghted** to be able to present to you our distinguished guests seated here at the head table. Today's program will work in this way: I will call upon each of our 'quotologists' and **elicit** from them a line or three from their works that will illustrate a word from the root *lacere*. But before we begin, let's give a hearty round of applause for the great food from the Nellie Kelly **DELI**, our great neighborhood **DELIcatessen!**" (Drumroll and a hearty round of applause.) "Please welcome our first guest, the distinguished Pulitzer Prize–winning novelist, Ms. Edna Ferber."

E.F.: "Being an old maid is like death by drowning, a really **DELIghtful** sensation after you cease to struggle."

M.C.: "Thank you! That was great. Next, one of the world's most famous dramatists, George Bernard Shaw. This from *Arms and the Man*. Mr. Shaw."

G.B.S.: "Bulgarians of really good standing — people in our position — wash their hands nearly every day. So you see I can appreciate your **DELIcacy**."

M.C.: "Most appropriate, G.B.S. Thank you. Now from France, Monsieur Jean-Paul Sartre. From his book *Words*. Sir."

J-P.S: "At the time, a refined family had to include at least one **DELIcate** child. I was a perfect subject because I had some thought of dying at birth."

M.C.: "Exquis! Merci! Next, from England, Douglas Dunn, his line from a review in the *Listener*. Mr. Dunn."

D.D.: "A **dilettante** is a product of where wealth and literature meet."

M.C.: "Touché! as Monsieur Sartre might say. Jolly good show. Now from Tin Pan Alley, the inimitable Cole Porter! His line is from his song 'It's Delovely' from his hit musical, *Red Hot and Blue*! Mr. Porter."

C.P.: "It's delightful, / It's **DELIcious**, / It's **DELEctable**. . . ."

M.C.: "A great triple play if I ever saw one! And now the renowned composer Igor Stravinsky with a line from *Poetics of Music*. Sir."

I.S.: "Poussin said quite correctly that 'the goal of art is **DELEctation**.'"

M.C.: "Meaning 'pleasure,' right? And now, ladies and gentlemen, our last participant this afternoon, Emily Brontë, who has some words for us from her masterpiece, *Wuthering Heights*. Miss Brontë."

E.B.: "My love for Heathcliff resembles the eternal rocks beneath: — a source of little visible **DELIght**, but necessary."

M.C.: "A big hand, ladies and gentlemen, for all our 'quotologists,' and a good afternoon to you all."

☛ ***Once uPUN a time***, a few years after the Watergate political scandal rocked the nation's capital, unsubstantiated rumors began floating around Washington that several hundred pastrami sandwiches had been pilfered from the Senate kitchen. Reporters immediately labeled it "Deli-gate"!

*But not: delineate [linea, threat, line], to draw, portray; light [AS lecht], illumination; not heavy.

*Combining forms: de-, di-, away; e-, out.

*Antonyms: delectable — disagreeable, tasteless, unappealing, unappetizing; delectation — displeasure, disappointment; delicacy — toughness, crudity, tactlessness; delicate — gross, inelegant, strong, healthy, glaring, careless; delicious — unpalatable, inedible, unpleasant; delight — disgust, distaste, bore, drag; delighted — disgusted, displeased; delightful — repulsive, depressing, distressing.

When a missile, rocket, or spacecraft reenters through the atmosphere, the nose cone or protective surface is **abLATed** by the intense heat: ab-, away + lated, carried, hence, burned, heated, melted. Surgeons may remove abnormal growths by **abLATion**.

When the pages of a manuscript are put in their proper sequence or order, they are **colLATed**, that is, brought or carried together. (The graduate student collated the pages of Dr. Fern's latest textbook.) This also occurs when two or more sets of data are merged by a computer operator. The act of doing this is called a **colLATion**, which is also the the name of a light meal or snack, as well as the practice in a monastery of reading Scripture at the close of day.

Something that is **colLATeral** is secondary, subordinate, ancillary. (These stories are merely collateral to Hemner's major literary goals.) The word also means confirming, supportive, substantiating, additional. (The new witness's collateral evidence influenced the jury.) As a noun it means security, guarantee, bond, surety, pledge. (Marc had to give his watch as collateral for the money he borrowed.)

When two or more things correspond, relate, parallel, or connect, they **correLATe**. (The attorney attempted to correlate the seemingly unconnected testimony of the various witnesses.) Hence **correLATion** is the mutual relationship of two or more items, parts, things; synonyms are interdependence, correspondence, reciprocity, give-and-take, and quid pro quo. (The CEO says there must be a positive correlation between the employees' performance and their pay.) Words that correspond to each other are said to be **correLATive**; examples are either . . . or, not only . . . but, and former . . . latter.

Medicines can be used to **diLATe** one's blood vessels and prevent clotting, thus the vessels are expanded, enlarged, widened. When one comments at length on a subject, he or she can be said to dilate on it. (Superintendent Oswell dilated on the importance of the honor code.)

To be **diLATory** is to be slow, tardy, delaying, procrastinating, dawdling, phlegmatic, and torpid. (The chess player's dilatory tactics infuriated his opponent.)

To **eLATe** others is to make them happy or proud. (This good news will elate your folks.) Thus **eLATed**, they will be joyful, exultant, exhilarated, jubilant, and ebullient, and one can hope that their **elATion**, their exaltation/exultation, ecstasy, delight, and rapture will be lasting.

*LATUS,
carried: LAT*

When the football quarterback throws a **LATeral** pass, he throws it sideways or to the side. When an employee is moved to a new position, it can be a demotion, a promotion, or a lateral move. (Barnley was disappointed that his move was lateral rather than the upgrade he had hoped for.) We learn about the lines marking the **LATitudes** (north and south) and longitudes (east and west) from maps and globes. **LATitude** is also used in the sense of having freedom from narrow restrictions; it means having leeway, liberty, indulgence, and elbowroom. (The students at Oxham Academy have more than the usual amount of academic and social latitude.) A **LATitudinarian**, therefore, is one whose conduct, ideas, interests, and opinions are not restricted and confined; such a person would be said to have a **LATitudinous** outlook.

An **obLATe** object is flattened at the poles; a football is an oblate spheroid. In the Roman Catholic church an oblate is a lay person who performs special religious work. An **obLATion** is a religious offering. (''Bring no more vain oblations; incense is an abomination unto me.'' Isaiah 1:13.) A **preLATe** is a high-ranking member of the clergy.

To **reLATe** a story is to narrate, tell, describe, recite, recount, or convey it. (Despite painful memories, Belle tried to relate the story of that terrifying hour.) To relate, say, Belle's story to one's own life is to connect, join, link, bring together, correlate the two. (I could not help relating Belle's experience to my own.) Two beings or objects that are **reLATed** are joined, linked, united; when two ideas or occurrences are related, they are thought to be relevant, connected, or affiliated. (Why Kyle felt that his unhappy childhood was related to his D– in computer science was beyond me.)

A **reLATion** or **reLATionship** is a connection, tie-in, link, bond, coupling, matuality, or liaison. (There is no relation between our store and the national chain of the same name.) A relation is a kin. (I think she's a very distant relation of mine.) It is a reference, application, regard, or bearing. (Your comments have absolutely no relation to the book we were discussing.) It is a telling, narration, report, description. (Kim's relation of Mom's reaction to the new styles at the fashion show was hilarious.) Relations are also connections between peoples and countries. (She'd make a good Secretary of State, she's very strong on foreign relations.)

As a noun, a **reLATive** is also a kin, of course. As an adjective, it means relevant, pertinent, apropos, germane. (My work record was not relative to the demands of the position, after all.) It also means comparable. (Relative to the other apartments we've looked at, this is a real bargain.) And it means related and correlated. (Zack is keen on political science and various relative fields.)

Albert Einstein's theory of relativity is said to be incomprehensible to all but a few people, but he himself described it this way: ''When a man sits with a pretty girl for an hour, it seems like a minute. But let him sit on a hot stove for a minute — and it's longer than any hour. That's **reLATivity**.''

SuperLATive is an adjective meaning peerless, supreme, nonpareil, matchless, utmost, and top-notch. (Uncle Emmett's a superlative bridge player.)

As a noun it can refer to a person or thing of the utmost degree; it also refers to exaggerated expressions of praise. ("I appreciated all those superlatives," the speaker said following his introduction, "and agree with everyone of them.")

To **transLATe** a foreign language into one's own is to convert or render it. Sometimes we suggest that the technical expert translate his or her jargon or nomenclature into more common terms. But one can also try to translate one's wishes into deeds. There are a number of ideas about how the **transLATions** of great works of literature should be done. Here are two: "There is no translation except a word-for-word translation," George Moore. "The best translations . . . are those that depart most widely from the original," Edmund Wilson.

Note: **LegisLATe**, *-ion, -ive, -or, -ure*, etc., come in part from *latus*; they are discussed under *lex*, law. See page 92.

*But not: latent [latere, to be hidden], dormant, potential; relay [laxus, slack], carry forward.

*Combining forms: ab-, away; col-, cor-, together; di-, apart; e-, out; ob-, toward; pre-, before; re-, back; super-, above; trans-, across.

*Antonyms: correlate — contradict, oppose; *dilate* — shrink, wane, contract, reduce, compress; *dilatory* — active, quick, diligent, brisk, eager, prompt, assiduous, sedulous; *elated* — gloomy, mournful, dejected, depressed, blue; *elation* — melancholy, misery, sadness; *relate* — separate, set apart, dissociate, be irrelevant; *related* — independent, isolated, nonconsanguineous; *relation* — isolation, disconnection, separateness; *relative* — autonomous, unique, inapplicable, inappropriate, irrelevant.

LAUDARE,
to praise: LAUD

To **LAUD** is to praise or extol; it is also a hymn of praise and, as **LAUDs**, a morning prayer. A **LAUDatory** speech is one that is filled with praise. (Burkly was embarrassed by the laudatory remarks the governor made about him.) Something that is **LAUDable** is deserving of praise. (It was, Robin felt, a laudable idea, but she wasn't sure the town was quite prepared for it.) A **LAUDation** is an act of **LAUDing**; it is an encomium, a eulogy, a tribute, a testimonial.

College seniors who can boast of (but never do so openly, of course) high grade-point averages often keep one eye on the standings of their peers. They would like to hit the top, **summa cum LAUDe**, graduating with highest distinction, or the next notch, **magna cum LAUDe**, graduating with great distinction, or, at the very least, **cum LAUDe**, graduating with distinction. Lots of their classmate say they will be quite satisfied just to graduate.

*Once uPUN a time in an area of the country where the word lord is served up minus the ''r,'' the proprietor of an ancient inn delighted in telling the tale of an ancestor who, upon opening his door one night during the Revolutionary War and seeing a man in a red coat, cried out, "Oh Laud, a Tory!" and fainted dead away.

☞   *But not: applaud [plaudere, to clap hands], to show approval by clapping.

☞   *Combining forms: cum, with; magna, great; summa, highest.

☞   *Antonyms: laudable — contemptible, ignoble, execrable, reprehensible; laudatory — belittling, abusive, scornful.

LEGARE, to bind, choose, send: LEGA, LEGE, LEGI

An **alLEGEd** embezzler is one who someone believes has stolen money but has not been convicted of the crime; in other words, one who is purported or supposed or said or thought to have done wrong. (The suspect **alLEGEdly** milked the company of more than $20,000. The **alLEGAtions** were made by two former employees who asked to remain anonymous. Today's lead editorial in the *Herald* **alLEGEs** that McCat did not act alone.)

Professors in a **colLEGE** are **colleagues**, persons with whom one has chosen to work. A workplace that has a **colLEGIal** atmosphere is one in which a group of colleagues share the responsibilities with minimal supervision from above. A **colLEGIan** is a student in a college, one who may or may not choose to wear **colLEGIate** apparel or to be active in either **intracolLEGIate** or **intercolLEGIate** activities.

A **LEGAte** is an envoy, an emissary, often one **deLEGAted** (appointed, authorized) by the pope. A **LEGAtion** is a **deLEGAtion**, that is, a diplomatic minister and his or her staff, as well as its official headquarters. A **LEGAcy** is anything handed down from the past. (Quincy had hoped for an inheritance of $$$, but his grandfather's principal legacy to him was his uncommon integrity. As a result the poor chap was **reLEGAted** to the lower regions of his social group.)

☞   *But not: allegiance [OF liege, vassal], loyalty; league [ligare, to bind], an association; legend [legere, to read], myth.

☞   *Combining forms: al-, to; col-, together; de-, from; inter-, between; intra-, within; re-, away.

LEGEIN [Gk], to gather, speak: LEXI, LOG, LOGUE

A **LEXIcographer** is a writer of dictionaries; he or she is involved in the gathering of the words of a language, along with their definitions and, often, their etymologies, in the creating of a **LEXIcon**. The emphasis of such a book is **LEXIcal**, that is, it is concerned with the words of the language rather than the grammar.

A **cataLOG** (also **cataLOGUE**) is a listing of items available for sale or use. **Eclectic** means diverse, broad, catholic, selective, liberal, comprehensive. (This year's catalog of outstanding photography will be an eclectic one, for it will feature a vast range of artists and techniques.)

A person suffering from **aLEXIa** is word-blind and unable to read. **DysLEXIa** is an impairment of the ability to read, but it can be overcome or compensated for. (One of the world's great geniuses, Albert Einstein, was **dysLEXIc**, as was Vice President Nelson Rockefeller.)

A **dialect** is a variety of a language that is set apart by geography or social differences. (I asked the man for a bottle of soda, and he didn't understand my dialect; he asked me if I meant tonic, dope, pop, a soft drink, or sody water.) **Dialectics** is the practice of examining statements by question and answer. A **diaLOGUE** (**diaLOG**) is a conversation, chat, interview, palaver, or bull or rap session, whereas a **monoLOGUE** (**monoLOG**) is a one-person show, soliloquy, lecture, sermon, diatribe, or tirade. The **DecaLOGUE** is the Ten Commandments.

An **anaLOGUE** (**anaLOG**) is something analogous or similar to something else. Shakespeare based many of the plots of his plays on actual events, and the accounts and books that these were found in are called analogues. (Three are several analogues for the story of *The Tempest*, Shakespeare's last play, and from these he borrowed both ideas and details.)

A **proLOGUE** (**proLOG**) is an introduction or preface to a literary work; in the theater it is delivered before a performance. An introductory essay to a book is sometimes called a **prolegomenon**. An **epiLOGUE** (**epiLOG**) comes at the end as a supplement or postscript of sorts. A **traveLOGUE** (**traveLOG**) is a talk or visual presentation of someone's travels.

*But not: brogue [Ir *brog*, shoe], a strong Irish (or other) accent; *electric* [*electrum*, amber], dynamic, exciting; *rogue* [perh. *roger*, obs. word for a beggar], scamp, scoundrel, vagabond; *vogue* [It *vogare*, to sail], current fashion.

*Combining forms: a-, without; *cata-*, thoroughly; *deca-*, ten; *dia-*, between; *dys-*, bad; *ec-*, out; *epi-*, in addition; *mono-* one; *pro-*, before.

*Antonyms: eclectic — narrow, limited, specialized; *epilogue* — prologue, preface; *monologue* — colloquy, give-and-take; *prologue* — epilogue, postlude, sequel, aftermath.

LEX, law:
LEG

Something that is **LEGitimate** is **LEGal**, lawful, licit, just, valid, **LEGit**, okay. (I am the legitimate owner of that car. The court ruled that the teachers' demands were legitimate.) An **illLEGitimate** act is **illLEGal**, unlawful, and improper; sometimes it can be **LEGitimized, LEGalized**, and justified. An illegitimate child is born outside of a legal marriage. A **paraLEGal** is an attorney's assistant, but not a person licensed to practice law.

The **LEGislative** body of Nebraska is unicameral; all the other state **LEGislatures** or General Assemblies or General Courts consist of two houses. In most cases the **LEGislators** will be senators or representatives, although in some states they are called delegates. Some dictionaries identify a woman member as a **LEGislatrix** or **LEGislatress**, with plurals of **LEGislatrixes, LEGislatrices**, and **LEGislatresses**, but studies show that most men can't pronounce the words, most women won't answer to them, and most everybody thinks that **LEGislation** should be enacted to **LEGislate** the words out of our language.

Voting is a **priviLEGe** that all citizens of the United States should take advantage of. People who live in countries with democratic governments are the **priviLEGed** ones.

A friend who is **loyal** is true, devoted, and staunch, whereas one who is **disloyal** is false and perfidious. "**Loyalty** to petrified opinion," said Mark Twain, "never yet broke a chain or freed a human soul."

☛ *Once uPUN a time* an officer said to the young man he had just stopped, "Son, that was an illegal turn you made back there at the corner." To which Tony Teen replied, "Gosh, I've never even seen one. How was I supposed to know?" "Seen one what?" the officer asked. "What you said," the teen replied. "You know, an ill eagle."

☛ *But not: delegate* [*legare*, to appoint], deputy; *law* [AS *lague*, a code of rules], rule, statute; *legible* [*legere*, to read], readable.

☛ *Combining forms: dis-*, not; *il-*, not; *-late*, to propose; *para-*, subsidiary; *privi-*, one's own.

☛ *Antonyms: disloyal* — steadfast, scrupulous, punctilious, conscientious, resolute; *illegal* — permissible, rightful, litigious, juristic, statutory, de jure; *illegitimate* — warranted, constitutional, reliable; *legal* — prohibited, banned, outlawed, unlicensed; *legalize* — proscribe, outlaw, interdict; *legitimate* — illicit, spurious, invalid, unprecedented, unfathered; *legitimize* — repudiate, inculpate; *loyal* — treacherous, two-faced, apostate; *loyalty* — perfidy, treachery; *privileged* — disadvantaged, downtrodden, exploited, deprived.

LIBER,
free: LIB

When we see or hear the word **LIBeral** in today's news, it is almost invariably a description of someone's political persuasion. Such considerations aside, a liberal helping of mashed potatoes is abundant, a liberal donation to a charitable organization is generous, a liberal attitude toward immigrants is tolerant, and taking a liberal view toward certain rules or regulations tends to be on the less strict and more broad-minded side.

An **ilLIBeral** attitude, on the other hand, tends to be narrow, bigoted, intolerant, stingy, and miserly. To **LIBeralize** a company policy or a municipal ordinance, for instance, is to loosen or broaden it.

On July 4, 1776, Thomas Jefferson declared that all men "are endowed by their creator with certain unalienable rights; that among these are life, **LIBerty**, and the pursuit of happiness." In 1934 the Italian dictator Benito Mussolini held a funeral for liberty, saying, "We have buried [its] putrid corpse." Actually, it lives on, but, as columnist Molly Ivins has written, we still must "vote, write, speak, work, march, sue, organize, fight, struggle — whatever it takes to secure the blessings of liberty to ourselves and our posterity."

For to **LIBerate** is to set free from whatever: bondage, ignorance, poverty, prejudice, unfairness, discrimination. The women's movement is dedicated to securing full economic, educational, legal, social, and vocational rights, equal to those of men, for women, or, as writer/lecturer Cathy Handley put it,

"Women's **LIBeration** is to find you're an individual." On June 6, 1944 (known thereafter as D-Day), Dwight D. Eisenhower, commander in chief of Allied forces in Western Europe, **delivered** a message by radio: "A landing was made this morning on the coast of France. . . . This landing is part of the . . . plan for the liberation of Europe."

Some months later a G.I. is reported to have said as he stood in the ruins of a French village, "We sure **LIBerated** the hell out of this place." Such is war. And such was the **deliverance** or salvation or liberation of Europe.

A **LIBertarian** believes in the doctrine of free will and advocates complete liberty of conduct and thought. What a **LIBertine** is, however, is not so easy to pin down: "1. a person who is morally or sexually unrestrained, esp. a dissolute man; a profligate; rake. 2. a freethinker in religious matters. 3. a person freed from slavery in ancient Rome.'

Livery is the uniform worn by servants and the care of horses and companies that rent out carriages and/or cars. Among the words that are close in kin are the **deliverers** who make **deliveries** and the **delivery** trucks they make them in.

But not: livery [AS *lifer*, liver], resembling liver.

Combining forms: de-, down, away; *il-,* not.

Antonyms: liberal — penurious, sparse, reactionary, conservative, die-hard, biased, prejudiced, rigorous, literal; *liberalize* — tighten, constrict; *liberate* — capture, imprison, enclave, immure; *liberation* — servitude, subjugation, domination; *libertine* — puritan, ascetic, celibate, abstainer; *liberty* — oppression, denial, taboo, ban, proscription, propriety, discretion, timidity.

IlLITERacy is a greater problem in America today, studies show, than it was fifty to seventy-five years ago. While our language has increased in its size and complexity — the 1987 *Random House Dictionary* includes "over 50,000 new words and 75,000 new meanings" — the electronic media have captured the attention of millions who might otherwise be reading books, magazines, and newspapers. A functional **ilLITERate** is one who reads at approximately the fourth-grade level. That means that he or she **LITERally** cannot read a "help wanted" newspaper ad, the caution labels on a car battery, the weather warnings that run silently across the bottom of the TV picture, or the 23rd Psalm — as it appears in *The Living Bible*, "Because the Lord is my Shepherd, I have everything I need! He lets me rest in the meadow grass and leads me beside the quiet streams."

There are many degrees of **LITERacy**. People who can read the four samples referred to above are **LITERate**, but if that is a measure of their skill, they are on the bottom rung of the ladder. On the next step up is one who can read with some proficiency the news magazines and the editorial and opinion pages of the daily paper. Above that is the person who is well read (keeping in mind here Mark Twain's aphorism, "The man who does not read good books has no advantage over the man who can't read them"). And on the top step is

*LITTERA,
letter of the
alphabet: LITER*

he or she who can be called **lettered**, meaning learned, highly educated, and qualified to stand among the **LITERati**, the intelligentsia. They are **LITERary** folk, those who not only can and do read the classics, but often teach and write about them as well. Classics are the works of lasting value that are the subjects of the lectures delivered in World **LITERature** 372, 8 A.M., M-W-F.

The **LITERal** meaning of **obLITERate** is to blot out or efface **letters**, not the letter-perfect ones written on **letterheads** and then folded into envelopes, but those of the alphabet. Today it means to destroy, eradicate, extirpate, or deracinate. **AlLITERation** is the repetition of the initial letters of several words. (You should hear Sally try to say "She sells sea shells by the seashore.") **AlLITERative** sounds are often heard in a program of perfectly pronounced poetry of Edgar Allan Poe.

☞ ***But not:*** *lettuce* [*lac*, milk], salad green; *liter* [Gk *litra*, pound], liquid metric measure; *litter* [*lectus*, bed], trash, waste.

☞ ***Combining forms:*** *al-*, to; *-head*, upper part; *il-*, not; *ob-*, away; *-perfect*, flawless.

☞ ***Antonyms:*** *illiterate* — taught, instructed, informed, educated, schooled, knowledgeable; *letter-perfect* — garbled, inexact, distorted, misquoted; *literal* — incorrect, erroneous, inaccurate, sloppy, hazy, careless, poetic, romantic, imaginative, figurative; *literally* — vaguely, figuratively, more or less; *literary* — uneducated, untutored, unenlightened; *literate* — ignorant, uninformed, unschooled; *obliterate* — make, create, build, preserve, restore, stet.

**LOCARE,
to place: LOCA**

"Glamorous Lisa Tomuch," the news release said, "is now on **LOCAtion** in the **LOCAlity** of Buxton, Devonshire, for the filming of 'The Lieutenant's Story,' the **LOCAle** of which is the famous Cat and the Fiddle Pub. 'The **milieu** there is perfect for this story; I can think of no better atmosphere anywhere,' Director Leslie Limey said.

"**LOCAls** may audition for bit parts beginning Tuesday. Applicants are advised that they may have to **reLOCAte** when the second half of the movie is shot. Everyday clothing may be worn in **lieu** of army garb.

"The 10:06 **LOCAl** pulled by **locomotive** #66 should be taken to Ayre. The hiring office is **LOCAted** on the village common."

As an adjective, *local* has many meanings, many of which are pejorative, that is unfavorable, negative, unpleasant, and disparaging. "We have all attended the local schools" is neutral. On the other hand, " I doubt if anyone big's ever heard of Sal; she's just a local celeb, you understand" may well be taken to mean limited, confined, narrow, small-town, parochial, provincial, and insular.

A **LOCAlism** is a custom, a word or phrase, a pronunciation, or a manner of speaking that is generally limited to a particular place or area. Drivers in one rural area may greet oncoming neighbors with a "thumb-up" from a hand on the steering wheel, while in another they may raise a couple of fingers or wave the whole hand. City drivers generally tend to keep all of both hands on the wheel when not phoning, tuning the radio, changing the tape, or making a fist.

To **LOCAte** is to settle, situate, unearth, pinpoint, track down. To **alLOCAte** is to set aside, assign, apportion, earmark, mete; one's **alLOCAtion** is one's share. To **colLOCAte** is to arrange in proper order. (When we put all the papers together, we had to collocate the numbered pages.) To **disLOCAte** is to put out of joint, as one's shoulder, and to upset or throw out of order, (''Through centuries of despair and **disLOCAtion**, we had been creative, because we faced down death by daring to hope,'' wrote Maya Angelou). To **reLOCA**te is to move to another place or to move again.

Locomotion is the act or power of moving from one place to another. A **locus** is old hat to geometry students. It is a place, location, spot, area, and its plural is **loci**. To **LOCAlize** is to position, place, locate, fix, establish. (The seismologists localized the quake as occurring along the San Andreas fault.)

But not: loco [Sp *loco*, insane], crazy; *locust* [*locusta*, grasshopper], cicada, tree; *purlieu* [*pur-*, through + *aler*, to go], an outlying part of a town.

Antonyms: local — broad, general, worldly, cosmopolitan, sophisticated, urbane, exotic; *localize* — broaden, amplify, widen, expand; *locate* — lose, conceal, dislodge, leave, decamp, depart, abondon, vacate; *locomotion* — immobility, inactivity, inertia, stasis.

LOGOS [Gk], word: LOG, LOGY

When we talk **LOGic**, we talk words. That is, logic has to do with reasoning, and we reason with words. A **LOGical** statement ''sounds'' right, is reasonable, rational, clear, coherent, valid, and cogent. An **ilLOGical** assertion is fallacious, wrong, invalid, implausible, perhaps not at first sight, but certainly after an objective examination. ''If everyone would get out and vote, I know our party would win the election'' is an obviously unreasonable, irrational, and illogical argument, and one does not have to be a trained **LOGician** to see the fallacy.

The form of reasoning known as a **sylLOGism** [Gk *syl-*, together] can be reduced from words to letters or other symbols. If A is B and B is C, then A is C. That's logical:

>   All cats are mammals.
>   Trixie is a cat.
>   Therefore, Trixie is a mammal.

However, if we say A is B and C is B, therefore A is C, that's bonkers:

>   A beaver lives in a lodge.
>   Jayson and Alicia Franklin live in a lodge.
>   Therefore, Jayson and Alicia Franklin are beavers.

Obviously absurd reasoning. No rational being would accept that conclusion. Right? Wrong:

>   An atheist does not go to church.
>   Lauri and Larry Lee do not go to church.
>   Therefore, Lauri and Larry Lee are atheists.

Maybe the two of them are, but that line of reasoning does not prove it.

The **LOGistics** of an enterprise, military or otherwise, is the planning, the organizing, and the working out of a project or operation. (Once we got the logistics of the trip straightened out, we had smooth sailing.)

A company's **LOGotype** or **LOGo** is its symbol or trademark used in advertising and on the product itself; tests show that many long-standing logos are now recognized even with the product name omitted. **LOGO** is a programming language used to teach children how to use computers. A **LOGogram** [Gk *gramma*, something written] is an abbreviated symbol for a frequently used word or phrase: the ampersand (&) stands for *and*; other symbols appear on the top line of the keyboard.

A logogram is also a simple form of the word game we call an anagram [Gk *ana-*, back]. Here's a sample: make as many words as you can from, say, North America (math, merit, rice, etc.) Other names for word games are **LOGogriph** [Gk *griphos*, riddle] and **LOGomachy** [Gk *machia*, battle]; the latter also means a dispute about words. **LOGodaedaly** [Gk *daidalos*, skillful] is the arbitrary or capricious coinage of words: *blizzard, flumadiddle, rowdy* are notable examples, and, now, for the first time ever in print, *impoopable*, adj., incapable of becoming exhausted or pooped out.

''Shakespeare used 17,677 words in his writings,'' Bill Bryson says in his fascinating book *The Mother Tongue*, ''of which at least one tenth had never been used before. Imagine if every tenth word you wrote were original.'' Here's a baker's dozen of Shapespeare's: barefaced, leapfrog, monumental, majestic, obscene, frugal, dwindle, gust, hint, hurry, countless, excellent, and summit.

The wings of a bird and those of an airplane are **anaLOGous**; they are also **homoLOGous** [Gk *homo-*, same]. An **apoLOGetic** [Gk *apo-*, defense] person is full of regret and remorse; he or she may also be, often needlessly, on the defensive. (There's no reason for you to be apologetic; you gave it one hundred percent.) To **apoLOGize** is to retract or confess or repent one's act or statement. An **apoLOGia** is usually a written work explaining or defending or justifying one's motives or actions. (The former Gestapo functionary's book is a whining, self-serving apologia that will convince no one.) To **euLOGize** (Gk *eu-*, good, well] is to praise someone to the skies.

Those words now lead us into the copious *-logy* category (**anaLOGY**, expression of similarity; **apoLOGY**, expression of regret; **euLOGY**, expression of praise). These and the following words have a general reference to speech or writing or collections or something related.

AnthoLOGY [Gk *antho-*, flowers], a collection of selected writings, such as essays, poems, short stories, by one or more authors.

DoxoLOGY [Gk *doxo-*, honor, glory], (l.c. hymn of praise to God; (cap.) hymn beginning ''Praise God from whom all blessings flow.''

EtymoLOGY [Gk *etymos*, true, real], derivation of a word; account of the history of a certain word.

NeoLOGY [Gk *neos*, new], a neologism (a new word) or an example of it.

PhraseoLOGY [Gk *phrasis*, style], manner or style of an expression, e.g., legal phraseology.

TautoLOGY [Gk *tauto*, the same], needless repetition of words, redundancy, verbiage, e.g., widow woman, hot water heater, my own personal opinion, to continue on, consensus of opinion.

TerminoLOGY [*terminus*, boundary, limit], terms used in a specific field, nomenclature, jargon, cant, lingo.

TriLOGY [Gk *treis, tria*, three], group of three literary or dramatic compositions, e.g., John Dos Passos's *U.S.A.* consists of three novels.

There is another and larger group of words that employ *-logy*; these are names of bodies of knowledge and sciences (although the scientific credentials of a few of these are a bit suspect).

AnthropoLOGY [Gk *anthropos*, human being], science dealing with the origin, evolution, and development of humans, including the study of their beliefs, customs, etc.

ArcheoLOGY [Gk *archaios*, ancient], scientific study of the cultures of historic and prehistoric peoples by analysis of their artifacts and other remains.

AstroLOGY [Gk *astron*, star], study that deals with supposed influences of celestial bodies on the lives of human beings.

BioLOGY [Gk *bios*, life], science of life and life processes.

CardioLOGY [Gk *kardio*, heart], study of the heart and its function.

ChronoLOGY [Gk *chronos*, time], science of arranging time in periods and historical events in their proper sequence.

ConchoLOGY [Gk *konkhe*, shell], branch of zoology dealing with mollusks and shells.

CosmoLOGY [Gk *kosmos*, universe], branch of philosophy dealing with the origin and structure of the universe.

DemonoLOGY [Gk *daimon*, divine power], study of demons or the belief in them; belief in demons.

DermatoLOGY [Gk *dermato*, the skin], medical science dealing with diseases of the skin.

EcoLOGY (Gk *oikos*, house], science that deals with the relationships between organisms and their environments.

EntomoLOGY [Gk *entomos*, notched], branch of zoology dealing with insects.

EpistemoLOGY [Gk *episteme*, knowledge], philosophy that examines the origin, nature, limits of human knowledge.

EthnoLOGY [Gk *ethnos*, culture, people, race], branch of anthropology that deals with the characteristics and cultures of racial and ethnic groups.

ExobioLOGY [Gk *exo*, outside + *bios*, life], study of life beyond the earth's atmosphere.

GeneaLOGY [Gk *genea*, race], study of ancestry and pedigree.

GeoLOGY [Gk *geo*, the earth], science that deals with the origin and structure of the earth.

GynecoLOGY [Gk *gyneco*, woman], branch of medicine that deals with the female body.

HagioLOGY [Gk *hagios*, holy, sacred], branch of literature dealing with saints, e.g., the biographies of saints.

HematoLOGY [Gk *haimat*, blood], study of blood, its nature and diseases.

HerpetoLOGY [Gk *herpeton*, creeping thing], branch of zoology dealing with amphibians and reptiles.

HistoLOGY [Gk *histos*, web (of a loom)], biological science that deals with the structure of plant and animal tissue.

HoroLOGY [Gk *horo*, hour], science of the measurement of time and the making of timepieces.

IchthyoLOGY [Gk *ichthys*, fish], branch of zoology dealing with fishes.

IdeoLOGY [Gk *idea*, form, notion], body of ideas that reflect the social needs and goals of individuals, groups, classes, or cultures.

LexicoLOGY [Gk *lexikos*, words], study of formation, meaning, and use of words and idioms.

MartyroLOGY [Gk *martys*, witness], branch of knowledge dealing with the lives and histories of martyrs.

MeteoroLOGY [Gk *meteoron*, a thing in the air], study of the atmosphere and the weather.

MethodoLOGY [Gk *hodos*, way, road], study of the principles and procedures of a branch of knowledge.

MycoLOGY [Gk *mykes*, mushroom, fungus], branch of biology dealing with fungi.

MythoLOGY [Gk *mythos*, story], study of or collection of the myths of a certain group of people.

NeuroLOGY [Gk *neuron*, nerve], medical study of the nervous system and its disorders.

NumeroLOGY [*numerus*, number], study of the occult meanings of numbers, as with the numbers of the year of one's birth, and their influence on one's life and future.

OncoLOGY [Gk *onkos*, mass], medical branch that deals with tumors, including the origin, development, diagnosis, and treatment of cancer.

OntoLOGY [Gk *einai*, being], philosophical study of reality and being.

OphthalmoLOGY [Gk *opthalmos*, eye], medical science that deals with the functions and diseases of the eye.

OrnithoLOGY [GK *ornis*, bird], zoological science that deals with birds.

OroLOGY [Gk *oros*, mountain], study of mountains.

PaleontoLOGY [Gk *palaios*, ancient], study of ancient forms and fossils.

PathoLOGY [Gk *pathos*, suffering], medical study of the nature of disease.

PenoLOGY [Gk *poine*, penalty], study of crime prevention and prison management.

PharmacoLOGY [Gk *pharmakon*, drugs], science of drugs, including their nature, preparation, and effects.

PhiloLOGY [Gk *philos*, loving], study of literary texts and written records to establish authenticity.

PhrenoLOGY *[Gk phren*, mind], practice based on the belief that certain mental faculties and character traits are indicated by the shape of the skull.

PhysioLOGY [Gk *physis*, nature], biological science of life processes by which animals function.

PsychoLOGY [Gk *psyche*, breath, spirit, mind], science of mental powers and functions.

RadioLOGY [Gk *radius*, beam], science dealing with x-rays and nuclear radiation for medical purposes.

SeismoLOGY [Gk *seismos*, quake], study of earthquakes and their phenomena.

SocioLOGY [*socius*, fellow, companion], study of the origin, evolution, and characteristics of human society.

SpeleoLOGY [Gk *spelaion*, cave], exploration and study of caves.

TechnoLOGY [Gk *techne*, art, skill], application of technical improvements in industry, commerce, etc.

TheoLOGY [Gk *theos*, god], study of the nature of God and of religious truth.

ToxicoLOGY [Gk *toxon*, bow], study of the nature and effects of poison.

ZooLOGY [Gk *zoion*, animal, living being], study of the origin, evolution, structure, and classification of animals.

But not: *monologue, prologue, travelogue*, etc.; see *legein*, p. 92.

LOQUI,
to speak:
LOCU, LOQU

"Who you voting for?" Ardley asked his friend Zacharia. "Me, I like the way Lomow talks — you know, everyday, common, ordinary. Like you and me."

"Ah, yes," Zacharia declared. "**ColLOQUial**, idiomatic, demotic, unsophisticated, vernacular."

"Whatever," Ardley said. "Doesn't throw around college words and says what he's got to say and that's it."

"I know what you mean," Zacharia stated. "No ostentatious **grandiLOQUence**, no high-flown, pompous, turgid, swollen language, and none of the **LOQUacious**, garrulous, verbose, gushy, prolix, non-stop speaking, replete with **circumLOCUtions**, or the wordy gobbledygook that characterizes the speech of so many who mount the stump."

"You took the words right out of my mouth," Ardley said. "Some of those guys talk like they got this wooden dummy on their laps, you know, going on like one of them Shakespeare guys talking all alone without nobody listening, like maybe they're talking in their sleep."

"Exactly!" Zacharia exclaimed. "Your analogy is most apt. Just like a **ventriLOQUist** talking out of his stomach, so to speak, his ventricle. And seemingly unaware that he is not alone, his **soliLOQUy** is like a monologue, a steady stream of words, rather than a **colLOQUy**, conversation, dialogue, discussion. And, yes, quite analogous to a **somniLOQUy**, the speech of a sleepwalker."

"Yeah!" Ardley said. "That's not Lomow, for sure. Like I said, he's down-to-earth, just like you and me."

"Well put. He has the gift of **eLOQUence**, the fluency, the appeal, the persuasion," Zacharia opined. "Yet his **eLOQUent** style is not that of one schooled in a half dozen stuffy courses in formal **eLOCUtion**. His speech is stirring, mov-

ing, striking, and forceful. Yet, oddly enough, I have concluded that his opponent, Oscar Hugo Himow, is more believable. I must cast my vote for him.''

''Yeah, me, too,'' Ardley said. ''Well, I enjoyed the **colLOQUium**, a conference like this one is always enlightening. Especially with an **interLOCUtor**
like you as a conversational partner. Your **LOCUtion** is firstrate, all of it, your
pronunciation, phrasing, wording, the whole shebang. And, too, I really appreciated your not engaging in **obLOQUy**, not a word of slander, rebuke,
calumny, nor opprobrium. All on a high level. Well, see you around.''

☛ **But not:* locus [*locus*, place], a locality; math term; *monologue* [Gk *mono*, sole
+ *logue*, *legein*, to speak], prolonged talk by one person.

☛ **Combining forms:* circum-, around; *col-*, together; *e-*, out; *grandi-*, great; *inter-*,
between; *ob-*, against; *soli-*, alone; *somni-*, sleep; *ventri-*, belly.

☛ **Antonyms:* circumlocution — brevity, terseness, conciseness, pithiness; *eloquent*
— inarticulate, hesitant, dull, tongue-tied, inexpressive, vapid, enigmatic; *loquacious* — tactiturn, reticent, silent, reserved, terse, quiet, conticent; *obloquy*
— praise, respect, adulation, eulogy, panegyric, esteem.

LUCERE,
to shine;
LUMEN, light;
LUC, LUM

Most of us who read more than we watch — and certainly *all* editors and
teachers — welcome writing that is **LUMinous** (You have written a concise,
luminous report!), **LUCid** (I appreciate your lucid explanation; it is both comprehensible and rational), and **pelLUCid** (Figgley's new book, alas, is not written in the sparkling, pellucid prose that distinguished her first novel).

Although under the entry for **transLUCent** the *Random House Unabridged Dictionary, Second Edition,* offers a sample sentence in which frosted glass is described as ''translucent but not transparent,'' the same dictionary gives as part
of its definition, ''clear, transparent.'' Clearly, **LUCidity** was neglected in that
instance. Other dictionaries, however, qualify as ''rare'' that definition or omit
it altogether.

When we **eLUCidate** something, we throw light upon it, make it lucid, and
just plain clear things up. (He: I believe my explanation has elucidated my
reasons for forgetting our anniversary. She: Oh? I didn't find it very **il-
LUMinating**, Elliott. Especially all that bunkum about **LUCifer** making you
forget! The truth is you've never been the same since you met that wealthy
LUMinary out in Hollywood!)

People who claim that they possess special intellectual or spiritual enlightenment are said to be members of the **ilLUMinati**.

To **LUCubrate** is to study hard, especially at night; thus **LUCubration** is
laborious study, also especially at night. It is likely that during such periods
— one hopes with sufficient **ilLUMination** — there will be some who try to
eLUCubrate, that is, produce something, such as a book, by long and intensive effort. If they do, and if it sells well, they will be hailed as **LUMinosities**,
intellectually brilliant, enlightened, and inspired.

Meanwhile, up in the heavens there's Sirius the Dog Star, the sixth nearest
to us and the brightest in the skies, with a **LUMinosity** twenty-three times

that of our sun. That would be too bright to read by, just as our moon is a bit too dim. But, then, whoever wanted to *read* by the light of that big old **LUCent** harvest moon, anyway?

*But not: lucre [*lucrum*, profit], money; *lucrative* [*lucrum*, profit], moneymaking; *lumbago* [*lumbus*, loin], a pain in the lower back; *lummox* [?], dolt, oaf.

*Combining forms: e-, out; *-fer*, to beat; *il-*, thoroughly; *pel-*, through; *trans-*, across.

*Antonyms: elucidate — muddle, confuse, perplex, obfuscate; *illuminate* — darken, obscure; *illuminating* — obscuring, puzzling; *lucent* — dim, murky, dull, opaque, dense; *lucid* — unintelligible, fuzzy, vague, enigmatic, irrational, muddled, incompetent; *luminary* — ordinary person, average citizen, nonentity, nonperson; *luminous* — abstruse, cloudy, subdued, dull.

LUDERE,
to play:
LUDE, LUS

The cord between the original meaning of this root and its present-day definitions is somewhat visible in a few of today's words and hardly at all in many others. People who allow themselves to be **deLUDEd** about their superiority are often "playing" with reality. They suffer from **deLUSive** beliefs. (What's so delusive, false, and unreal about my thinking that I'm twice as good as I really am?) There's nothing new about **deLUSions**; Cervantes' Don Quixote saw armies that were actually sheep and giants that were in fact windmills.

The cord can be sensed, too, in **ilLUSions**, the daydreams and fantasies that sometimes "play" with our senses of reality. (I know it's only an illusion, but our living room seems so much bigger now that one wall is all mirrors.) To experience an illusion is generally quite normal, whereas people with delusions on the scale of Don Quixote's have some mighty serious problems.

An **ilLUSory** idea is deceptive and misleading. (Coach told us before the game that thinking we're unbeatable because we're unbeaten is an illusory idea.) A magician, especially one who practices sleight of hand, is an **ilLU-Sionist**. (There wasn't any rabbit in that hat when he showed it to us!) To **disilLUSion** your friends is to shatter their illusions, to open their eyes as to what's what. (Petie said she hated to disillusion us, but we didn't have a chance in the world of winning the $10,000,000 sweepstakes.) Someone who is **disilLU-Sioned** is disappointed, disheartened, and downcast. (Sirwitz was dreadfully disillusioned when his painting did not get even an honorable mention.)

From there on the cord becomes all but invisible. To **alLUDE** to an event is to mention or speak of it. (The millionaire frequently alluded to the poverty of his childhood.) An **alLUSion** is the referring to or mention of a person or event. (The award-winner's speech was filled with allusions to Fitzgerald, Welty, and Hemingway.) Originally the word had the meaning of "to play beside," but there is little of that sense left today.

To **colLUDE** is to connive, conspire, or plot with another to do something. (Kate admitted that she had colluded with a clerk in the college office to change her math grade.) **ColLUSion** is a secret agreement, conspiracy, scheme, or machination for deceitful or fraudulent purposes. (It was proved during the trial that the employees had acted in collusion in trying to take over the corporation.) An example of a **colLUSive** agreement is one that would illegally increase or fix prices on a certain product.

Someone who **eLUDEs** the truant officers evades, escapes, and avoids them. That's what can happen with the answer or solution to a problem when we are not quite able to bring it to the light. (I kept thinking I had the answer, but then it eluded me again.) An **eLUSive** runner, whether on the football field or the Great Plains, is difficult to catch, just as an abstract concept can be.

PreLUDEs are preliminary comments, works, or events. (During her nightly prelude to her stand-up comedy act, Tizzy relaxed to the sounds of Chopin preludes on compact discs. During the **interLUDEs** that she had to endure while others were on stage, she paced the floor of her dressing room. It was a practice so pointless that eventually even she had to laught at her **ludicrous** habit.)

☞ *But not: exclusive* [*claudere*, to close], chic, select; *preclude* [*claudere*], to prevent the existence of something or make it impossible.

☞ *Combining forms: al-*, to; *col-*, together; *de-*, from; *dis-*, apart; *e-*, away; *il-*, against; *inter*, between; *pre-*, before.

☞ *Antonyms: illusory* — factual, real, authentic, practical, true, genuine, down-to-earth; *ludicrous* — sensible, logical, sad, doleful, grave, solemn, melancholy, sorry.

LUNA[L],
SELENE [Gk],
the moon: LUNA

We must suppose that the moon shone as brightly on ancient Greece as it did on Rome, but their word-legacies are strikingly different. From *Selene*, the Greek goddess of the moon, we get technical terms such as **selenography**, the study of the moon's surface, **selenology**, the branch of astronomy that deals with the moon, and a cluster of words that are largely confined to chemistry labs.

Across the waters of the Ionian and Adriatic seas, however, the words trickling down from *Luna*, the Roman moon goddess, were generally more people-oriented. Well, sort of, anyway. Folks who supposedly lived on the moon were called **LUNArians**, and the minds of some people were thought to be affected by the phases of the moon, resulting in **lunes**, fits of madness. Everytime there was a full moon, a bunch of **LUNAtics** came out of the **LUNAtic** closet. The **interLUNAr** period between the full and new moons was relatively pleasant and safe, the lunatics either back in the closet or in their normal phase.

Those words are no longer used in the technical sense of insanity or dementia; we employ them in a looser and wider sense, although one not necessarily less alarming. (''The world,'' said David Lloyd George, one-time British prime minister, ''is becoming like a lunatic asylum run by lunatics.'') Today we tend to lean toward the lighter vein of being a few bubbles off center, about ninety cents short of a dollar, or shy several beans in the pod. **LUNAcy** is a part of this group, too. (That's sheer lunacy, quitting his job six weeks before Christmas!)

''Lunatic fringe'' refers to members of a group that hold extreme or fanatical views. **SubLUNAry** denotes the vast area ''below'' the moon and refers to things terrestrial or pertaining to the earth; it is also used in the sense of mundane, worldly, or mortal.

Demilune refers to the half moon and, therefore, to a crescent or anything crescent shaped. We speak of the **LUNAr** month and module as well as the rover, the vehicle the Apollo astronauts used in exploring the moon's surface, of **LUNAte** or crescent-shaped bones or designs, and of **LUNAtion**, a period of approximately 29½ days between returns of the new moon.

Combining forms: demi-, half; *-graphy*, a description; *inter-*, between; *-logy*, the study of; *sub-*, below.

Antonyms: lunacy — sanity, rationality, lucidity, reason, prudence, common sense; *lunatic* — sane, rational, reasonable, sound, lucid, all there.

After the taking of the census every five years in ancient Rome, a purification ceremony took place; it was called a **LUSTRum**, and the word now means a period of five years. A ten-year period is called a decade [Gk *dekad*, a group of ten], twenty years is a score [ON *skor*, notch], and one hundred is a century [*centuria*, a group of one hundred soldiers]. A millennium is one thousand years [*mill*, thousand + *ennium*, year], and a myriad is the equivalent of ten millenniums [Gk *myriad*, ten thousand].

An **ilLUSTRious** person is eminent, famous, and renowned; an illustrious career is **LUSTRous**, distinguished, and exemplary. A lecture that is **ilLUSTRative** is explanatory, illuminating, and explicative. (After listening to all those boring, **lackluster** speeches, it was a great treat to hear Dr. Jane Long's illustrative talk. I felt it added **luster** to her already distinguished reputation.) To **ilLUSTRate** a book is to pictorialize, delineate, or ornament it — assuming, that is, that the **ilLUSTRations** are attractive and pertinent to the text. To illustrate a point is to clarify or simplify it or, perhaps, to highlight or emphasize it.

But not: illusion [*il-* + *ludere*, to play], a misconception; *lackadaisical* [from *lackadaisy*, a variant form of *lackaday*, an expression of disapproval, dismay, regret, or sorrow], mindless, indifferent; *lusty* [AS *lust*, pleasure], hearty, vigorous.

Combining forms: il-, thoroughly; *lack-*, without.

Antonyms: illustrious — obscure, unassuming, lowly, humble, infamous, notorious; *lackluster* — radiant, shiny, lively, vivid; *luster* — drabness, dullness; *lustrous* — dark, dim, drab, dull.

LUSTRARE,
to purify:
LUSTR

M

**MAGNUS,
large, great;
MAGN, MAJ**

When King John of England was forced to sign the **MAGNa Carta** on June 15, 1215, a great step forward was made in the cause of liberty. Today in democratic countries around the world the **MAJority** can call the shots. Although the English people refer to their monarch as His or Her **MAJesty**, the **MAJor** personage in their government is the prime minister.

In earlier times a Venetian nobleman was called a **MAGNifico**, but today a person of such wealth and power is termed a **MAGNate**. Our city governments are headed by **mayors**, and the person in charge of an enormous household, such as that of a monarch or other member of a royal family, is referred to as the **MAJor domo**.

When we got to college, we major in a field or subject, such as English, math, history, German, etc. In Speech 107 we learn to avoid speaking in the pompous style known as **MAGNiloquence**. In English we discover that people who talk of "**maximizing** one's attention span in a **maximal** learning environment" are speaking the nonsense language called gobbledygook. Students who aim for the **maximum** graduating honor, summa cum laude, are sometimes disappointed if they hit only the second level of **MAGNitude** or importance, **MAGNa** cum laude. In reality, these **maxima** (a plural of maximum) are both commendable. These are people who dream of someday creating their **MAGNum opus**, a great work of art or writing.

Sometimes words become chopped off; just as we have mini-markets and minivans, we have **maxi**-service in a restaurant, maxicoats for women, and maxi-taxis for small groups.

There are times, too, when we **MAGNify** people's qualities by using words that are gross exaggerations. "What a **MAGNificent** grass rake this is!" "Why, I think your left earring is simply **MAJestic**!" "Ms. Zilch is the most **MAGNanimous** person in the world; she gave a whole can of pork and beans to the Food for the Homeless drive!" This is often done to poke fun at others and is a favorite weapon of cartoonists and comedians.

A **maxim**, a saying, adage, proverb, or axiom, is a general rule or truth, such as Benjamin Franklin's "Early to bed and early to rise, makes a man healthy, wealthy, and wise."

☛ *But not:* magnet [Gk magneta, short for Magnes, the stone of Magnesia], thing or person that attracts; magnolia [after Pierre Magnol, F botanist], shrub and tree; majlis [Ar], Iranian house of parliament; maximite [after Hudson Maxim, its inventor], an explosive.

☛ *Combining forms:* -animous, soul; carta, charter; cum laude, with praise; domo, house; -ficent, -fico, -fy, to make; -loquent, to talk; opus, work.

*Antonyms: magnanimous — petty, mean, selfish; *magnificent* — humble, modest, ordinary; *magnifico* — nobody, cipher, pawn, lightweight; *magnify* — reduce, compress, disparage, belittle; *majestic* — lowly, grubby, squalid, humble; *major* — minor, lesser, smaller, secondary; *majority* — minority, few, nonage, immaturity; *maximize* — minimize, scale down, lessen; *maximum* — minimum, iota, minimal, least.

The **MALL** — that center where millions of Americans shop every day — owes its name to the ancestor of a popular lawn game. In the seventeenth century ''**pall mall**'' was introduced into London. A contemporary described it as a game ''wherein a round ball is struck with a mall [**MALLet**] through a high arch of iron, which he that can do at the fewest blows wins.'' Its descendant is, obviously, our croquet, a game that is now an intercollegiate sport.

In London pall mall was first played in alleys, one of which became so popular with the players that the street took on the name of the game. When young King Charles II (1630–85) and his courtiers discovered the pastime, he chose to move the playing field to a wide thoroughfare that ran through St. James Park.

Since mallets are wicked (wicket?) instruments, in order to keep them from becoming instruments of harm, this rule was posted: ''Noe persons shall after play carry their malls out of St. James Park without the leave of the keeper.'' (Except, we've got to believe, for young Charlie. Keepers tend to be rather **MALLeable** in the presence of royalty; as a matter of fact, they tend to be downright rubbery. They know they might be **mauled** if they get stubborn and unyielding.)

When those two thoroughfares were no longer used for the game, both the Mall of St. James Park and Pall Mall became promenades, that is, public places for leisurely strolling and, in time, the displaying of goods for sale.

And that's the way it is today in the mall — shops, scores of not-so-leisurely walkers, and no one playing croquet.

*But not: pall [*pallium*, cloak], a cloth that covers a coffin; something that covers, such as gloom or darkness; *pall* [form of ''appall,'' *pallidus*, pale], to decline, bore, satiate; *pell-mell* [*miscere*, to mix], helter-skelter.

*Antonyms: malleable — rigid, intractable, refractory, unmanageable.

In her novel *Parents and Children*, Ivy Compton-Burnett has two characters discuss the matter of obedience:

''She still seems to me in her own way a person born to **comMAND**,'' said Luce. . . .

''I wonder if anyone is born to obey,'' said Isabel.

''That may be why people command rather badly, that they have no suitable material to work on.''

To command, one must govern, rule, guide, order, or require, a difficult enough task at best; but as **comMANDer** one must also be leader, chief, direc-

MALLEUS,
hammer: MALL

MANDARE,
to order:
MAND, MEND

tor, captain, or boss. As a noun, command has two different meanings: 1. authority, power, supremacy (Need I remind you that Whiteside is in command here?); and 2. an injunction, fiat, order (Once the command was given, the children stopped talking). Dictionary definitions of ''command performance'' state that it is a play, ballet, opera, etc., that is presented at the request of a head of state. The phrase, however, has trickled down to other uses, particularly in regard to any social or business function that one is expected to attend. (You turned down the boss's dinner invite? Around here that's considered a command performance!)

ComMANDant is the title of the senior officer of the U.S. Marine Corps, the chief officer of a certain place or group, and the head of a military school. A **comMANDo** was a specially trained Allied military unit in World War II. To **comMANDeer** private property is to seize it for police or military use. (The officer commandeered a delivery truck to chase the getaway car.) Police and military units have **comMANDing** officers; a hockey team going into the third period ahead 6 to 0 has a commanding lead; a house high on a bluff overlooking the Mississippi River offers a commanding view. A **comMANDment** is an order, mandate, charge, precept, rule, edict, or decree.

To **comMEND** is to praise, extol, acclaim, eulogize, endorse, boost, approve. (The reviewers commended the actor's performance and the movie itself.) It also means to entrust, transfer, give, and hand over. (Ed's grandfather commended his two stores to Ed and his wife.) **COmMENDable** means praiseworthy, laudable, meritorious, deserving, and exemplary. (Generosity is a commendable trait.) ''Small matters win great **comMENDation**,'' Francis Bacon wrote, meaning approval, praise, approbation, encomium, and panegyric.

To **counterMAND** an order or command is to cancel, revoke, rescind, abrogate, or nullify it. (The lieutenant countermanded the sergeant's order.)

A **deMAND** is an order, injunction, requisition, exhortation, or ultimatum. (Mom's every demand was taken care of.) It is also a need or requirement. (There isn't a great demand for icemakers in Nome.) It has two meanings as a verb, as well: 1. to insist on, claim, press for, require (Our new principal demands strict obedience to the rules); 2. To need, require, necessitate, call for (It was a situation that demanded immediate action). The adjective **deMANDing** means exacting, taxing, tough, trying, onerous. (Brooks has applied to two of the most highly selective and demanding colleges in the country.)

A **MANDate** is a command, directive, writ, dictate, behest, instruction. (The president had a clear mandate from the voters to end the hostilities.) It is also a protectorate or dependency. (This island is a mandate of the United States government.) An order or rule that is **MANDatory** is compulsory, obligatory, imperative, requisite, binding, peremptory. (The commission proposed that two years of Latin and Greek roots be mandatory in all high schools.)

In Shakespeare's *Macbeth* King Duncan says, ''This castle [of Macbeth's] hath a pleasant seat; the air / Nimbly and sweetly **recomMENDs** itself unto our senses.'' Thus when we recommend a book to a friend, we endorse, promote, applaud, praise, and sanction it. But when the police officer recommends that we use extreme caution on the wet road, he or she advises, counsels, advocates, proposes, or suggests. A **recomMENDation** is an endorsement, approval, good word, commendation, and plug. (It was Professor Engers' recommendation that got me the scholarship.)

To **reMAND** is to send back; it is commonly used in sending a case back to a lower court and in sending an accused person or a prisoner back into custody. (The visiting judge ruled that the two prisoners who were awaiting trial be remanded to the state prison system.)

But not: commence [com-, with + initiare, to begin], to start; comment[com-, with + men, mind], remark; mendacious [mendax, false], lying, dishonest.

Combining forms: com-, thoroughly; counter-, against; de-, down, away; re-, back, again.

Antonyms: commend — condemn, disparage, censure, discredit; commendable — inferior, blameworthy, contemptible, culpable, execrable; commendation — blame, incrimination, disapproval, blackball; demanding — easy, simple, leisurely; mandatory — optional, voluntary, discretionary, volitional; recommend — denigrate, discourage, deter, remonstrate; recommendation — criticism, objection, aspersion, animadversion.

''I say, must you really catch the night rain? I mean, you're that short of water around here?''

''What? Night rain? No, no! I have to catch the night train!''

''It's that kind of oral confusion that, back around Chaucer's time, changed ''a napron'' into ''an **apron**.'' The same change took place with the snake we know today as ''an adder''; it was once ''a nadder.'' In detective circles this is known as ''The Case of the Sliding N.''

An early **map** of the world was known as a *mappa mundi*, most likely because such maps were drawn on pieces of cloth.

Napery is the linen (or cotton or synthetics) that covers our table, hence **napkin**, a small piece of cloth. Be warned, however, that in England it's a diaper and in Scotland a handkerchief or neckerchief.

A **mop** is a wadded-up piece of cloth or bundle of yarn used to wipe up a spill; to complete an action or operation today, we mop up. An obsolete meaning of mop was a rag doll, and from that may have come the word **moppet**, a small child.

But not: nap [AS hnappian], to doze; nap [D noppe], fuzzy surface on cloth.

As the old song sort of says, ''M'' is for *mother*:

Dutch	French	German	Greek	Italian	Russian	Spanish
moeder	mère	Mutter	mētēr	madre	mat	madre

MAPPA, napkin, cloth

MATER [L], METER [Gk], mother: MAT, METRO

It follows thus that "M" is also for **MATernal**, or motherly ("My maternal waitress advised me in the selection of my lunch," Arnold Bennett); **MATernity**, motherhood, pertaining to pregnant women; **MATRimony**, marriage, wedlock ("A lady's imagination is very rapid; it jumps from admiration to love, from love to matrimony in a moment," Jane Austen); **MATron**, a mature and dignified married woman, a female prison or hospital employee, a dame, a dowager ("The bashful virgin's side-long looks of love, / The matron's glance that would those looks reprove," Oliver Goldsmith); **MATronly**, maturely dignified, sedate.

A **MATriarchy** is a family, community, society, or state in which women have most of the authority. The acknowledged head is a **MATriarch**, although the word is also used to designate a highly respected older woman.

An original meaning of **MATrix** is "the womb," stemming from an earlier Latin meaning of a female animal kept for breeding purposes. Today it usually refers to a mold, cast, die, or template. It also means the place or point from which something else develops; as U.S. Supreme Court Justice Benjamin Cardozo once wrote, "Freedom of expression is the matrix . . . of nearly every other form of freedom."

A **MATriculant** is someone who **MATriculates** or enrolls in a college or university as a candidate for a degree to be obtained many semesters and student loans later. With sheepskin in hand, the graduate will be privileged to look back upon, sing about, and be solicited for funds by his or her **alma MATer**.

The mother city or parent state in a colony of ancient Greece was called a **METROpolis**. Because it was a principal place, a hub, or center of many activities, the citizens came to be regarded as **METROpolitan**, meaning urbane, cosmopolitan, well bred, and sophisticated. In short, **METROpolites**. Today some of those live in a **METROplex** (like Dallas–Fort Worth) have at their convenience a high-speed railway called a **METROliner** (Boston–New York–Washington, D.C.), watch ballgames in a **METROdome** (Minneapolis), and speed between work and home on the underground **METRO** (Washington, D.C., Paris, Montreal).

☞ *Once uPUN a time* a pixieish soothsayer came up with this long-range spring behavioral forecast: April pranks will bring Matrix.

☞ *But not: mate* [G *gemate*, companion], a spouse; *material* [*materia*, matter], substance; *metronome* [Gk *metro*, measure], instrument used in musical practice.

☞ *Combining forms: alma*, nourishing; *-arch*, ruler; *-dome*, roof shaped like an inverted bowl; *-liner*, plane, ship, or train operated by a transportation company; *-plex*, having parts; *-polis*, city, state.

☞ *Antonyms: metropolitan* — suburban, rural, countrified, rustic, bucolic.

MEDIUS,
middle: MEDI

MEDIum has varied meanings. If one's clothing is marked "medium," it is the size that is approximately in the middle, somewhere between S and XL.

A newspaper is a medium, channel, instrument, or agency of communication. One plural of medium is **MEDIa** (**MEDIums** is also acceptable), which refers to newspapers, magazines, books, radio, and TV, all of which are **means** of mass communication. A medium also means surroundings, environment, circumstances, conditions. (Icy water is not an ideal medium for goldfish.) Fortune tellers, soothsayers, psychics, and clairvoyants are called mediums, go-betweens, so to speak, between the real world and some other one. (The medium assured Aunt Agnes that Uncle Ulysses would tell her where the jewels were buried.)

A **mean** is a middle or **interMEDiate** point between higher and lower or larger and smaller quantities. This is also called the **MEDIal** or **MEDIan** point. The grassy dividing strip between the opposite lanes of a highway is called a median. An intermediate or middle school is one between the elementary and the high school. When people choose a course of action, they often settle for a mean between two extremes. "A means to an end," "by all means," "by any means," "by no means," and "by means of" are common expressions. A person of means is one who is wealthy, who is at the **meridian** of his or her career, and whose *milieu* (literally "middle place," see *locare*, page 96) is a cut or two above the average middle-class neighborhood. (Note: the "m" in A.M. and P.M. stands for **meridiem** (see also *dies*, page 43), the middle of the day, the point between *ante* and *post*.)

Sometimes disputes can be best settled by an **interMEDIary** or **MEDIator** who tries to **MEDIate** or settle the differences between the two sides. **MEDIation** is an important part of the democratic process even though it is not often that **imMEDIate** solutions are arrived at.

The Middle Ages are generally regarded as beginning with the fall of the Roman Empire in A.D. 476 and ending with the fall of Constantinople in A.D. 1453; this is the **MEDIeval** period. The area surrounding the **MEDIterranean** Sea was the center of much of the activity of those times.

Being average is one thing, but being **MEDIocre** is quite another. A song from the musical *The Sound of Music* urges us to "Climb Ev'ry Mountain," to ford the streams, follow the rainbows, and find our dreams. That's what it takes, the song says, to get to the top. But mediocre literally means "halfway up the stony mountain." Gave up. Chickened out. Settled for **MEDIocrity** and a way of life that results in a **MEDIocracy**, a form of government distinguished by its middling, average, so-so, second-rate leaders. But according to the poet Robert Frost, there is a choice: "The world is full of willing people; some willing to work, the rest willing to let them."

*But not: mean [AS *maenan*, to tell], to intend, have in mind; *mean* [ME *mene*, common], inferior, hateful; *medicate* [*medicare*, to heal], treat medicinally; *meditate* [*meditari*, to muse], contemplate; *middle* [AS *middel*].

*Combining forms: *ante-*, before; *dian-, diem-*, day; *-eval*, age; *im-*, not; *inter-*, between; *-lieu*, place; *-ocre*, stony mountain; *post-*, after; *-terran*, land.

☛ *Antonyms: immediate* — distant, indirect; *mediocre* — singular, outstanding, exceptional, impressive; *medium* — extreme, aberration; odd, different, unusual, extraordinary.

MENDUM,
defect, fault:
MEND

A **MENDacious** person has a defect or fault: lying, prevaricating, fibbing, falsifying, paltering, telling falsehoods. **MENDacity** is the tendency to lie; it is untruthfulness. It is also a lie, falsehood, equivocation, fib, deceit, prevarication. And by a small stretch of the imagination here, the word allows the mention of two examples of wordplay. The first is an Irish bull, a statement that has a built-in contradiction: ''Half the lies or mendacities our opponents tell about us are not true,'' Sir Boyle Roche. The second is a pun with play on the word *lie*, both to rest and to tell a mendacity: ''The tombstone is about the only thing that can stand upright and lie on its face at the same time,'' Mary Wilson Little.

A **MENDicant** is a beggar, a vagrant, a scrounger, a panhandler, a down-and-outer. He may be lectured about **MENDing** his ways, but it is, most likely, a difficult condition to **aMEND**, correct, ameliorate, rectify, remedy, or put right.

An **aMENDment** is a correction. (The city editor had to make several amendments to the new reporter's story.) It can also be a change or an alteration. (Two senators introduced amendments to the minimum wage bill.)

When an editor **eMENDS** a manuscript, he or she makes changes, corrections, or deletions. The alterations are called **eMENDations**.

When someone says, ''I tried to make **aMENDS** for the way I talked to her by sending her a dozen roses, but it was to no avail,'' that person is trying to compensate for the loss or injury or insult or misunderstanding that has occurred.

☛ *Combining forms: a-,* out; *e-,* out.

☛ *Antonyms: mendacious* — honest, veracious, creditable.

MERERE,
to earn: MERI

When a person is cited for **MERItorious** service, it is a reward that has been earned and is deserved, just as scouts earn **MERIt** badges and children merit gold stars for praiseworthy work or behavior. However, when our manners and attitudes become **meretricious** (from **meretrix**, a harlot, hence such synonyms as showy, flashy, tawdry, garish, specious, and spurious) well, when that happens to us, we begin to earn and deserve **deMERIts**.

A **MERItocrat** is a member of a **MERItocracy**, a system in which ability and talent are valued over class privilege and wealth. (We intend to turn our educational system into a meritocracy in order to help the able and talented assume roles of leadership in our society.)

Someone holding the title of **eMERItus**, as ''Distinguished Scholar Emeritus'' or ''Headmaster Emeritus,'' has retired from active duty but still holds his title on an honorary basis. If there are two, it's **eMERIti**. ''*His* title''? You got it. It's **eMERIta** for one woman, **eMERItae** for two or more. No kidding.

*But not: meridian [dies, day], zenith.

*Combining forms: -cracy, rule; e-, out; -trix, feminine ending.

*Antonyms: meretricious — genuine, tasteful, unobtrusive, decorous; merit — dishonor, shame, unworthiness; meritorious — disreputable, deplorable, reprehensible, flagrant, unworthy.

MIKROS [Gk], small: MICRO

There are many more *micro* words in our everyday world than there are those with its contrasting form, *macro*, meaning large, long, great. We have macrocosm, macroeconomics, and macrostructure but no handy household macrowaves, macroscopes, or macrophones.

Many homes today have a **MICROwave** oven for speedy cooking and a **MICROphone** for use with a tape recorder or a video camera. In the science labs at school there are **MICROscopes** to study **MICROorganisms** and perhaps **MICRObes** (disease-carrying microorganisms) and examples of **MICROcosms** (worlds in miniature). In the libraries there are often collections of **MICROfilms**. Students taking auto mechanics learn to use a **MICROmeter**, and in geography class they locate **MICROnesia** on maps and globes and read about Oceania, the Pacific islands of which it is a part, in their textbooks.

MICROlogy has two very different meanings. On the one hand it is the science dealing with the functions of microscopes in laboratories. But it also means the paying of undue attention to trivial matters. (You're telling me that you're not going to hire Pamela because she had a bit of dust on the outside of her attaché case?)

*Combining forms: -be, life; -cosm, world; -logy, the study of; -meter, measuring device; -nesia, islands; -organism, animal or plant; -phone, sound; -scope, to watch.

MISEIN [Gk], to hate: MISO

A **MISOgamist** is not someone who is simply leery of or uncomfortable with the idea of marriage; he or she has a deep-seated hatred of it. (Rebecca was an inveterate, unalterable **MISOgamic**; her inherent aversion to matrimony was Professor Fleet's classic illustration of **MISOgamy** in Abnormal Psychology 346.)

MISOgynism is the hatred of women. (The guy's a **MISOgynic** writer who portrays all his women characters as duplicitous hypocrites. If you knew about his early childhood, I think you might better understand why he's such a **MISOgynist**.) The counterpart is **misandry**, the hatred of men. (Julia is a **misandrist** because of her mother's bitter experiences.)

MISOpedia is the hatred of children, but when comedian W.C. Fields said, "Anyone who hates children and dogs can't be all bad," he did not earn a sufficient number of points to be classified as a genuine **MISOpedist**. He got laughs, and that was his objective.

A **MISanthrope**, as the play of that name by the French comic dramatist Molière demonstrates, is a hater of humankind and the society it has produced.

When Alceste, the play's hero, sees that the accepted forms of what we call civilization are nothing but hypocrisy, he becomes **MISanthropic**, gloomy, and disillusioned.

But our pet hates are not directed only at Homo sapiens. **MISOcainea** is an abnormal animus, adversion, abhorrence, and antagonism toward new ideas. **MISOneism** is the hatred or intolerance of anything new or changed. (By the time Dudley was approaching his eighth decade, he was a true **MISOneist**, clinging to the order of things as he had known it for so long.) **MISOlogy** is the hatred, dislike, or distrust of argument, of enlightenment, of reason and reasoning. (There was no way that a **MISOlogist** such as he took pride in being was ever going to make it as a philosophy major.)

There is some balance here. A philanthropist is an altruistic, magnanimous, and benevolent person, and philogyny is the liking or love of women. Philander started out with a similar meaning, but a funny thing happened on the way to today. The word comes from the Greek *philandros*, referring to the love of a man by a woman, to "loving one's husband," but in medieval ballads and romances Philander became the name of a male who flirted with females, the word mistakenly taken from the Greek root, and that's the way philanderers are always going to be.

☞ *But not: mis-* [AS *mis*], ill, mistaken, wrong, as in *misbehaviour, mischief,* and *misdemeanor; misorient* [*oriri*, to rise, hence the east, sunrise], to orient or accustom improperly; *mysophobia* [Gk *mysos*, uncleanliness; *phobia*, fear, dread of], abnormal fear of uncleanliness.

☞ *Combining forms: -andry*, man; *-anthrope*, humankind; *-cainea*, new, recent; *-gamy*, marriage; *-gyny*, woman; *-logy*, reason; *-ne*, new; *-pedia*, child.

MOLERE,
to grind:
Mill, MOL

An **eMOLument** is profit or salary or fees or tips from employment. Its original meaning, "a **MILLer's** fee for grinding grain," still lingers: people talk of grinding out a living, a grind is a job or task that is tiresome and boring, and the all-A student who gets there by dogged perseverence is sometimes referred to as a grind.

A **MILL** may be a large factory for the **MILLing** of paper or steel or textiles or a small kitchen appliance such as a coffee mill. We often associate the milling process with especially difficult times in our lives. (Harry's really been through the mill since Sara's death.) The **MILLstones** that grind the grain into flour, down by the old **MILLstream**, enter our lives, too. (What a millstone around their necks that second mortgage has been.) We speak of the output of a mill as being ordinary, so-so, unimpressive. (I'd say it's nothing special, just run of the mill.) Our twelve **MOLars** grind, too. Imitation or mosaic gold is called **orMOLu**, a gold powder that is used in gilding, that is, making something look like gold.

A **moulin** is a naturally formed vertical shaft in a glacier, but *moulin* is also the French word for mill, and the Moulin Rouge ("red mill") in Paris is a dance hall that opened in 1889 and was made famous by the drawings of Toulouse-Lautrec.

To **imMOLate** is to offer as a sacrifice, especially to a god. When a sacrificial victim was about to be burned up in ancient times, the body was sprinkled with holy meal, ground to a powder. In modern times when one sacrifices his or her life for an ideal, it is called **self-imMOLation**.

*But not: emollient [*mollis*, soft], softening; *mill* [short for *millesimus*, thousandth], one-tenth of a cent; *millennium* [*mille*, thousand + annus, year], a period of one thousand years; a hoped-for time of peace and prosperity.

*Combining forms: e-, out; *im*-, upon; *or*-, gold.

MORS, *death:*
MORT

A **MORTal** is a human being, a creature subject to death. As an adjective the word has a wide variety of meanings: 1. Deadly, relentless, implacable, inexorable, irreconcilable (Howell spent a large part of his life running from Tarkel, his mortal enemy); 2. Extreme, severe, grievous (All the time that he was the general manager I was in mortal dread of losing my job); 3. Possible, conceivable (Little Julie had every mortal thing that her heart could ask for); 4. Wearisome, tedious (The two wounded men lay in the muck for more than twelve mortal hours); 5. Causing death (It was not, as we had all feared, a mortal wound); 6. Spiritual death (In the eyes of the church, Bromlie had committed a mortal sin); 7. Very great, awful (By the end of the day, it was clear that the committee had made a mortal mess of the festival).

Besides referring to death, destruction, carnage, bloodshed, and extermination, **MORTality** means mankind, humankind, Homo sapiens, and humanity. **ImMORTality** is deathlessness and eternity, plus fame and glory. While no human being is **imMORTal**, we speak of certain quantities such as wisdom as being everlasting, and certain evils as being constant and perpetual. At the age of thirteen Joan of Arc, a French peasant girl, heard ''voices'' telling her to liberate her country from the English. Clad in white armor, she led a small army to victory, changing the trend of the Hundred Years' War. Charged later with witchcraft and heresy, she was burned at the stake when she was nineteen. In the twentieth century she was beatified and canonized by two popes and **imMORTalized** by people around the world.

When a living plant or animal is **moribund**, it is dying. When one has been **MORTified**, horribly embarrassed and humiliated, one would just as soon *be* dead. It also means to discipline oneself. (He mortified himself by fasting for three days.) A wound that has mortified has putrified and become gangrenous; timely medical help may postpone one's visit with the **MORTician** at the nearby **MORTuary**.

To liquidate a debt by paying it off in installments is to **aMORTize** it. A **MORTgage** is the pledging of property as security for the repayment of money borrowed. And while **post-MORTems** are autopsies performed on a cadaver, they also can occur at the bridge table after a hand has been played, in the locker room after a 64 to 3 football loss, or on the way home from a party that turned unpleasant.

Memento mori is a Latin phrase meaning ''remember that you must die''; a human skull, for example, is a memento mori, a reminder of our mortality.

☞   ***Once uPUN a time*** a chef, seeking a catchy advertising slogan for his gourmet restaurant, altered Shakespeare's ''Lord, what fools these mortals be!'' to ''Oh, what foods these morsels be!'' Within weeks there were lines of people waiting for tables.

☞   ***But not:*** *morgue* [F after the name of a building in Paris used to house unidentified bodies in the nineteenth century], place where bodies are kept; *mortarboard* [*mortarium*, bowl for mixing certain powdery materials and the mixture], the square cap worn by graduates who wear gowns; *remorse* [*mordere*, to bite], regret, sorrow.

☞   ***Combining forms:*** *a-*, to; *-fy*, to make; *-gage*, a pledge; *im-*, not; *post-*, after.

☞   ***Antonyms:*** *immortal* — ephemeral, temporary, transitory, fleeting; *moribund* — potent, viable, vital; *mortal* — imperishable, lasting, incorporeal, undying; *mortify* — praise, exalt, extol, uplift.

N

CogNATe means related by birth, having the same ancestors. In the world of words, English and German are cognate languages; as are French, Italian and Spanish. The German *kalt* and *Milch* and the English *cold* and *milk* are, obviously, cognate words, related in ancestry. Within the English language we have, among many others, *time* and *tide*, which are first cousins: "Time and tide wait for no man" goes the cliché.

One's **NATive** land is the one in which he or she was born. Native means inherent, that is, belonging to a person by **NATure** or **NATivity**. Persons living in a country in which they they were not born can gain the rights and privileges of a citizen through the process of **NATuralization**. ("As a **NATuralized** American citizen I take my patriotism very seriously," Hazel Henderson.)

One's native tongue is, **NATurally**, the language one first speaks. (Although Margaret was born in Indonesia, but her native tongue is English; although it may seem so, that is not **unNATural**, for her parents were in the diplomatic corps.) Tourists hire native guides, note the native dress, shop for native pottery, and listen to native expressions. Persons with native ability may also be described as having **inNATe**, **NATural**, indigenous, and inborn talent.

A **NATion** is a group of people living under a unified government. One's **NATionality** is that of the country of which he or she is a citizen. Patriotism and **NATionalism** are synonyms, but one can be a patriot without the fervor that sometimes characterizes a **NATionalist**; the latter are not usually ardent **interNATionalists**. A **nascent** nation is one that is just emerging, beginning, developing, maturing.

When a person who wrote stories or poems, for example, during high school begins to write again after years of inactivity, he or she experiences a rebirth, a regeneration, a revivial, or a **renascence**. It can also be called a **renascent** interest.

Similarly, the period of about A.D. 1350 to 1650, between the Middle Ages and modern times, is known as the **Renaissance** because it was a great revival of learning, literature, and art in Europe.

The word **NATal**, relating to birth, is commonly seen in **preNATal** and **postNATal**, referring to the before and after care of a **pregnant** woman. A **neoNATe** is a newborn child, and **neoNATal** pertains to such children. **Noel**, the yuletide season, a Christmas carol, and a male given name, comes from the birth of Christ and as *noël* means Christmas in French. **Nee** is an everyday newspaper word; "Mrs. Key, nee Lee" tells us that Mrs. Key was born Miss Lee.

Pregnant has a number of important uses in addition to meaning with child, having a baby, expecting, in a family way, and *enceinte* (French). It also means filled, fruitful, creative, imaginative, significant, meaningful. (The members of the committee came up with a number of ideas that were pregnant with possibilities.)

Each year we could rightfully celebrate our ''natal day'' instead of our ''birthday,'' but it would involve changing all those cards one finds in stores, and few of us are **naive** enough to think that would ever happen. Maybe when we were young and **puny** (weak, anemic) **naifs** (inexperienced, naive people), but not now when we have learned that **naiveté** is a word meaning simplicity, inexperience, childishness, innocence, foolishness, and, even, simplemindedness.

☛ *But not:* nasal [*nasus*, a nose], of the nose; *natant* [*natare*, to swim], swimming, floating; *natty* [perh. var. of *neat*], spiffy, neatly dressed.

☛ *Combining forms: co-*, together; *in-*, in; *neo-*, new; *post-*, after; *pre-*, before; *pu-*, after; *re-*, again.

☛ *Antonyms: cognate* — dissimilar, distant, different, unrelated; *innate* — acquired, learned, extrinsic, superimposed; *naive* — artful, worldly, wise, calculating; *naiveté* — urbanity, sophistication, savoir-faire; *nascent* — dying, ceasing, waning, ending; *native* — imported, alien, foreign; immigrant, foreigner; *natural* — studied, guarded, purposeful, disingenuous, factitious; *naturalized* — alien, noncitizen, outsider, foreigner, stranger; *unnatural* — artless, simple, unaffected, benign, humane, merciful; *pregnant* — trivial, senseless, dull, barren, sterile, arid; *puny* — weighty, sizeable, considerable, significant.

NEKROS [Gk], corpse: NECRO

People who have an abnormal fear of death are afflicted with **NECROphobia** or thanatophobia; if they have an aberrant attraction to corpses, their affliction is **NECROphilia**. But if they have **NECROmimesis**, a state in which they believe themselves to be dead, they might be said to be in need of professional help. Actually, it could be worse; for if they also are afflicted with **NECROlatry**, which is worship of the dead, then they would be pretty heavily into a weird form of narcissism, which is excessive self-love and vanity.

Then there's **NECROmancy**, a state in which people believe they are communicating, can communicate, or have communicated with — guess what — the dead. It is a kind of magic or sorcery that is practiced by a witch, no doubt on nights when the moon is hidden behind menacing clouds and within the confines of a cemetery. If it is a big enough graveyard and is the reposing place of people from ancient times, it is called a **NECROpolis**, literally ''city of the dead,'' a tourist attraction of rather dubious popular appeal.

The rest of the group reside on another floor. **NECRObiosis** is the death of tissue or cells caused by disease or aging; **NECROsis** is the death of living tissue in one's body and has an even scarier cousin: gangrene. **NECROpsy** is another word for an autopsy, and a **NECROlogy** is a list of persons who have died in a certain place or time; such registers are often kept in churches or monasteries, while newspapers and magazines frequently list the names of those who have died during a recent period.

Combining forms: -biosis, mode of life; *-logy*, study of; *-mancy*, divination, prophesying; *-osis*, abnormal state; *-philia*, unnatural attraction; *-phobia*, fear; *-polis*, city.

Several centuries ago the word **nephew**, the common term that refers to the son of a sister of brother, was used by churchmen not only in regard to those genuine nephews upon whom they bestowed churchly favors, but for quite different purposes as well. Roman Catholic clergy who fathered illegitimate sons and daughters referred to them as their nephews and **nieces**, thus hoping to avoid any suspicions that they had broken their vows of celibacy, chastity, abstinence.

NEPOS, grandson, nephew; NEPTIS, granddaughter niece

Out of this emerged the word **nepotism**, one that has spawned such synonyms as favoritism, patronage, prejudice, bias, partisanship, and discrimination. It is the practice of showing favoritism to members of one's family when making political appointments or business advancements or promotions. Actress Ilka Chase called it ''a $10 word meaning to stow your relatives in a soft berth''; Thomas Jefferson described it as ''perverting public office into private property''; and an anonymous punster said it was ''putting on heirs.''

But not: nepho-, combining form meaning cloud, hence, *nephometer*, a device for measuring the amount of cloud cover in the sky.

Antonyms: nepotism — fairness, detachment, impartiality, evenhandedness.

With the help of the prefix *in-* we have several ''harmless'' words from this root:

NOCERE, to harm; NOXA, harm: NOC, NOX

''There are few ways in which a man can be more **inNOCently** employed than in getting money,'' Samuel Johnson. Guiltlessly, naively, unoffendingly.

''Ralph wept for the end of **inNOCence**, the darkness in man's heart, and the fall through the air of the true, wise friend called Piggy,'' William Golding. Naiveté, purity, guiltlessness, chastity, simplicity, sinlessness.

''Ah! some love Paris, / And some Purdue. / But love is an archer with a low I.Q. / A bold, bad bowman, and **inNOCent** of pity. / So I'm in love with / New York City,''' Phyllis McGinley. Blameless, harmless, sinless, upright, impeccable, inculpable, ingenuous.

''After an existence of nearly twenty years of almost **inNOCuous** desuetude [disuse] these laws are brought forth,'' Grover Cleveland. Safe, mild, moderate, inoffensive, painless, dull, banal, trite, bland.

Without the negative prefix the mood changes:

''What we call progress is the exchange of one **nuisance** for another nuisance,'' Havelock Ellis. Bother, vexation, annoyance, irritation, pest, burden, affliction, thorn, aggravation.

''Of all **NOXious** animals . . . the most noxious is a tourist. And of all tourists the most vulgar, ill-bred, offensive and loathsome is the British tourist,'' Francis Kilvert. Injurious, harmful, destructive, unwholesome, pernicious, lethal, virulent, deadly.

''I know no method to secure the repeal of bad or **obNOXious** laws so effective as their stringent execution,'' Ulysses S Grant. Offensive, disgusting, repulsive, repugnant, abhorrent, revolting, invidious, reprehensible, pernicious, abominable.

''Oh, these **NOCuous** mosquitoes!'' Everyone. Harmful, bothersome, noxious.

☞ ***But not:*** *inoculate* [*oculus*, eye], inject a needleful of serum as a disease preventative.

☞ ***Combining forms:*** *in-*, not; *ob-*, toward.

☞ ***Antonyms:*** *innocence* — guilt, impurity, corruption, turpitude, reprehensibility, cunning, guile, disingenuousness, worldliness; *innocent* — guilty, culpable, reprehensible, impure, wily, iniquitous, nefarious, vicious, worldly, sophisticated, scheming, offensive; *innocuous* — noxious, harmful, bad, injurious, deleterious, pernicious; *nocuous* — harmless, benign, safe; *noxious* — wholesome, beneficial, salubrious; *nuisance* — delight, pleasure, happiness, joy; *obnoxious* — likable, acceptable, engaging, seemly, fit, congenial, welcome.

NOTARE,
to mark:
NOTA, NOTE

The **deNOTAtion** of a word is what we find in a dictionary. It is the direct or explicit meaning or meanings of the word: ''**NOTAry public** — a person legally authorized to authenticate contracts or take affidavits.'' As Sgt. Joe Friday used to say on TV's *Dragnet*, ''Just the facts, ma'am.''

The **conNOTAtion** of a word is not what the makers of the dictionary give to you, it is what you — and your experiences — give to the word. Recall for a moment how your Uncle Moshe, a notary public who lived next door when you were a kid, used to play catch with you on the driveway between your houses on summer evenings, and then one afternoon you **NOTEd** he wasn't there anymore. His sign was still in the front window, his hat on the chair by the door, his notary seal and **NOTEpad** on his desk. But he was gone, never to **NOTArize** a signature again. Dead or alive, you never knew.

That's the connotation of ''notary public'' to you; it's yours and yours alone, never to be completely shared with anyone else. What does the memory or thought of ''winter'' convey? To one person it might be sitting in front of a blazing log fire, the smell of popcorn in the air, but to another it could be the terrifying experience of trying to find a haven in a blinding snowstorm. ''Home?'' Is it a place of warmth, care, and love? Or one ravaged by abuse and hate?

It's a double-laned street, the **deNOTAtive** lane for what a word **deNOTEs**, the **conNOTAtive** lane for what it **conNOTEs**. That's what brings words to life (with the **NOTAbly** sad exception, of course, of the case of Uncle Moshe, his life now filed away at the courthouse under ''**NOTAries** public — Missing'').

NOTEd and **NOTAble** people are those who have made their marks. When we make a **NOTAtion**, we make marks on a paper. It is **NOTEworthy**, too, that we also have **bank NOTEs, musical NOTEs, footNOTEs,** and **keyNOTE**

speeches, which sometimes seem **NOTA bene**, to go on forever. (That Latin phrase means mark well, note well, or take notice.)

An **anNOTAtion** is an explanatory note made in a book alongside the text itself. There are **anNOTAted** volumes of the works of Shakespeare and, even, *The Annotated Alice* (the seven-year-old girl who fell down the rabbit hole into Wonderland), with notes in the margins explaining, for instance, that the names of the courses that the Mock Turtle took in school were really puns: ''Mystery, ancient and modern'' being history and ''Fainting in Coils'' being painting in oils.

But not: NOTA, an acronym formed from ''None of the Above''; *notice* [*noscere*, to get to know], to observe.

Combining forms: *an-*, to; *bene*, well; *con-*, together; *de-*, down; *foot-*, bottom; *key*, main; *public*, general, open; *-worthy*, deserving.

Antonyms: *notable* — little known, unknown, anonymous; *notably* — inconspicuously, indistinctly, invisibly; *noted* — notorious, infamous, obscure; *noteworthy* — insignificant, unremarkable, undistinguished.

O

OCULUS,
eye: OC

Not only has this root given us a strange hodgepodge of words, but some of their paths have been rather extraordinary, too. Take the word for those branched horns on the male of the deer family — **antlers**. The first three letters come from *ante-*, before, plus *ler*, from *ocular*, of the eye, thus "before or in front of the eyes." In Middle English it was *auntelere*.

PinOChle is the name of a card game; the word most likely came to us through a mixed bag of French, Swiss-French, and Swiss-German words for eyeglasses.

The eye of a potato is the bud from which a new plant grows. When a tree shoot is grafted onto a root stock to grow a new tree, a bud of new growth is used. This is the path that led to our word **inOCulate**, to inject a serum containing a small amount of "germs" in order to make the recipient's body immune to those germs. Remember this the next time the doctor's needle is about to pierce your skin; it will make it less painful.

When someone tries to **inveigle** us into doing something, we're being enticed, tricked, fooled, tempted, seduced, beguiled, cozened, or bamboozled. In Latin it meant "eyeless," *ab-*, without + *oculis*, eyes, hence, blinded, we got tricked.

Those holes in your shoes that the laces go through are grommets or **eyelets** (the ends of the laces, incidentally, are called aglets). The French word for eye is *oeil*, so their word for the little hole was *oeillet*. Someplace along the line after the word got into our language it evolved into what we have today.

A **monOCle** is one of those single lenses that British movie actors sometimes wear, and **binOCulars** are for birdwatchers and sports fans and two eyes.

An **OCulist** is an eye doctor, **OCular** pertains to the eyes, and *eye* doesn't stem from **OCulus** after all. It derives from the Anglo-Saxon *eage*.

☞ ***But not:*** *occult* [*occulere*, to cover over], hidden, secret; *octet* (Gk *okta-*, eight], company of eight singers; *octuple*, a shell rowed by a crew of eight; *octuplets*, a group of eight; *octuplicate*, to make eight copies of, to multiply by eight.

☞ ***Combining forms:*** *ant-*, before; *bi-*, two; *in-*, without; *mono-*, one.

ODIUM,
hatred

In May, 1776, John Adams wrote the following to his wife Abigail in regard to the colonies' plight: "There is something very unnatural and **odious** in a government a thousand leagues off." Odious means hateful, abhorrent, loathsome, nauseating, abominable. He was referring to the monarchy of King George III over there in London, of course.

In William Congreve's play *The Way of the World* a gentleman says, "I chiefly made it my own care to initiate her very infancy in the rudiments of virtue, and to impress upon her tender years a young **odium** and aversion to the very sight of men." Odium means hatred, enmity, detestation, abhorrence, opprobrium.

An anonymous student wrote in his daily journal: "Once again Dr. —'s lecture produced an unbearable **ennui**, but no one in the class has the nerve to tell him what dreadful boredom, tedium, languor, and lassitude he continually dribbles forth."

Ralph Waldo Emerson wrote this poem after a trip to Cape Cod:

> I wiped away the weed and foam,
> I fetched my sea-born treasures home;
> But the poor, unsightly, **noisome** things
> Had left their beauty on the shore,
> With the sun and the sand and the wild uproar.

Things noisome are unwholesome and unhealthful, like the stench from a garbage dump.

Annoy can be traced to the Latin phrase *in odio*, literally meaning "in hatred." To annoy may mean simply to bother, tease, or chafe someone, but it can also boil up to provoke, harass, exasperate, disturb, gall, rile, ruffle, vex, and plague. And that can mean trouble.

In Chapter 6 of Lewis Carroll's *Alice's Adventures in Wonderland* Alice pays a visit to the Duchess, who is holding a baby in her arms and singing "a sort of lullaby" that goes like this:

> Speak roughly to your little boy,
> And beat him when he sneezes:
> He only does it to annoy,
> Because he knows it teases.

In *Pudd'nhead Wilson* Mark Twain wrote, "Few things are harder to put up with than the **annoyance** of a good example." Approximately two thousand years before that, Ovid, a Roman poet, wrote in *Ex Ponto*, "It is **annoying** to be honest to no purpose."

***But not:** annotated* [*nota*, a mark, note], supplied with explanations; *noise* [*nausea*, seasickness], sound; *odeum* [Gk *oideion*, song place], hall or theater for dramatic or musical performances.

***Combining forms:** an-*, in; *en-*, in.

***Antonyms:** annoying* — pleasant, agreeable, soothing, comforting, mollifying; *ennui* — stimulation, animation, excitement, eagerness, enthusiasm; *odious* — agreeable, pleasing, entrancing, attractive, likable, charming, entrancing; *odium* — honor, respect, regard, esteem, repute, deference.

In about 1870 Ernst Haeckel, a German biologist, coined the word *okologie*, which became **oECOlogy** in English before the "o" was dropped; its literal meaning is "study of houses," but in this case it may be more fitting to say, "the study of our house," meaning the planet Earth. There have been many spin-offs from the word, such as **ECOcatastrophe, ECOcide** (referring to oil

OIKOS [Gk], house: ECO

spills and chemical dumping), **ECOfreak** (describing an overly zealous environmentalist), and **ECOhazard** (something that is considered dangerous to a habitat).

Charity, it is said, begins at home; so does **ECOnomy**, etymologically, at any rate, for the Greek root *oikonomia* means household management. Beginning, Intermediate, and Advanced **ECOnomics** are college courses that some students claim require superhuman intelligence to get a C– in. **ECOnomic** and **ECOnomical** are adjectives, and their meanings overlap at times, but they are not always interchangeable. Both mean frugal, thrifty, and money-saving (We always buy this brand for economic/economical reasons), but most of us would be uncomfortable with ''Economic shoppers love Chedley's bargains'' and ''Senator Villet criticized the administration's economical policy.''

To **ECOnomize** is to skimp, scrimp, stint, conserve, husband, and be parsimonious. The practice of economy is frugality, husbandry, prudence, austerity, thrift, and providence. When **ECOnomists** speak of the nation's economy, they mention financial structure, monetary resources, productive power, and financial management, but ordinary folks who are not especially well off **ECOnomically** often refer to it in words that are not printable in the family newspaper.

Understandably, a number of words pertaining to affairs of the church come from *oikos*. A **diocese** is a district of churches presided over by a **diocesan** bishop. A **parish** is a part of a diocese that has its own church; it is also any local church and its field of activity, and in Louisiana it is a county. (Pointe à la Hache, Louisiana is the seat of Plaquemines parish.) The **parishoners** of the church are the congregants. **Parochial** pertains to parishes and parish schools. It also means having very narrow, provincial, insular views, and **parochialism** is ignorance and extreme narrowness of interests and attitudes. **Ecumenical** means universal or worldwide; the ecumenical movement is a largely Protestant attempt to achieve universal Christian unity, and an ecumenical marriage is one that is inter-denominational or interreligious, that is, between two people of different religions.

☛ ***But not:*** *diorama* [F *di(a)*, through + *(pan)orama*], a three-dimensional scene against a painted background.

☛ ***Combining forms:*** *dio-*, completely; *-logy*, study of; *-nomy*, managing; *par-*, near.

☛ ***Antonyms:*** *economic, economical* — extravagant, spendthrift, wasteful, imprudent, prodigal, improvident, lavish, ample, expansive, elaborate, expensive, exorbitant, high-priced; *economize* — squander, waste, dissipate, misuse; *economy* — extravagance, wastefulness; *ecumenical* — local, regional, limited, circumscribed, confined.

***OPINARI,
to think: OPIN***

To have an **OPINion** is to have a view, a conviction, an assessment, an idea. To express it is to **OPINe**, although the word is largely confined to comic use today. (''Well, now, that's zactly what he orta do,'' the old settler opined.)

An **OPINionated** or **OPINioned** person is often regarded as being obstinate, pigheaded, obdurate, inflexible, bullheaded, dogmatic, bigoted, and overbearing. (Let's not ask him to be a judge in the essay contest; he's far too opinionated.)

One can find many opinions about the worth of opinions. The Greek philosopher and **OPINionator** Plato remarked that, "Between knowledge of what really exists and ignorance of what does not exist lies the domain of opinion. It is more obscure than knowledge, but clearer than ignorance." Bertrand Russell, a British Nobel Prize winner and **OPINionist**, said, "The fact that an opinion has been widely held is no evidence whatever that it is not utterly absurd." And Ambrose Bierce, an **OPINionative** American journalist, held that, "A prejudice is a vagrant opinion without visible means of support."

*But not: Op-Ed [Op(posite the) Ed(itorial)], newspaper page; *opinicus* [?], a monster having the head, neck, and wings of an eagle, the body of a lion, and the tail of a bear; *pinion* [*penna,* feather], bird's wing; to shackle.

P

PAIS [Gk],
child: PED

PEDiatrics is the medical branch that deals with children; it is also known as **PEDology**. A **PEDiatrician** is a physican who specializes in that field. **PEDodontics** is the branch of dentistry that deals with the care and treatment of children's teeth; a **PEDodontist** is the specialist to whom children go. **OrthoPEDics** is the surgical branch of medicine that deals with bone deformities, diseases, and injuries; **orthoPEDic** surgeons most frequently work with the young, particularly in the correction of crippling impairments or diseases.

The word **encycloPEDia** is a word that did not get the correction it needed when it was young. In brief this is what happened: The intended meaning was based on the Greek *enkuklios paideia*, meaning a circular or well-rounded education. But somewhere along the line the *paid* became *paed* and then *ped*, thus going around from "circle" to "child." Persons with **encycloPEDic** minds are rare, as they often tell us.

PEDagogics is the art of teaching; educational cynics argue that both the word and definition are becoming archaic. In ancient Greece a *paidagog* (**PEDagogue**) was a child's tutor. An educational idea is **PEDagogic** or **PEDagogical**. (Miriam's revolutionary pedagogical scheme was to allow her children to read anything they wanted to.)

The meanings of the rest of the words that stem from *pais* tend to have a pejorative effect or force, that is, a connotation that is disparaging, belittling, or derogatory. A **PEDant** used to be defined as a schoolmaster; today it's a "thumbs down" word that describes one who makes a show of scholarship or learning. By any other name: egghead, highbrow, show-off, dogmatist, plodding academician. When you ask a question of one, be prepared for a **PEDantic** answer: pompous, bookish, overly meticulous, nitpicking, erudite, like everything you wanted to know and a whole lot more. Such is the stuff of **PEDantry**.

Then there's **PEDerasty**, an abnormal man-boy relationship; the **PEDerast** being a **PEDophile**, a word used by psychiatrists to describe an adult who is sexually attracted to young children; the attraction is called **PEDophilia**.

☛ *But not: peddling [ped, a basket], trifling, piddling; pedestrian [pes, foot], dull; pediculosis [pedis, louse], infestation of lice.*

☛ *Combining forms: cyclo-, circular, general; en-, in; -erast, love; -gogue, to lead; -iatric, medical; -logy, body of knowledge; -odont, having teeth; ortho-, correction of deformities; -philia, unnatural attraction.*

☛ *Antonyms: encyclopedic — limited, confined, specialized, specific, circumscribed; pedantic — pithy, succinct; comprehensive, general; vague.*

126

When people come down with the flu, they tend to let others know that they are not feeling up to **PAR**. When they are playing a round of golf, they are delighted when they shoot below par. Par is a measure, a guideline, a standard that is used whether one is in a sick bed with 102 degrees of temperature and the blinds drawn or out on the links on a sunny day when cool breezes waft across the fairways. **ComPARisons** are being made in these examples: How does one feel at 98.6 degrees as **comPARed** with 102? How does one feel with 72 strokes compared with 76 or 86 or 96? Whether it's better to be up to par or below par depends upon the game.

Something that is **comPARable** is similar, like, cognate, analogous, commensurate, tantamount. (Oh, I think life in a town this size is quite comparable to that in a metropolis, although I suspect that such comparisons are rather superficial.) **ComPARative** means relative, approximate. (Janice may be a comparative newcomer in politics, but she has demonstrated that she is a **comPARatively** quick learner.) In grammar the comparative forms of good, near, friendly, and thoughtful are better, nearer, more friendly, and more thoughtful. Anything that is said to be **incomPARable** is matchless, unrivaled, **peerless**, unsurpassed, excellent, and **nonPAReil**. (Only a sight of such incomparable beauty could have inspired Wordsworth to write that poem.)

PARity is equality, equivalence, correspondence, similarity, analogy. (The Ministers of Finance met in Paris to seek parity in value in the currencies of the two countries.) **DisPARity** is difference, gap, inequality, inconsistency, incongruity. (There exists a "shocking disparity between the rich and the poor," Adlai E. Stevenson.)

To **disPARage** someone or something is to belittle, discredit, deprecate, criticize, put down. (Please, let's not disparage good manners. I'm afraid cousin Clem's remarks disparaged our whole family.)

Susan Glaspell's short story "A Jury of Her **Peers**" is about a jury of Martha Hale's friends and neighbors, meaning her equals, fellow citizens, and colleagues. **Peer** and **compeer** are synonyms, but the latter also means a close friend, comrade, companion. (Only her compeers knew of her plans.) In Great Britain and Ireland a peer is a member of the nobility, or the **peerage**, and if a man is a duke, marquis, earl, viscount, or baron.

When two people have a dispute over, say, where their property lines are, the **pair** may have to call upon an **umpire** to settle the question. *Umpire* is derived from the French *nompere* (*nom*, not + *per*, equal), that is, a kind of higher authority, one not equal to the disputing parties. Over the years "a nompere" became "an umpire."

Persons who bet at the horse races usually do so on the **PARimutuel** ("to make equal") system, in which those holding winning tickets divide the total amount bet according to how much each wagered. Those who take their winnings plus the original bet and gamble it all on the next race **PARlay** their bet. One need not be at the racetrack to parlay something. (The young couple parlayed their talents into a successful business partnership.)

PAR, equal,
peer: PAR

☛ ***But not:*** *disparate* [*parare*, to prepare], dissimilar; *parity* [*parere*, to bear], ability to give birth; *parley* [Gk *ballein*, to throw], conference; *peer* [perh. *appear*], to look.

☛ ***Combining forms:*** *com-*, together; *dis-*, apart; *in-*, not; *-mutuel*, mutual; *non-*, not; *um-*, not.

☛ ***Antonyms:*** *comparable* — different, unlike, unequal, dissimilar; *comparatively* — nearly, approximately; *disparage* — esteem, value, appreciate, cherish; *disparity* — accord, unity; *incomparable* — pedestrian, lackluster, second-rate, ordinary; *nonpareil* — average, mediocre, commonplace, usual; *parity* — difference, inequality, diversity; *peerless* — inferior, humdrum, run-of-the-mill, so-so, banal.

PARERE,
to give birth to,
to come in sight:
PAR

As **PARents** we are fathers or mothers, progenitors, procreators, dams (mothers), sires (fathers), ancestors, and antecedents. But we are much more, too: as part of our **PARental** position, we are prototypes, models, and exemplars. With **PARenthood** come many responsibilities. (Martin's father claims that Martin is a young man of very distinguished **PARentage.**) The current "in" word for parenthood, rearing, and upbringing is **PARenting**. (The worst moments of parenting for me were having to lie to my children about the Easter bunny and the tooth fairy and Santa, and then having to tell them that I had lied.)

A **biPARous** birth is one in which two offspring are brought forth. (Bim and Tim L., Dolly and Molly R., and Jack and Zack D. all have biparous parents.) In a **uniPARous** birth only one offspring is produced, and a **multiPARous** birth produces more than one. **FetiPARous** animals bear young before they are truly developed, and thus often carry them in a pouch. (In science today we learned that kangaroos and opossums are fetiparous marsupials.) Birds and most reptiles and fishes are **oviPARous**, that is, they produce eggs that hatch after being expelled. Most mammals are **viviPARous**, bringing forth live young rather than eggs. A **viper** is a venomous snake that is so named because some of them give birth to live young, but when Philip Wylie wrote *Generation of Vipers* he was referring not to snakes but to spiteful, evil, treacherous human beings.

AntePARtum and prenatal, as well as **postPARtum** and postnatal, are synonymous words, meaning before birth and after birth, respectively. **PARturition** is the act or process of giving birth to a child.

The catalog of songs, plays, skills, tricks, and such that an actor or a theatrical group can perform is a **repertoire**. A **repertory** theater or company is one that produces a season of several works year after year. Such a theater produces, brings forth.

When Shakespeare's Macbeth says, "Thou canst not say I did it. Never shake thy gory locks at me," he is speaking to an **apPARition**, one that **appears** to him to be the ghost of Banquo, the general he has just had three murderers do away with. The ghost's **appearance** is but momentary; it soon **disappears** as mysteriously as it had come. It is **apPARent** to those with him at the royal banquet that "his Highness is not well," but Macbeth **apPARently** recovers, saying, "I drink . . . to our dear friend Banquo, whom we miss," at which point the ghost **reappears**. The audience finds the scene quite **transPARent**, obvious, understandable, overt, and plain, for it has witnessed several scenes that those at the banquet can know nothing about.

When students become overwhelmed by the large number of characters in a novel, play, or short story, many teachers list the names and roles they play on the chalkboard or on a **transPARency** to put on an overhead projector.

Once uPUN a time two weary parents began pronouncing and spelling "parental" as "parent-toll," because of the toll (cost, price) that the bringing up of nine kids had amounted to.

But not: paranoia [Gk *paranoia*, madness], a mental disorder characterized by delusions, etc.; *parentheses* [Gk *parenthesis*, a putting in beside], the marks ( ) used to set off an explanatory or qualifying element.

Combining forms: ante-, before; *ap-*, toward; *bi-*, two; *dis-*, away; *feti-*, fetus; *multi-*, more than one; *ovi-*, an egg; *post-*, after; *pre-*, before; *re-*, again; *trans-*, across; *uni-*, one; *vivi-*, alive.

Antonyms: apparent — uncertain, doubtful, veiled, covered up, obscure, hidden, imperceptible; *appear* — vanish, be uncertain, be doubtful; *appearance* — departure, passing, vanishing; *transparent* — covert, hidden, profound, complex, opaque, murky, clouded, subtle, wily, devious.

PATER [L & Gk], father: PATRI, PATRO

"I am delighted that you **PATROnize** my store," said the shopkeeper, "but I hate it when you patronize me." The first use means to shop at, trade with, or buy from and is a word with a kind of neutral, evenhanded, impartial connotation. The second use of the word, however, carries a load of unpleasant, pejorative baggage; it means to put down, talk down to, act in a superior way to, treat haughtily. **PATROnizing** people never win blue ribbons or gold medals.

PATROnage is versatile, too. The shopkeeper welcomes his customers' patronage. Most charitable organizations owe their existence to the support, backing, and patronage of their donors or **PATROns**. In politics patronage is the granting of political appointments, contracts, and favors; a synonym is *porkbarreling*.

PATRIot is another word that carries a double load. One who loves his or her country is a patriot; Stephen Decatur, an American naval hero, stated the case for **PATRIotism** when he said in reply to a toast, "Our country, right or wrong!" But, wrote Thomas Paine, a hero of the American Revolution, there is, unfortunately, "the summer soldier and sunshine patriot." One who displays a conspicuous or boastful and aggressive kind of patriotism may be called a flag-waver, chauvinist, jingo, or jingoist.

A **comPATRIot** is a person of one's own country, a colleague. An **exPATRIate** is one who has been banished from a country or one who initiates the move to another country. Many American writers chose to live as expatriates in Paris after World War I.

A **padre** is usually addressed or referred to as "father."

In Great Britain only **PATRIcians** are entitled to sit in the House of Lords; a cynic once wondered how in the world they could find that many people who are noble, imposing, dignified, genteel, well-bred, and aristocratic. Well, their **PATRImony** probably helped; a hefty inheritance from one's father tends to do that, especially if one's father was the **PATRIarch** of a very wealthy family. It may help, too, to inherit a highly respected **PATROnymic**: Daddy's good name.

The word **perpetrate** has negative connotations. What demented soul perpetrated this crime? Who perpetrated this tasteless magazine? I'll tell you what: the **perpetrator** is an egregious transgressor, outlaw, culprit, wrongdoer, and offender!

Paternal advice is fatherly. (The coach said he wanted to give me some paternal counseling about my problems, but it sounded to me like a bunch of **patter**.) **Paternalism** is an attitude or practice in a business or government agency in which management treats the employees as a father would his children; it is often resented. **Paternity** is fatherhood. (We never could establish the paternity of the puppies; the **pattern** of spots was our only clue.)

☞   ***But not:** expatiate* [*spatium*, space], discuss at length; *patter* [*pat*, to tap gently], gentle tapping, as with little feet or raindrops; *pope* [GK *pappas*, father], head of the Catholic Church.

☞   ***Combining forms:** -arch*, ruler; *com-*, together; *ex-*, out of; *noster*, our; *-nymic*, a name; *per-*, thoroughly.

☞   ***Antonyms:** patrician* — commoner, plebeian, proletarian, peasant, hoi polloi, philistine; vulgar, bourgeois, lowbrow; *patriot* — subversive, traitor; *patriotism* — treason, subversion; *patronizing* — humble, tactful, discreet, respectful.

PECCARE,
to stumble, sin:
PECCA

In the spring of 1843 British forces under the command of Sir Charles Napier defeated the armies of Sind (today a province of Pakistan) and annexed the area to what was then British India. It has been reported that Sir Charles sent a war dispatch back to the London magazine *Punch* consisting of four words: "**PECCAvi** — I have Sind." Although it broke the unspoken rule for puns (if they have to be explained, forget it), it was considered acceptable on the grounds that most people would not know that a peccavi is a confession of sin, with the literal meaning, I have sinned, which he had.

A **PECCAble** person is liable to sin; a **PECCAnt**, one who has apparently already done so, for he or she is guilty, wrong, and sinful; and a **PEC-CAtophobic** is one who lives in mortal fear of sinning.

An **imPECCAble** individual is that rare bird who is not only faultless and flawless, but also not liable to sin and incapable of sin. We have, however, found it expedient to break this impossible standard into achievable parts. (Well, look at Stanley, would you. Absolutely impeccable dishwashing technique!) There is also one other out. A **PECCAdillo** is a very minor or slight sin — you know, like a white lie, a trifling slip, a bit of a lapse, an indiscretion, a *faux pas*. (Surely I will be forgiven *that*. Just a teeny-weeny peccadillo, don't you know.)

*But not: *peccary* [Sp *pecari*], a piglike, hoofed animal; a javelina.

*Combining form: *im-*, not.

*Antonyms: *impeccable* — imperfect, defective, impaired, compromised; *peccant* — saintly, spotless, moral, righteous, pure.

For about thirteen centuries Europeans who were well-enough educated to be able to write used quill **PEN**s made from bird feathers, hence the name. A **PEN**na is the normal bird feather, different in shape from those known as down and plume feathers. The small **PENknives** that many people carry were originally designed to make and sharpen quill pens. By the mid-nineteenth century pens made of metal had become popular, and the birds of Europe became much more friendly. A pseudonym or *nom de plume* is also known as a **pen name**, one used only for writing.

PENNA,
feather: PEN

Feathers enable wings to function, and if flags are to be noticed and attract attention, they need to be able to move much like the wings of a bird. That is why the names of some flags were taken from *penna*: A **PENnon** was once borne on the lance of a knight; today it is usually tapered or triangular. A ship's flag, used for identification and signaling, is a **PENnant**, as is the long, tapering flag that is symbolic of a league championship in baseball.

Winning the pennant is like reaching the **pinnacle** of a lofty peak. To bind or cut off the wings of a bird is to **pinion** them; it also means to shackle or restrain someone. (The guards quickly pinioned the prisoner's arms.)

When knights wore helmets, they also liked to wear a colorful plume of feathers on them; it was called a **panache**. And someone daring enough to wear feathers while fighting a battle was undoubtedly a person of great style and flair. Cyrano, the hero of Edmond Rostand's famous play entitled *Cyrano de Bergerac*, is a man with an extremely large nose. As he lies on his back, dying, his nose pointing heavenward, he declares that there is one thing that he can call his own, "Et c'est . . . mon panache" (And that is . . . my panache). Which is that nose of his. Today the word signifies style, verse, dash, spirit, brio. The feathers have long been forgotten.

*But not: *pen* [AS *penn*], an enclosure; *penchant* [*pendere*, to hang], a strong liking for something; *pentad* [Gk *pent-*, five], a period of five years.

*Antonyms: *panache* — apathy, lethargy, indolence, languor; *pinnacle* — minimum, nadir, depths, zero, zilch, zip.

PES, foot:
PED

To **imPEDe** something is to slow it down; to **exPEDite** something is to speed it up. **ImPEDimenta** is cumbersome baggage or paraphernalia that slows us down at the airport, for example; it is an **imPEDiment** to our progress. An **exPEDitious** move is a prompt and speedy one. (The crisis called for expeditious action.) The word **exPEDient** is two-faced: it means suitable and practical on the one hand and selfish and conniving on the other. (Sonia thought it expedient to take notes at the meeting. The city council's move to raise their own salaries was an expedient one.) As a noun an expedient is an advantage, a benefit. (Advertising in the paper has been an expedient to our business.)

Early **exPEDitions** marched on their feet. If it was a military move, so did the foot soldiers, the **peons** and **pawns**. And maybe their cousins, the **pioneers**, went along, for that word was once spelled *peonier*.

PEDals and **PEDometers** were nonexistent way back then, and perhaps **PEDicures** were rare except for ladies of Cleopatra's standing (or sitting?). But at the foot of the mountains there were always the **piedmonts, PEDestals** stood outside the amphitheaters, **centiPEDes** and **milliPEDes** scurried about (underfoot, of course), and **trivets** had all three feet firmly planted on the tables.

There has always been respect for bloodlines, that is, our (and our neighbors') ancestry, lineage, and extraction. That our ancestors were sometimes hard put to come up with new words is illustrated by **PEDigree**. The word comes from the Middle French *pié de grue*, literally, ''the foot of a crane,'' the lines the toes made in the sand apparently seeming similar to those on a chart showing the descent of us **biPEDs**. People who own livestock and dogs are often interested in the pedigree of their **quadruPEDs**, too.

Cap-a-pie means head to foot. A **pied-à-terre** is a secondary or temporary residence; its literal meaning is ''one foot on the ground.'' Prospective renters look for one that has been recently **revamped**: new paint, wallpaper, and carpeting. A **vamp** is a part of a shoe, and shoes often are in need of repair, and that's where today's word came from. **Impeach** traveled down this road, too; the word that means to accuse a public official of misconduct or even to remove him or her from office once meant to fetter, to put shackles on one's feet. **PEDestrian** came the same way; while it has always named one who walks, it long ago opened up a branch office, becoming an adjective and meaning plodding, dull, so-so, and insipid. (Dr. Thikrik's commencement speech was so pedestrian it reminded us of someone caught at a red light that never changed.)

And then there's **sesquiPEDalian**, referring to words that seem as though they are a foot and a half long. Columnist Molly Ivins, striking out at people who insist on implementing instead of beginning or starting and facilitating rather than speeding up or simplifying, raised the battle cry, ''Person the barricades! Combat sesquipedalian pomposity!''

☞   ***But not:*** *foot* [AS *fot*]; *pawn* [OF *pan*, a pledge], security for a loan; *pedant* [Gk *paidos*, child], one who shows off learning; *peddler* [ME *ped*, basket], seller of small items; *podiatrist* [Gk *pous*, foot], foot doctor; *vamp*, coquette, [short for vampire].

Combining forms: bi-, two; *cap*, head; *centi-*, hundred; *-cure*, to care for; *ex-*, out; *-gree*, crane; *im-*, in; *-meter*, measure; *milli-*, thousand; *-mont*, mountain; *quadru-*, four; *re-*, again; *sesqui-*, one and a half; *-stal*, standing piece; *-terre*, earth; *tri-*, three.

Antonyms: expedient — detrimental, impractical, inadvisable, fruitless, unselfish, altruistic, ethical; *expedite* — retard, hinder, block, obstruct; *expeditious* — dilatory, sluggish, inefficient, leisurely; *impede* — facilitate, abet, promote, further, aid; *impediment* — aid, assistance, encouragement, help, benefit; *pedestrian* — imaginative, exciting, fascinating, compelling, significant, remarkable; *pioneer* — imitate, follow; disciple; *sesquipdalian* — terse, succinct, concise, trenchant, laconic, epigrammatic.

PETERE,
to seek:
PET, PETU

An **apPETite**, says a Jewish proverb, "is something you always bring to someone else's table." It is also hunger, thirst, desire, hankering, fondness, longing, and craving. For what? For food, knowledge, power, love, companionship — for whatever is **apPETizing**, tempting, alluring, enticing, desirable, or tantalizing. An **apPETence** is an intense desire, a strong, overpowering appetite; it is also used in the sense of a propensity, that is, a natural tendency, leaning, proclivity, bent, penchant, taste. (Cardinals have an appetence for sunflower seeds.) An **apPETizer** is a small portion or sampling that whets one's desire for more. (The appetizers, bits of cheese on tiny crackers, made me ravenous for dinner. The short preview of the new sitcom was an appetizer for the coming season.)

CentriPETal force seeks or is directed toward the center; it is what keeps a train on a track or a motorcycle upright when it goes around a curve; this is the opposite of centrifugal force, which we see in action during the spin-dry cycle of a washing machine (see *fugere*, to flee).

To **comPETe** is to contend, contest, oppose, strive, vie. (Ying's dream is to compete in the next Olympic Games.) **ComPETition** is opposition, rivalry, conflict, struggle. (Prices should go down now that Brind's Food Store has some competition.) It is one's rival, contender, adversary, opponent, **comPETitor**. (Our chief competition for the championship is Duling High.) It is also a contest, race, match, encounter, bout. (An international panel judges the figure-skating competition.) A person who is **comPETitive** has a strong desire to succeed and may also be combative and aggressive. A business that is not competitive usually has difficulty surviving.

"**ComPETence**," says Dr. Laurence Peter in *The Peter Principle*, "like truth, beauty and contact lenses, is in the eye of the beholder." What the beholder looks for is ability, skill, expertise, efficiency, and know-how. The author also claims that in most organizations employees tend to rise on their own level of **incomPETence**, like the excellent teacher who is "promoted" out of the classroom to the position of principal — where he or she is **incomPETent**.

ImPETUous people and actions are impulsive, hasty, brash, unpremeditated, precipitate, and capricious. (Quitting that job in a snit was an impetuous act that I really regret. Only impetuous Felipe could fall in love so many times.) It also means violent, moving with great force, relentless, inexorable. (The heavy rains were accompanied by impetuous winds.) **ImPETUs** is an impulse, a moving force, a stimulus, an incentive, a spur. (The skater's impetus sent her crashing into the wall. Rose needs an impetus to study.)

Things **perPETUal** are everlasting, eternal, endless, and enduring — if we view them as useful or worthwhile. However, they are interminable, ceaseless, incessant, and unremitting if we wish they'd go away. It is the difference between enduring love and interminable telephone solicitations that **perPETUally** harass us. To **perPETUate** something is to preserve it or to extend, prolong, protract, or immortalize it. (The eternal flame is intended to perpetuate his memory.) **PerPETUity** is the state of being perpetual or eternal or everlasting. (An anonymous donor bequeathed this land to the museum in perpetuity.)

As a noun a **PETition** is a request or appeal that people are asked to sign, often for clemency for a prisoner or to repeal a law that is considered unfair. As a verb it means to pray, appeal, ask, seek, or supplicate. (The homeowners petitioned the city council for a change in the zoning ordinance.) When some people don't get their way, they tend to become **PETUlant**, that is, irritable, cross, sullen, impudent, or surly and may take on a dozen or so other ill-tempered, ill-natured attitudes.

To **propitiate** is to mollify, appease, pacify, placate, or conciliate. (The mayor tried to propitiate the angry taxpayers.) A sign or condition that is **propitious** is favorable, promising, auspicious, felicitous, and encouraging. (It looks as though we'll have propitious weather for the carnival.)

To **repeat** is to say something again, to iterate or reiterate, or to echo, mimic, or imitate. Another meaning is to retell, recite, recount, reveal, or quote. (Mimi repeated what she had heard to her friends.) A person who repeats a course or grade is a **repeater**, as is one who commits a crime after having been convicted of another, a recidivist. It is also a type of gun and clock. **Repeated** (adj.) and **repeatedly** (adv.) mean said, done, made, etc., over and over (Despite repeated warnings, he still came late. We tried repeatedly to reach them by phone.)

RePETition has a similar meaning: restatement, replication, recurrence, retelling. (Repetition may be an effective learning method, but it certainly is dullsville.) **RePETitious** and **rePETitive** are usually interchangeable; they both mean redundant, wordy, prolix, pleonastic, tautological, as well as boring, tiresome, monotonous, and dull. (That last lecture series was repetitious [-ive] in capital letters.)

☞ ***But not:*** *aperitif* [*aperire*, to open], a small alcoholic drink to stimulate the appetite before a meal; *petrel* [? from *St. Peter* in allusion to his walking on water], small sea bird, also called Mother Carey's chicken; *petunia* [F *petun*, tobacco], flowering plant.

☞ ***Combining forms:*** *ap-*, to; *centri-*, center; *com-*, with; *im-*, into; *in-*, not; *per-*, through; *pro-*, forward; *re-*, again.

Antonyms: appetite — aversion, distaste, repugnance, surfeit, loathing; *appetizing* — unpalatable, distasteful, repellent, unsavory, nauseating; *competence* — ineptitude, inability; *competent* — inept, deficient, lacking, maladroit, klutzy, gauche; *competitive* — aiding, cooperative, collaborative, mutual; *impetuous* — patient, prudent, cautious, wary, moderate, leisurely; *incompetent* — deft, apt, efficient, expert, proficient; *perpetual* — finite, temporary, discontinuous, ephemeral, transient, transitory, fleeting; *perpetuate* — terminate, cut off, discontinue, finish, exterminate, annihilate; *petulant* — pleasant, agreeable, gracious, complaisant, amenable; *propitiate* — anger, irritate, provoke, vex, incense, exasperate; *propitious* — ominous, threatening, unfavorable, sinister, disheartening, baleful; *repetitious* — fresh, new, varied, interesting, concise, pithy, terse, succinct.

PIUS,
devoted: PI

Many Renaissance artists sculpted statues of the **PIeta** showing the dead Christ lying in the lap of his mother, but the most famous is the marble masterpiece by Michelangelo (c. 1500) in St. Peter's Basilica. It is viewed each year by hundreds of thousands of devote and **PIous** pilgrims as well as secular, nonreligious, and **imPIous** tourists. Some are there in hopes of **exPIating** their sins of **imPIety** and becoming renewed with godliness, reverence, and **PIety**.

When a family is down-and-out, its condition is **PIteous, PItiful,** and **PItiable**; it is also heart-rending, distressing, and touching. As we pass by, we give them a **PItying** glance. Pitiful has another face, too: mean, contemptible, and despicable. (What a pitiful trick that was to play on your best friend!)

A **PItiless** person is merciless, ruthless, inexorable, and implacable, one without a **PIttance** or shred or iota of common decency. **PIty** is both a verb (Oh, how we pitied them as they watched all their possessions go up in smoke) and a noun ("But yet [said Shakespeare's Othello as Iago pushed him toward the murder of Desdemona, his wife] the pity of it, Iago!, O! Iago, the pity of it, Iago!")

But not: piebald [*pie*, a magpie, a bird with black and white plumage], having patches of black and white or other colors; said of a horse; *pitted* [*puteus*, a well, pit], marked or scarred with pits.

Combining forms: ex-, out; *im-*, not.

Antonyms: impious — respectful, reverent; *piety* — infidelity, apostasy, blasphemy, faithlessness; *piteous* — delightful, happy, joyful, pleasant; *pitiful* — fortunate, prosperous, flourishing, commendable, dignified, laudable, admirable; *pittance* — abundance, sufficiency, bounty, excess; *pity* — apathy, disdain, indifference, scorn, inhumanity, ruthlessness, cruelty.

PLACARE,
to calm: PLACA

• Following a succession of scandals, the administration realized that it must try to **PLACAte** public opinion. Pacify, soothe, assuage, propitiate, conciliate.

• It was the **imPLACAbility** of his racial prejudices that finally was his undoing. Rigidity, inflexibility, intransigence.

• When management assumed a more **PLACAtory** stance, the impasse was finally broken. Conciliatory, peaceable, reconciling, irenic.

• Our commencement speaker used what she called the **imPLACAble** movement of the universe as her point of reference. Uncompromising, relentless, inexorable.

• The plant manager found that the supposedly irate workers were quite **PLACAble**, and the dispute was quickly ended. Peaceable, conciliatory, accommodating.

☞ *But not:* placard [F *plaquier*, to plaster, plate], poster, sign.

☞ *Combining form:* im-, not.

PLEBES [L],
DEMOS [Gk],
the people: PLEB,
DEM, DEMO

The *plebs* of ancient Rome and the *demos* of ancient Greece were the common people, the populace, but some of the words that stem from these two have followed divergent paths. For instance, whereas a **DEMagogue** in Athens was a popular leader of the people, today the word was a pejorative or negative and derogatory connotation. **DEMagoguery** is described as the attempt to arouse the emotions, fears, and prejudices of the populace.

PLEBes are members of the freshman classes at Annapolis and West Point, and a **PLEBiscite** is a direct vote by the people of a country on a public question. But a person with **PLEBeian** ideas and tastes is said to be base, coarse, common, low, lowborn, lowbrow, mean, obscure, ordinary, uncultured, undistinguished, and unrefined, to mention a few.

However, not all the words from these roots are so highly charged. **EnDEMic** means growing naturally, indigenous, native. (These plants are endemic to the region.) An **epiDEMic** refers to something that is extremely prevalent, spread over a large area. (The flu is reported to have reached epidemic proportions. An epidemic of break-ins has alarmed the citizens of our town.) A **panDEMic** outbreak is one that covers a much larger area, even the entire globe. **DEMOphobia** is a mental disorder in which one has an abnormal fear of or aversion to crowds. **DEMOgraphy** is the science of the statistics of a population — births, deaths, marriages, gender, age, ethnic origin, occupations, diseases, and much more.

A **DEMOcrat** is a person who believes in the political equality of everyone; hence, the form of government that we know as **DEMOcratic**, the one about which the distinguished Winston Churchill said, ''No one pretends that **DEMOcracy** is perfect or all-wise. Indeed, it has been said that democracy is the worst form of government except all those other forms that have been tried from time to time.''

A political candidate who adjusts his or her language to fit the crowd that gathers outside the office doors or factory gates may be making an effort to be **DEMOtic**, that is popular, common, of the people. (Senator Hassel's failure to develop an acceptable demotic touch has hurt his campaign.) The word pertains to the everyday, current form of language, the vernacular, the speech patterns and vocabulary of the people. (Dr. Ruth owes much of her popularity to her keen ear for the rhythms and idioms of ordinary folk.)

But not: demo [*de-,* + *monstrare,* to show], a demonstrator, such as a car; *indemnify* [*in-,* not + *damnum,* harm], to protect against loss; *pandemonium* [the principal city in Hell in Milton's *Paradise Lost,* where all the demons were], bedlam, chaos, tumult.

Combining forms: -agogue, leader; *-cracy,* to rule; *en-,* in; *epi-,* among; *-graphy,* form of recording; *pan-,* all; *-phobia,* abnormal fear; *-scite,* to know.

Antonyms: democratic — autocratic, despotic, highfalutin', snobbish; *demotic* — exclusive, private, notable, aristocratic, elitist, highborn; *endemic* — alien, foreign, naturalized; *epidemic* — contained, limited, isolated; *pandemic* — esoteric, exclusive, local, parochial, sporadic; *plebeian* — elite, aristocratic, patrician, cultured, noble, refined, blue-blooded.

POLItics is the science or art of **POLI**tical government; it is the practice of conducting political affairs. That's the way dictionaries and students enrolled in **POLI sci** 309 look at it. Will Rogers, a humorist and newspaper columnist whose sayings are still published daily, more than a half century after he died in an airplane crash, saw politics differently:

"Politics has got so expensive that it takes lots of money to even get beat with."

"The more you read about politics, the more you got to admit that each party is worse than the other."

"If you ever injected truth into politics you would have no politics."

When Rogers wrote those words, he was not attacking the American **POLI**ty or form of government. What he did was mock politics, **POLI**ticians (or **POLI**ticos), and those who engage in **POLI**ticking, that is, promoting themselves or their **POLI**cies at every turn. He did it by making fun of them and holding them up to ridicule. But the world of politics wasn't his only target; he also aimed his pen at big business, communist **POLI**tburos, and the military, as well as snobs, speechifiers, hero-worshippers, and all others who he felt took themselves too seriously.

He was not **POLI**tic or discreet, but only those who were his enemies could have called him **IMPOLI**tic or tactless. His humor was his strong suit, and the American **body POLI**tic — the people as a whole — ate it up. Certainly no one ever accused Rogers of being a**POLI**tical, that is, being neither involved nor interested in politics.

In ancient Greece a city-state was known as a **POLI**s, the most famous of which is the **AcroPOLI**s of Athens with its Parthenon. A large cemetery in those days was known as a **necroPOLI**s, and a **metroPOLI**s was the mother city of a colony. Today the latter is any large, busy city with its surrounding **metroPOLI**tan area, which, in turn, may be but one of several that comprise a **megaloPOLI**s. Small wonder that it's almost impossible to **POLI**ce the place

POLIS [Gk],
city: POLI

adequately, from either the standpoint of patrolling, regulating, protecting, and safeguarding (The captain doubted that he had sufficient personnel to police such a large event on short notice) or that of cleaning, straightening, and tidying (The scouts were asked to police the area after the picnic). Noun synonyms are authorities, patrol, force, troopers, constabulary, gendarmerie, cops, and fuzz.

A **cosmoPOLItan** is a person who feels at home in many places, a citizen of the world, taking pride in being free of provincial prejudices and narrow thinking. **CosmoPOLIte** is a synonym; coincidentally, it is also the name of a butterfly otherwise known as the painted lady.

☞ *But not: polish* [*polire*, to polish], to make smooth; *polite* [*polire*], courteous.

☞ *Combining forms: acro-*, height; *-buro*, bureau; *cosmo-*, world; *im-*, not; *mega-*, large; *metro-*, mother; *necro-*, dead.

☞ *Antonyms: cosmopolitan* — narrow, local, insular, provincial, parochial; *impolitic* — prudent, diplomatic, shrewd, judicious, artful; *metropolitan* — rural, rustic, bucolic; *police* — neglect, disarray, mess, dilapidate; *politic* — rude, blundering, rash, careless.

PORCUS, hog, pig: POR

Had an errant arrow not hit King Harold II in the eye at the Battle of Hastings in 1066, felling him and shattering the morale of his troops and enabling the French-speaking William the Conqueror to lead his Norman army on to London, where he was crowned king of England, our language would be far different today.

Not only would we be shopping for meaty pigchops and plump pig roasts, our politicians would be busying themselves trying to pass pigbarrel legislation. **PORkchoppers**, officials, legislators, and others who are primarily interested in personal gain from their positions of power, would be known as pigchoppers. Hat manufacturers would be pushing for the return of the pigpie snap-brim, pigupines would roam the woods with their needle-sharp quills, the sight of pigpoises breaking the surface of the sea would delight boaters, and the fashionable would dine off pigelain plates — **PORkpie, PORcupine, PORpoise**, and **PORcelain**, respectively.

The Anglo-Saxon words were those of the field; in addition to *pigge* (pig), there was *cealf* (calf), *deor* (deer), *cu, bole, oxa* (cow, bull, ox), and *sceap* (sheep). But the more civilized and sophisticated newcomers from across the English Channel brought words for the table. As pig turned into **PORk**, so calf became veal; deer became venison; cow, bull and ox became beef; and sheep became mutton. And thus men whose side whiskers are narrow at the top and broad at the jawline wear muttonchops instead of sheepchops.

The connection between our **PORcine** friends and the name of the material used in the making of porcelain dinnerware and Dresden figurines is said to have come about because of the resemblance of the shape of a highly polished seashell called *porcellana* in Italian to the curved back of a **PORca**, pig.

Resemblances have often played major roles in the coinage of words. The porcupine was a *porc d'espine* in Middle French, so called because it looked like a thorny pig, and the porpoise was a porcopiscis from its resemblance to what they fancied a sea hog would look like.

Once uPUN a time a little boy got an aquarium for his birthday. He put guppies and minnows and a frog in it, but only a short time passed before he accidentally tipped it over, shattering the glass and scattering its occupants. "What a mess!" his father said. "And not even paid for yet!" "But gee, Papa," the little boy said, "I didn't do it on porpoise!"

But not: porch [*porticus*, portico], veranda.

A substance that can be ground into a **POWDER** is **PULVERable** or **PULVERizable**, and when it has been so processed, it has been **PULVERized**. But imaginative writers have expanded the word's uses; some of its synonyms are crush, brind, demolish, annihilate, mince, destroy, trample, triturate, and comminute. (Weasels pulverize Tech 73–2! The veteran comic pulverized the holiday audience. The tornado pulverized the campsite.)

Powder may take the form of dust, grain, sand, grit, meal, flour, or efflorescence. (A layer of yellow, **POWDERy** pollen from the pine trees covered the lawn chairs.) As a verb it means to dust, scatter, sprinkle, strew, spread, spray, or dredge. (Mike dredged the fish with a powdery mix of cracker crumbs and flour before frying.) Weather personnel speak of powdery clouds, and skiers rejoice when a fresh, loose powder snow covers the slopes.

GunPOWDER, clipped to "powder", is used in a number of combinations: powder burn, charge, chest, flask, horn, keg, magazine, man, mill, and monkey. In the ballad "Oliver's Advice" Valentine Blacker, a British soldier, recorded these words that Oliver Cromwell, the one-time lord protector of England, Ireland, and Scotland, gave to his troops: "Put your trust in God, my boys, and keep your powder dry."

But not: pow [?], expression imitative of noise, as "socko! bam!"; *powwow* [Algonquian, Indian conference, from *medicine man*], conference of or with Native Americans; *wow* [?], expression of amazement, wonder, etc.

PULVIS, dust:
POWDER,
PULVER

It is interesting to note that among the lesser definitions of the verb **point** is to **PUNCtuate**, as in writing. Several centuries ago the insertion of points, dots, and straight and wiggly lines to indicate pauses in writing was referred to as **pointing**. As we often point at or point out an object to direct one's attention to it, so punctuate is commonly used for emphasis (The boy's tears punctuated his tragic story) or to emphatically interrupt at intervals (The flashes of gunfire punctuated the darkness of the night).

A **pointed** remark is one that is directed at someone (The principal's pointed remarks made Harry and Merry squirm); one that is **point-blank** is plain and blunt (Mrs. O said point-blank that Tommy was never to enter her house

PUNGERE,
to point, stab:
PUN, PUNC

again); **pointers** are pieces of advice (The editor gave us pointers on how to organize our themes). **Pointy-headed** is a disparaging term used to describe stupid, idiotic, pretentious, self-important people.

A **PUNCtilious** person is finicky, fussy, meticulous, and very, very precise, one who broods and frets about the fine points, the nuances, the niceties, the **PUNCtilios** — of **PUNCtuation**, clothes, or any number of other things. (Oh, dear me, I really don't know whether to use a comma here or not or whether to wear my blue tie or the yellow one. Decisions, decisions!)

Being **PUNCtual** is important, too: "**PUNCtuality** is the politeness of kings," said Louis XVIII of France. But then again, maybe not: "Punctuality is the virtue of the bored," said the novelist Evelyn Waugh.

We have all had unpleasant experiences with **PUNCtures**, whether by means of a nail in our tire or a needle in our arm. Here's another look at the matter: "There was a faith-healer of Deal / Who said, 'Although pain isn't real, / If I sit on a pin / And it punctures my skin, / I dislike what I fancy I feel.' "

PUNChy is a word that is an explicit example of language confusion. Which of the following two meanings is the real one? 1. dazed and befuddled, as from two many blows to the head, **PUNCh-drunk**; 2. forceful, dynamic, cogent, vigorously effective ("Punchy prose! Action-packed best-seller candidate!"). Which one? Both of the above.

PUNgent and **poignant** remarks may be caustic and stinging, causing pain and distress. This could result in the speaker's having the feelings of shame, remorse, and anxiety that we call **comPUNCtions**. (The thief obviously had no compunctions about stealing the poor family's food.) If the culprit does feel guilt, then an apology might help **exPUNge**, blot out, eradicate, or obliterate it. We smell the pungent reek of a cigar and taste the pungent **punch** of a jalapeño pepper, but similar complications do not usually result.

A **pivot** is a fulcrum or swivel; as a verb it means to rotate or to hinge on or be contingent on. (Our winning this game pivots on Joe's kicking foot.) Synonyms of **pivotal** are decisive, vital, crucial, and critical. (I haven't made up my mind about the job; this is a pivotal moment in my life.) **Pounce**, meaning to jump or leap, also comes from *pungere*, as does **PUNCheon**, the name of both a heavy timber and a stamping tool.

Then there's **PUN**, and here's a celebrated sample. About two hundred years ago when Thomas Hood, a British poet and humorist, became ill, he sensed that an undertaker he was acquainted with was becoming uncomfortably interested in his health. Thinking that the man seemed anxious to earn a livelihood by seeing that Hood's ashes were stashed away in a vase or urn, he phrased it this way: "I fear he is too eager to urn a lively Hood." Small wonder that there was talk of nominating Hood for the "Pun Gent of the Year" award.

☞ ***But not:*** *punch* [perh. Hindi *panch*, from Sanskrit, *panca*, five (there were originally five ingredients: spirits, water, lemon juice, sugar, and spice], a sweetened drink; *pundit* [Skt *pandita*, learned, wise], learned person.

Combining forms: -blank, white center of a target; *com-,* greatly; *ex-,* out.

Antonyms: pointed — vague, aimless, irrelevant, inappropriate; *pointless* — telling, meaningful, productive, valid, logical, sensible, sharp; *punchy* — alert, clearheaded, mild, tepid; *punctilious* — careless, casual, slipshod, negligent; *punctual* — tardy, late, undependable, irregular; *punctuate* — minimize, understate, de-emphasize; *pungent* — bland, tasteless, unpalatable, weak, unstimulating, uninteresting, mild, moderate, soothing, dull, inane, vapid.

Q

QUALIS,
of what kind:
QUAL

One of the ongoing discussion topics of today is about what is called the **QUAL**ity of life, that is, the character, the nature, the flavor of daily life. Where is living most suitable to a certain individual, in the inner city, a suburb, a small town, a megalopolis, an exurb, or a rural area?

There are those who say that in order to **QUAL**ify, be eligible or fit to debate the subject one must have sampled several of the options. Others do not believe that such **QUAL**ifications, requisites, conditions, or requirements are necessary, claiming that a person who has lived in one place all his or her life is perfectly **QUAL**ified, suited, capable, and competent to voice an opinion.

However, qualified has another meaning: limited, restricted, and conditional. ("Any opinion Archie expresses is bound to be a qualified one," Edie argued, "considering his limited experiences. Therefore, I feel that he is unfit, ineligible, and **unQUAL**ified to join the debate.")

But unqualified also has an entirely different meaning: not modified, restricted, or limited (Latisha warrants our unqualified praise), absolute and out-and-out (You, sir, are an unqualified liar).

In grammar a **QUAL**ifier is a modifier, such as an adjective or an adverb, as well as a word that expresses degree or intensity. (After our *rather* long hike through the *somewhat* dense underbrush, I felt *very* weary.) One who survives the **QUAL**ifying heats, rounds, or tests in a competition becomes a qualifier. (Maria is one of the qualifiers for the finals; Andy was **disQUAL**ified.) A **QUAL**itative style, change, or list would be concerned with "how good?" rather than "how much?" (which is quantitative).

☞ ***But not:*** *qualm* [?], pang of conscience, uneasiness.

☞ ***Combining forms:*** *dis-*, not; *un-*, not.

QUANTUS,
how many,
how much:
QUANT

It happened at a political debate shortly before a recent election. One of the incumbent's supporters claimed that his candidate's twenty-four years of elective and appointive federal service **QUANT**ified him as one of the nation's most responsible leaders.

" 'Quantify,' yes," a woman in the audience said, " 'qualify,' no. There's an enormous distance between the two. It's the distance and the difference between **QUANT**ity and quality, and that's the difference between numbers and merit."

Had Mark Twain been there, he might have offered his quip about the nature of quantity: "I must have a prodigious quantity of mind; it takes me as much as a week, sometimes, to make it up." It is volume, extent, mass, aggregate, amount, magnitude.

QUANTitative pertains to the measurement of quantity. (The missionary said he hoped the shipment of foodstuffs would not have any quantitative limitations.)

A **QUANTifier** is a word or number that indicates the amount or size of something. (*Much* of the crowd, estimated to be approximately *seventy* strong, hooted and jeered at *several* of the speakers.)

QUANTum (pl. **QUANTa**) refers to the amount of something. (Professor Sachs remarked on the tiny quantum of knowledge we have of the universe.) A **quantum jump** (or leap) is a term from physics that has made its way into other areas. (The CEO spoke of the quantum jump in the company's productivity.)

But not: *quandary* [?], dilemma; *QANTAS* [acronym for Queensland and Northern Territory Aerial Service], Australian airline.

1. **quibble**, to argue over minor points, especially by using evasive, ambiguous arguments, to equivocate, bicker, carp, cavil. (The oppositions' **quibbling** over a dozen irrelevant, minor points served only to delay the passage of the bill.)

quorum, the number of members of a group required to be present in order to transact business. (Irwin got to the meeting just in time to make it a quorum.)

2. **quasi**, seeming, almost, virtual. (Laverne is technically not a member of the organization; she's what we'd call a quasi member.) As a combining form, and usually hyphenated, it has the meaning of close-but-not-quite-there. Thus something that is quasi-scientific is not truly scientific, but it does resemble the real thing. Depending upon the intent of the user, it may take on the meaning of pseudo, bogus, or counterfeit. (Lincoln never did that; the book you got that from is quasi-historical fiction). *The Random House Unabridged Dictionary, Second Edition*, lists nearly one thousand *quasi-* entries, ranging from *quasi-absolute* to *quasi*-zealous. The word **quasar**, the name given to the starlike objects thought to be the most distant and luminous in the universe, is a blend of *quas(i)* and *(stell)ar*, nearly a star.

3. **quondam**, former, one-time, erstwhile. (Both Cecilia and Albert are quondam general managers at Sylvester's.)

But not: *Quasimodo*, Salvatore, Italian poet, 1901–68, Nobel Prize for Literature, 1959.

Antonyms: *quasi* — real, genuine, true, authentic.

QUI, who;
QUAM, how;
QUOM, when

As Henry, Prince of Wales, and Sir John Falstaff, his boon companion, play with words in Shakespeare's *Henry IV, Part I*, Falstaff says, ''How now, how now, mad wag! what, in thy **quips** and thy **QUIDdities**?'' The quips are the witticisms, wisecracks, puns, jokes, gags, epigrams, and ripostes that they exchange; the quiddities are the trivial, quibbling distinctions they make as they argue.

The literal meaning of **QUIDnunc** is ''what now?'' Hence it is gossip, idle talk, hearsay, tittle-tattle, or small talk. And as a person it is a gossiper, busybody, scandalmonger, magpie, or yenta.

QUID, what,
something: QUID

A **QUID pro quo** (something for something) is the substitution or return of one thing for another. (At Vic's school the quid pro quo is the exchange of the students' maintenance work for their education.)

In Spain **hidalgo** is a man of the lower nobility; in South America he is one who is highly esteemed or owns considerable property; in central Mexico it is the name of a state.

☛ *But not: quid* [var. of *cud*, the portion of food that a cow, for one, returns from the first stomach to the mouth to chew again, AS *cwudu*], a portion of something to be chewed but not swallowed, as with tobacco; *quid* [?], British slang word for one pound sterling.

QUOT,
how many:
QUOT

QUOTa is short for **QUOTa pars**, how great a part? In 1921 Congress passed the Quota Act, instituting limits on immigration to three percent of each nationality that lived in America in 1910; it was repealed in 1965. The United States government has also long employed quotas on goods and services that are exported or imported. Synonyms are part, share, allotment, percentage, portion.

The quantity resulting from the division of one quantity by another is called the **QUOTient**. One's intelligence quotient (IQ) is obtained by dividing an individual's mental age (as determined by the score on an intelligence test) by the chronological age and multiplying the result by one hundred. So with the Achievement Quotient (AC). The DQ or Desire-Determination-Drive Quotient employed by those who find the IQ culturally biased does not use this mathematical formula.

QUOTidian [*quot* + *dies*, day] reports are those that are made every day. A quotidian fever recurs daily. Because happenings or events that occur with regularity tend to become common, quotidian has also come to mean commonplace, ordinary, as usual. (We expected to see another boring, quotidian flick, but it turned out to be super, a real sleeper.)

To **QUOTe** a person is to repeat a statement he or she has made in writing or speaking. (Look, I'm quoting the truant officer verbatim, word for word, snarl for snarl!) What is quoted becomes a **QUOTation**; they fill thousands of pages of the scores of books devoted to them. (Scudley was surprised to find that the play about the Bible was so full of familiar quotations.)

Some remarks are **QUOTeworthy** and **QUOTable** and some are not. (Yes, I heard what the senator said, but it's not what my paper considers quotable stuff.) They may be irrelevant and uninteresting or, sometimes, inappropriate, unsuitable, and unprintable. ("The surest way to make a monkey out of a man is to quote him," Robert Benchley.)

☛ *But not: quoth* [AS *cwethan*, to say], said.

☛ *Combining forms: -dian*, day; *-worthy*, deserving.

R

A king is the chief male authority in a country that still supports a **ROYal** family. He is a monarch or sovereign who gained his position by heredity and expects to hold it for life. Royal refers to a king and his family, court, and society; among its synonyms are kingly, queenly, princely, **REGal**, noble, majestic, and purple. The size of the world's **ROYalty**, that is, those people holding royal status or power, has dwindled immensely during the twentieth century, but from time to time a **ROYalist**, a supporter of a king or a monarchy, pops up in the news, often to say that he knows a good man who's available to **reign** should a vacancy occurs.

Many of the words of that system are still with us, however. Authors and composers and owners of mineral and oil rights, for example, still receive **ROYalties**, their portion of the income from their works or properties. We speak of people receiving the royal or red carpet treatment, secretly hoping to stumble onto the royal road to success, dreaming of a royal flush when we play poker, and complaining that Cousin Iodine is once again being a royal nuisance or pain.

Shoppers for kitchen and other household products are familiar with **REGal** and **REGina**, brand names chosen by their manufacturers because they mean, respectively, befitting a king and befitting a queen. Regina, queen, is a female given name, as **REGis** and **Rex**, king, are for males. Apartment complexes are sometimes given exalted (and pretentious) names such as Chateau **ROYale**.

REGalia refers to the ceremonial insignia, emblems, or dress of a high office, order, or position, as well as fancy and dressy clothing. (Everyone will be wearing formal party regalia tonight.) To **REGale** people is to entertain, amuse, please, delight, charm, or entrance them. (The juggler regaled the carnival crowd.) It also means to feast and wine and dine. (The local brass regaled the visitors with a sumptuous banquet.)

A **viceROY** is a king's deputy appointed to rule a province or another country, which is known as a **viceroyalty**; his wife is a **viceREINE**; and they are described as being **viceREGal**.

REGicide refers to the killing of a king or to the person who commits the crime.

REGnant, reigning, ruling, usually follows the noun it modifies, as in ''a queen regnant,'' in much the same manner as the official title of a reigning queen: Elizabeth Regina. The children of the state of Arkansas learn that their state's motto is **REGnat populus**, ''The people rule.'' The highest honor for a professor at such British universities as Cambridge and Oxford is to hold a **REGius** Chair, an appointment traditionally made by the ruling monarch. **REGulus** is a first magnitude star in the constellation Leo. Students of European history know that an **interrex** was the person who stepped in when an **interREGnum** occurred, that is, the period between the end of one king's reign and the onset of the next one's.

☞ *But not: regular* [*regere,* to rule], usual; *roy* [Scots Gaelic word meaning red], a male given name; *sovereign* [OF *soverain*], ruler.

☞ *Combining forms: inter-,* between; *vice-,* deputy.

☞ *Antonyms: regal* — common, low; *regale* — bore, tire, economize; *royal* — plebian, crude, vulgar, base, coarse.

RIDERE,
to laugh:
RID, RIS

In the chapter entitled "The Mock Turtle's Story" in *Alice's Adventures in Wonderland,* Alice and the Mock Turtle are discussing their schooling. When Alice tells him that she learned French and music, the Mock Turtle says that his school offered those courses, too, but he couldn't afford the cost: "I only took the regular course." Which was, he goes on to say, "Reeling and Writhing" and "the different branches of Arithmetic — Ambition, Distraction, Uglification and **DeRISion**."

As we know, all laughter is not the same; sometimes it is fun, but sometimes it is cruel. Mockery, scorn, heckling, sneering, and contempt are synonyms of derision. (The stuck-up, snooty student came up with the wrong answer when called upon and so became the object of derision.) To **RIDicule** something or someone is also to poke fun in a contemptuous, nasty way; Alice Walker tells how the poetry of Phillis Wheatley, who was born free in Africa but became a slave in America, was "held up to ridicule for more than a century." To **deRIDe**, scoff or sneer at, taunt, mimic, humiliate, disparage all fit into the bin labeled **deRISive** words.

It's nice to know, however, that those whose laughter is mean-spirited often appear to be **RIDiculous** in the eyes of others. Now, ridiculous can carry the connotation of meanness, but much more often it is on the laughable, ludicrous, nonsensical, comical, screwball, ho! ho! side of the coin. (That is the most ridiculous, absurd, wild, screwy, crazy movie I've ever been to; you've just *got* to go see it!)

That's the side of the coin where **RISible** can always be found, right along with humorous, farcical, funny, amusing, facetious, and jocular. (Hey, he's no sourpuss; he's a risible person who enjoys a good laugh. The new sitcom on Monday nights is supposed to be risible, but I didn't see the humor.) **RISibility** is the ability to laugh, to see the funny side of life. (Wait'll you hear what happened to good old Smithew on his last fishing trip! I tell you, that'll tickle your risibilities!)

And last, there's **riant**, a word that's been at home in crossword puzzles for a long time but really deserves to be pulled out into the open. It means cheerful, laughing, smiling, pleasantly mirthful, and we need all of those attributes we can get. Have a riant day!

☞ *But not: uprising* [AS *risan*], a revolt.

☞ *Combining forms: de-,* completely.

☞ *Antonyms: derision* — approval, commendation, kudos; *derisive* — respectful, appreciative, admiring, deferential; *ridicule* — esteem, praise, honor, encourage, hearten; *ridiculous* — sensible, sober, sound, serious, logical; *risible* — grave, stern, doleful, sad, somber.

The Latin word *ripa* means "that which is cut out by the **RIVer**." When one traveled in ancient times, the river was often the artery and the bank or shore was the place of **arRIVal** and departure. (We hope to **arRIVe** in Rome by Wednesday.)

People who settle along the shore of a body of water live in **riparian** homes or **RIVerside** apartments and have, by law, riparian rights, entitling them to fish and to make use of the water for power or irrigation. The world's **RIVieras**, French and otherwise, owe their name to this root.

People who have achieved the goal or position that they have been working toward are said to have **arRIVed**. However, an **arRIViste**, one whose rapid rise has been at the expense of integrity and honesty, is regarded as a parvenue, social climber, pretender, nouveau riche, and upstart. Gossip may well center on whom and how many this vulgarian sold down the river or sent up the river. "Down the river" came to us from the days when slaves were sold to plantation owners down the Mississippi, where harsh treatment awaited; it meant to betray, let down. "Up the river" originated from the journey up the Hudson River from New York City to Sing Sing Prison at Ossining.

RIPA, bank, shore: RIV

*But not: drivel [AS *dreflian*], gibberish, slobber; *driver* [AS *drifan*], chauffeur, golf club.

*Combining form: ar-, to.

It seems odd that **Rivulet**, a small stream or streamlet, **derives** from *rivus* but the word *river* does not. So it seems with **RIVAl**, a word that shares that **deRIVAtion**. Somewhere way back in time a form of the root apparently had to do with two men having to share a rivus or stream, and we all know what can happen then. A **RIVAlry** can result, like who can catch the biggest fish, and out of that can come the Big Annual Contest, to be followed by the ceremony where some celebrity awards what could become the coveted Golden Dorsal Fin statuette. From such happenings are great **RIVAlries** born.

RIVUS, brook, stream: RIVA

Another **deRIVAtive** of this root is **unRIVAled**, meaning peerless, supreme, unparalleled, and tops. (Mac's new assignment offered unrivaled opportunities to make new friends.)

*But not: riven [ON *rifa*, to split, tear], split apart, as a log; *rivet* [OF *river*, to attach], attach, hold one's attention.

*Combining forms: de-, down; *un-,* not.

When a material or substance is worn away by **corROSion**, the **corROSive** agent is usually a chemical action; when the surface of the earth is worn away by **eROSion**, the **eROSive** agent is usually water, waves, or wind. In a less

RODERE, to gnaw: ROD, ROS

technical sense, a corrosive wit is caustic, scathing, harsh, sarcastic, cutting, sharp, and cruel. (If you ask me, it was his corrosive wit that meant curtains for that marriage.) Historian Bernard De Voto wrote of the "manners and miserliness that **corRODe** the human spirit." Supreme Court Chief Justice Earl Warren said that "when the rights of any . . . are chipped away, the freedom of all **eRODes**." Another writer was concerned about "the corrosion of the faith and the corruption of moral standards," while still another complained that his father's commitment to salvaging his nearly bankrupt company was eroding their family life. Not exactly water, waves, wind, and chemicals.

RODents are mammals with four continually growing incisors; they're beavers, chipmunks, mice, rats, and squirrels — all expert gnawers. But no matter how gifted the gnawer, there always remains a rough, uneven, erosive edge. Ask a beaver, however, if it's uneven, and he'll say, "Gnaw!" every time.

A **RODenticide** is a substance for killing rodents. Perhaps that's what Ralph Waldo Emerson had in mind when he supposedly said something about the man who builds a better rodenticide will have the world beating a path to his door.

☛   ***But not:*** *corroborate* [*roborare*, to make strong], confirm; *morose* [*morosus*, fretful], gloomy.

☛   ***Combining forms:*** *-cide*, act of killing; *cor-*, completely; *e-*, off.

☛   ***Antonyms:*** *corrosion, erosion* — upkeep, repair, maintenance, preservation; *corrosive* — courteous, soft-spoken, soothing, pleasant.

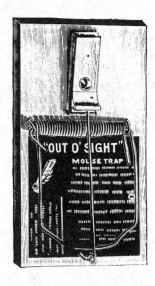

S

To **SALUte** someone is to greet, welcome, hail, honor, praise, and congratulate that person, although not necessarily all at the same time. In Rome one says "Salute!" (sa loo' tay) as a toast or to one who has just sneezed; in Spanish-speaking countries the wrod for such occasions is **SALUd** (sa lood'). These words are cognates, kindred, related, and of the same family, just as are our *sneeze*, the Anglo-Saxon *sneosan*, the German *niesen*, the Dutch *sniezen*, and the Danish and Swedish *snysa*. (In Berlin a sneeze brings out a hearty "Gesundheit!" [G *gesund*, sound, as in health]. Hereabouts the echo of a sneeze is often "Bless you!" And such pleasant responses are, as they say, nothing to sneeze at.)

Salus explains why the **SALUtation** (the "Dear People:" part of a letter) comes at the beginning and why the **SALUtatory**, the **SALUtatorian**'s speech at Commencement exercises, is always the first one on the program. The other student speech, coming an hour or so later, is the "So long!" said by the valedictorian [*vale*, farewell + *dicere*, to say].

The goddess of health in ancient Rome was **SALUs**. She left us with **SALUbrious** and **SALUtary**, twins that mean promoting or favorable to health, hence curative, beneficial, wholesome, healthful. (Whetherford found it necessary to move to a more salubrious/salutary climate.)

But not: salacious [*salire*, to leap], lewd, obscene; *Saluki* [after *Saluq*, ancient city of Arabia], breed of dog similar to the greyhound.

Antonyms: salubrious, salutary — debilitating, deleterious, harmful, detrimental.

If a book you are reading describes a man as being **SANGuine** about the future of the human race, he is being cheerfully optimistic. If it is about children who live in the northern hemisphere and have sanguine complexions, they no doubt have rosy, ruddy cheeks. If it is a book written a century or so ago, and the battle between warring factions has turned sanguine, that means the blood is flowing.

SANGuinary is the generally preferred word for bloody and bloodthirsty. Thomas Paine urged in *The Rights of Man* that we "teach governments humanity. It is their sanguinary punishments which corrupt mankind." A solider writes from the front about "this bitter and sanguinary war that is waged under inconceivable conditions." A newspaper editorializes about "the wave of sanguinary and murderous crime that is sweeping our community."

ConSANGuineous refers to kinship, to being related by blood and ancestry. A person exhibiting **SANG-froid** (in French, literally, "cold blood") is composed and imperturbable. (The robbers carried off the heist with complete and incredible sangfroid.) **SANGria**, a cold drink made of red wine, fruit juice, sugar, soda water, and fruit slices, is so called because of its bloodlike color.

SALUS,
health: SALU

SANGUIS,
blood: SANG

149

☞ *But not: sang, past tense of sing (AS singan].

☞ *Combining forms: con-, together; froid, cold, frigid.

☞ *Antonyms: sang-froid — discomfiture, uneasiness, agitation, nervousness; sanguine — pessimistic, morose, gloomy, somber, pale, pallid, wan.

**SAPERE,
to taste,
to be wise: SAV**

A **SAVant** is a learned scholar, a person of humongous knowledge, a pundit, and guru. In the movie *Rain Man*, Dustin Hoffman plays the role of Raymond, an autistic "idiot savant," a psychiatric term describing a mentally defective person who has exceptional skill in a special field, such as music or math. (In the movie a box of toothpicks was spilled onto the floor, and in a second or so Raymond counted them, all 495!)

A **sage** is a wise and learned philosopher, an intellectual who is sometimes referred to as an egghead. A **sapient** person is scholarly and judicious, whereas one with a full load of **SAVvy** radiates know-how, common sense, and practical, street-wise knowledge. As a verb, savvy means to know and understand; as an adjective, it means shrewd, canny, and perspicacious.

An **unSAVvy** person is a hopeless nerd. One endowed with **SAVoir-faire** is self-assured, tactful, poised, and diplomatic.

An **unSAVory** person is offensive and obnoxious. Unsavory food is bland, flat, and tasteless; when it's **SAVory** and **sapid**, it's palatable, piquant, toothsome, appetizing, and delicious.

Insipid food also is flavorless and bland; insipid books and movies are dull and boring; insipid people are namby-pamby blahs. To **SAVor** life (flowers, travel, friends, sunsets, books, etc.) is to relish it, to appreciate it, to enjoy it; only **Homo sapiens** have that privilege.

☞ *But not: sagacious [sagax, wise], astute; sage [salvia, safe], an herb; sagebrush [salvia], a shrub; savage [silvaticus, of the woods], primitive man; savior [salvare, to save], rescuer.

☞ *Combining forms: faire, to do; homo, man; in-, in; un-, not.

☞ *Antonyms: insipid — savory, delicious, exciting, provocative; sapid — bland, unpalatable; savant — dolt, ignoramus, lowbrow; savoir-faire — awkwardness, clumsiness; unsavory — pleasing, upright, virtuous.

**SCALA,
ladder: SCAL**

The verb **eSCALade**, meaning to climb or **SCALe** ladders to reach a higher level (To get to the fortified encampment, the warriors escaladed the series of cliffs by means of ladders), is undoubtedly the word that the inventors of t he **eSCALator** had in mind when they adopted it as their trademark. Fitting word, too, for the mechanism is actually a continuously moving ladder. Only a nit-picking perfectionist would argue that there is no "down" in the definition of the original word. All loyal readers of the society columns know that there are as many downs on the social escalator as there are ups; it is also a fact that many of the **upSCALe** get a kick out of an occasional visit to a store that caters to the **downSCALe**. On the other hand, about forty years after **eSCALate** was given birth (The president announced that the sending of more troops did not indicate that he was **eSCALating** the war), someone came up with **de-eSCALate**.

La SCALa, the name of one of the principal opera houses of the world, is properly Teatro Alla Scala, Italian for "Theater at the Stairway." It was built in 1776 by the Empress Maria Theresa of Austria. A stairway is a series of steps, and that is what a scale is, as, for example, the numbers on a thermometer.

Some corporation headquarters are organized so that the upper **echelon** executives' offices are on the top floors of the building. (Wilfrid always intimated that his office was upper echelon, nineteenth floor or higher.)

But not: scale [ON *skal*, bowl], a weighing device; *scale* [OF *escale*, husk], skin outgrowth as on fish, etc.; *scaloppine* [OF *escalope*, shell (of a nut, snail, etc.)], pounded slices of veal breaded and sautéed, as *scaloppine alla Marsalla*.

SCIRE, to know: SCI

The evolutionary paths that some words have followed would baffle the best hound dog in the hunter's pack. Take **nice**. Today's meanings are varied, but they're crystal clear to us in all their guises. Agreeable, desirable: I like your new car, really nice. Friendly, pleasant: That new kid on the block seems like a nice sort. Precise, accurate: This desk you built is a nice piece of workmanship. Respectable, virtuous: Well, I do hope you've found a nice girl for a change. Proper, suitable: That was not a very nice thing to say to Reverend Windee. Refined, fastidious: Nice people don't spit — not in the house, anyway. And in an ironic sense of bad, inappropriate: "You're a nice one to be telling me how to act," she said, but not very **nicely**.

That's today. Now for where it came from: *ne-*, negative + *scire*, to know, hence, ignorant, incapable. From there it passed into French with the meaning of silly, simple, simpleminded. In time it crossed the English Channel, perhaps with William the Conqueror, and by the time Chaucer used it in the fourteenth century, it bore the sense of wanton, lewd, lascivious.

So the word moseyed along, stopping at "coy, shy, reluctant" and then "unimportant, trivial," before taking on, in the eighteenth century, its meaning of "pleasing," but it was not fully accepted until the 1934 publication of the *Merriam-Webster New International Dictionary, Second Edition*. **Nicety** (usually plural) came along with it. (They quickly learned to appreciate the **niceties** of the affluent life.) To which was added, much later, the term **nice-nelly**, a prude. (Hey, I'm telling you, she's no nice-nelly.)

One's **conSCIence** is the inner sense of knowing what is right and wrong; a decade before the start of the Civil War, Frederick Douglass, an escaped slave, wrote ". . . [I]t is not light that is needed, but fire . . . the conscience of the nation must be roused"). A **conSCIentious** person is one who heeds that inner voice. (We've always trusted our attorney; she's extremely conscientious.) Something that is **unconSCIonable** is unscrupulous, unprincipled, preposterous, monstrous, unreasonable, immoral, and unethical. (Did you hear that in the same period that the company laid off 13,000 employees the brass split more than $50,000,000 among themselves? Now that's unconscionable!)

A **conSCIous** act is one that is deliberate and intentional. (It didn't seem to be a conscious insult; my impression was that it was a slip of the tongue.) **ConSCIousness** is awareness. (Voyd's every action is motivated by his class consciousness.) One who is **self-conSCIous** often appears to be ill at ease, diffident, uncomfortable, embarrassed, and uptight. (When Hazel realized that she was the only woman in slacks rather than a dress, she became acutely self-conscious.) **SubconSCIous** pertains to the mysterious down-deep mind, the one psychoanalysts probe. (Two weeks after Hamm enrolled in Beginning Psychology, he started in: "Way down deep in my parents' subconscious, they hate me. I'm serious.") An **unconSCIous** impulse or act is one that is not premeditated or planned out; it is unwitting, inadvertent, involuntary, fortuitous. (Man, did you see that shot? Fifty feet out and never touched the rim! Unconscious!) One can be temporarily devoid of consciousness, as the result of an accident, for example. (The paramedic examined the *unconscious* man.)

OmniSCIent people know everything and take pride in their **omniSCIence**, their infinite, total knowledge, gifts that are often figments of their own imaginations. Those who are **preSCIent** claim to have the gifts of foresight, clairvoyance, premonition, prophecy, and **preSCIence**, a word that is almost always mispronounced

and inevitably misunderstood. One who is **neSCIent** is ignorant or, at least, agnostic.

A **plebiSCIte** is a direct vote taken on a matter of public importance, such as a determination of autonomy or affiliation with another country. (A 1935 plebiscite in Saarland determined that the state would be reunited with Germany.) See also *plebes*, page 136.

A **SCIence** is a branch of knowledge dealing with facts arranged systematically and showing the operation of general laws. (Biology is the science of life, or living matter.) Over the ages we've broadened its application considerably to include the meanings of skill, art, craft, dexterity, expertise, method, finesse, and discipline. (Starting my ancient jalopy by parking it on a hill probably seems nutty, but I've got it down to a science now.) Something that is **SCIentific** is empirical, demonstrable, systematic, verifiable, tangible, or technical. (Of all the members of the department, only Dr. Schwann truly epitomized the scientific spirit.)

An **unSCIentific** experiment or report or analysis does not conform to the principles of science. (My device for measuring wind speed at the airport was bounced — "Look up **SCIolism**," was the comment. I did. It means "superficial knowledge.") Examples of **SCIolists** are the phrenologists who read the shape of one's head and the palmists who study the lines on one's hand. **SCI-fi** is short for science fiction, and nobody asks you to believe that.

☞ ***But not:*** *scintillating* [*scintilla*, spark], vivacious, witty; *sciosophy* [Gk *skio*, shadow + *sophy*, wisdom], supposed knowledge.

Combining forms: con-, together; *ne-, ni-,* not; *nelly,* female name; *omni-,* all; *pre-,* before; *sub-,* under; *un-* not.

Antonyms: conscientious — unreliable, negligent, heedless, irresponsible, slovenly, sloppy; *conscious* — asleep, insensible, unaware, dead, oblivious; *consciousness* — impassivity, insensibility, ignorance, unawareness; *nice* — disagreeable, unkind, cold, distant, miserable, awful, dreadful, mean, coarse, ill-bred, vulgar, sloppy, boorish, gauche; *nicely* — carelessly, sloppily, unpleasantly, unattractively; *nicety* — coarseness, crudeness, slovenliness, roughness; *omniscient* — fallible, ignorant, unknowing, limited, nescient; *prescience* — hindsight, retrospect, afterthought, postscript; *scientific* — spiritual, intuitive, ineffable, transcendental, noumenal; *self-conscious* — confident, relaxed, easy-going, spontaneous, secure, trustful.

In "Bartleby," Herman Melville's first published short story, the **SCRIvener** who worked in the narrator-lawyer's office was a law-copyist whose amusing and startling reply to almost anything his employer asked him to do was, "I would prefer not to." Professional copyists lost out to the typewriter and other marvels that came into being a century ago. Today they might be clerks or court reporters or notaries public or possibly **SCRIbes**. A **SCRIbbler** is a hack, an inferior writer. A piece of **SCRIp** is temporary money or a certificate to be used when trading at a company store.

The literal meaning of **manuSCRIpt** is "written by hand," a definition that seems a bit strange today, when almost no professional writers use pen or pencil. That's what the copyists did for many centuries, dipping Chinese brushes or Egyptian reeds or quills fashioned from bird feathers into ink and writing on papyrus, parchment, and eventually paper. Monks preserved the learning of early eras when they wrote in **SCRIptoriums** in their monasteries, often copying **SCRIpture**. Others, later, sat at **eSCRItories**, an elaborate writing desk or secretary.

In 1883 Mark Twain donned his pioneer's hat when his *Life on the Mississippi* became the first typewritten manuscript to be submitted to a publisher. A **SCRIpt** is the manuscript of a play or movie; it also refers to the characters and letters that are used in handwriting.

A **superSCRIpt** is a letter or number written above the line; a **subSCRIpt** is written slightly below. A **postSCRIpt** is a message written after one has signed a letter, usually headed by P.S. To **inSCRIbe** is to autograph a book or picture, or to write, etch, or engrave. The result is an **inSCRIption**. To **tranSCRIbe** is to note, write down, copy, or record. A **tranSCRIpt** is a written copy, as of one's academic record. A **tranSCRIption** is a recording, as of a program or notes from dictation.

A **preSCRIpt** is a rule or law or ordinance. **PreSCRIptive** grammar is concerned with the "correct" and "incorrect" rules such as not ending sentences with preposition (What else am I going to end a question with?) and never splitting infinities (I am going to *really* study for this exam!). **DeSCRIptive** gram-

SCRIBERE,
to write: SCRI

mar, on the other hand, is concerned with the observation and study of how the language actually works.

To **proSCRIbe** is to prohibit, forbid, or outlaw; hence a **proSCRIbed** area is one to which access is restricted because of possible danger or because it is private property. To **circumSCRIbe** an area or an activity is to enclose or limit or draw a line around it. (His meager education circumscribed his dreams. Before we left on our trip, we circumscribed all the major cities in red on our map.)

To **aSCRIbe** is to credit or attribute. (I ascribe my good health to the exercises I do. That painting has been ascribed to several artists, I fear.) A **conSCRIpt** is someone who has been drafted through military **conSCRIption**. To **subSCRIbe** to an idea or proposal is to concur or agree with it; to subscribe to a cause is to contribute to it; to subscribe to a document is to sign it; to subscribe to a magazine is to order and pay for a **subSCRIption**.

A physician orders or **preSCRIbes** medicine, usually with a **SCRIbble** on the **preSCRIption** form.

If one attempts to **deSCRIbe** a book that has been pegged by the reading public as being **nondeSCRIpt**, one ends up with "uninteresting, ordinary, usual, insipid, dull," all perfectly good adjectives, if a trifle on the negative side. Hence the **indeSCRIbable** can indeed be translated into a **deSCRIption**.

☞ *But not: scrimmage* [ME *scarmishe*, skirmish, minor battle], football practice session; *scrimp* [Scand], economize drastically.

☞ *Combining forms: a-*, to; *circum-*, around; *con-*, with; *de-*, down; *in-*, not, on; *manu-*, by hand; *non-*, not; *-orium*, place for; *post-*, after; *pre-*, before; *pro-*, before; *sub-*, under; *super-*, above; *tran-*, over.

☞ *Antonyms: descriptive* — abstract, general, vague; *nondescript* — distinctive, extraordinary, unusual, vivid, unique, unforgettable; *proscribe* — approve, sanction, allow, permit, encourage; *subscribe* — reject, dissent, be opposed.

SECARE,
to cut: SECT

When somethng is **biSECTed**, it is cut into two equal parts; if it's **triSECTed**, the result is three equal parts, but if it's **disSECTed**, it will most likely be cut close to the part of the plant or animal that the **disSECTor** wishes to examine, analyze, or study. (In math class today our teacher showed us how to bisect angles with **biSECTors** and trisect rectangles. In Francisco's biology class the teacher discussed the **disSECTion** of the frogs they will work on tomorrow. In English a guest speaker dissected several of the students' poems.) A **secant** is a straight line that **interSECTs** a curve at several points. **ViviSECTion** is the act of dissecting a living animal for scientific purposes.

To **interSECT** is to cut or divide by passing through or across. (The proposed highway would intersect our town.) An **interSECTion** is the place where two lines cross. (Our school is located at the intersection of two major city streets.) The point at which a road **biSECTs** is where it forks. (There's a fine restaurant at the point where Sycamore Street bisects.)

Large school classes are often divided into **SECTions**; a **SECTional** sofa is made up of two or more parts; a **SECTor** is a part of a circle (Yes, please, I would like an ample sector of that blueberry pie, thank you), as well as a division of a city (That sector is in dire need of new water lines), a nation's economy (''The private sector has a central role to play in any credible strategy to reduce unemployment,'' Coretta Scott King), and a military operation divided into zones, theaters, or spheres of action (After the armistice a wall divided the American sector from that of the Soviets).

A **segment** is a portion or section of something that naturally divides, as a segment of an orange. (We'll study the history of the feminist movement in chronological segments.)

InSECTs are invertebrate animals with a divided, three-part body. Moles feed on them and are thus **inSECTivorous**; however, most human beings do not, at least intentionally, and they thus employ **inSECTicides** at the sight of the site of an ant.

Risk, risky, and **risqué** are said by some etymologists to come from *secare*. A risk is a danger, peril, or jeopardy as well as to endanger, imperil, or jeopardize. (It was far too great a risk; I dared not risk my family's safety for that.) A situation that is risky is unsafe, precarious, perilous, parlous, chancy, and dicey. (It's a risky drive in good weather, but with ice on the road? No way!) A risqué remark or story is one that may range from indecorous and indelicate to bawdy, salacious, vulgar, and smutty. (I don't know if the kids should see this movie — it's a little risqué.)

A **scion** is a cutting of a twig or shoot to be used for grafting or planting; it also means a descendant. (The two men at the end of this table are scions of an infamous gambling family.) **Notch**, the cut on a stick that people once kept score with, whether of a game or of the number of rainy days in the spring, came down a twisty path from *secare*, as did **sickle**, a cutting tool.

*Once uPUN a time two people were discussing the closing of the *Times*, a venerable afternoon newspaper. ''Yup, my daddy owned it for years,'' said one. ''Then when the bottom of the economy fell out, advertising dried up, circulation plummeted, and he lost it all. And so did his children.''

''Hmm,'' the other said. ''Seems I've heard about you for years. That means you're a scion of the *Times*. Right?''

*But not: sect [*sequi*, to follow], a denomination.

*Combining forms: bi-, two; *-cide*, killer; *dis-*, apart; *in-*, in; *inter-*, between; *vivi-*, alive; *-vorous*, to devour.

*Antonyms: risk — security, protection, safety; risky — certain, sure, guarded, secure, safe; section — whole, totality, all, entirety.

SEMINarians are students who specialize in theology and religious history at a **SEMINary**, a special school that prepares them for the ministry, priesthood, or rabbinate. Many of their advanced classes, as in many colleges and uni-

*SEMEN,
seed: SEMIN*

versities, are **SEMINars** — small, usually informal classes in which students and teachers exchange information and hold discussions. **SEMINal** ideas are creative, original, germinal, and productive, the ''seeds'' that tend to influence the development of future events. (One of the seminal ideas that came out of the French Revolution was the concept and ideal of social equality.)

Semen is the fluid from the male production organ that carries the sperm or seed. **InSEMINation** is the sowing or implanting of seed; artificial insemination is a common practice among raisers of livestock. Both **SEMINation** and **disSEMINation** pertain to the sowing of seeds; the latter has broader meaning, such as the spreading or broadcasting of ideas. (Jefferson's political philosophy has been **disSEMINated** throughout the world.)

Birds who feed mainly on seeds are said to be **SEMINivorous**.

☛ *But not:* dissemble [*similis*, similar], to pretend, conceal; *semester* [*sec*, six + *mensis*, month], a school period.

☛ *Combining forms:* dis-, apart; *in*-, in.

☛ *Antonyms:* disseminate — contract, narrow, shrink; *seminal* - hackneyed, sterile, useless, worn-out.

SENEX, old, old man: SEN

That the average age of our **SENators** is considerably greater than that of our representatives is natural considering the Latin root the word springs from. The Roman **SENate** was a council of elders; so is that of the United States. It is also called the upper or **SENior** legislative body, senior meaning older. Those having **SENiority** have been in the chamber the longest and are often the oldest.

Sir and **sire** are male terms of respect in English, as are **SENhor** in Portuguese, **SEÑor** in Spanish, **signor** and **signore** in Italian, and **monsieur** in French. **Monseigneur** is a French title of honor reserved for princes, bishops, and the like; its literal meaning is ''my sir''' or ''my lord.'' **Monsignor** is a title conferred upon certain high-ranking prelates.

Old age has its drawbacks, of course. A person who is **SENescent** is growing old; since that would apply to everybody from Day One on, its sense is ''aging.'' (Young people don't age; they grow up and get older.) A **SENile** person is weak and infirm, often mentally and physically; the condition is called **SENility**.

To sire is to father an offspring; a sire is the male parent of a quadruped. As a verb it means to beget and, as a kind of spin-off, to author. (Our tireless author has sired another tired novel.)

A feudal lord was called a **seigneur** or a **seignior**. One who assumed lordly airs in those days was called *sirly* (sir-like) meaning lordly (lord-like), which eventually came to mean arrogant, rude, and ill-mannered and to be spelled **surly**. (Dad says surly behavior is now reserved for waiters and parking attendants. Yes, **sirree**!)

But not: sirocco [Ar *sharq*, east], dry, dusty wind from northern Africa.

Antonyms: senior — junior, apprentice, underling, newcomer, stripling, tadpole; *surly* — amiable, civil, courteous, gracious.

As a transitive verb, to **asSEMBLe** is to fit or connect or piece something together. (If I had read the instructions, I could have assembled this model in half the time. I've done all the research; now I have to assemble the information for my term paper. The foreman assembled a new crew.) As an intransitive verb it means to meet, congregate, convene, gather. (The student body will assemble in the auditorium immediately after lunch.)

An **asSEMBLy** is a convocation, a gathering, a roundup. It is also the putting together of, say, a complicated mechanism. (We'll need a few extra hands for the assembly of the glider.) In some legislatures, it is the name of the lower house, hence the members are **asSEMBLymen** and **asSEMBLywomen**. And it is a signal, often by bugle, for troops to fall in.

An **asSEMBLage** is the act of **asSEMBLing**; it is the aggregate or collection of the gathered people or things; it is also a form of sculpture in which unrelated, often discarded items are composed into a whole.

An **enSEMBLe** is the entire outfit of clothing of a person. (Now if I had a new hat, my ensemble would be complete.) It is a set of furniture, a theatrical troupe or company, or a musical group. (Tomorrow we'll hear the Warsaw String Ensemble.)

A **SIMULcast** is a program that is broadcast **SIMULtaneously** on radio and television, or on two or more channels or stations, or in several languages. **SIMULtaneous** happenings exist or occur at the same time. (Visitors to the General Assembly of the United Nations can twist a dial on their headsets and hear what the speaker is saying in simultaneous translations of five different languages.)

But not: dissemble [*similis*, like], to pretend, feign; *resemble* [*similis*], be similar to; *simulate* [*similis*], to imitate.

Combining forms: as-, to; *en-*, in.

Antonyms: assemble — disperse, separate, disband, dismantle, disconnect; *assembly* — dispersal, separation; *simultaneous* — staggered, distant, diachronous.

SIMUL,
together, at the
same time:
SEMBL, SIMUL

When school heads arrange the year's activities and holidays, they make up a **schedule**. In this country, the word is pronounced *skej'ool*; should some English or Canadian cousins be visiting, they would call it a *shed'yool*.

A **schism** is a breach or break or division, especially in a religious body, but it also occurs in political parties. A **schismatic** is a person who promotes such a break or who goes along with it.

A **SCHIZophrenic** or **SCHIZoid** is a person with mental disorders that are manifested in abnormal shyness or delusions or withdrawal or hallucinations or multiple or split personalities; in other words, a split from the world or

SKHIZEIN [Gk],
to split: SCHIZ

from reality. Both words are also adjectives. Psychiatrists call the disorder **SCHIZophrenia**; in the past it has also been called *dementia praecox*; its literal meaning is "split mind."

SCHIZy is an informal word used loosely to describe someone the speaker suspects may be on the brink of withdrawing behind the draperies or thinking he's Michael Jackson on tour in Japan. Or the purpose might be just to irk or bug a friend.

☞ *But not: scheme* [Gk *echein*, to have, hold], design, plan.

☞ *Combining form: -phrenia*, mind.

☞ *Antonyms: schism* — union, fusion, agreement, compromise, harmony.

SKOPEIN [Gk], see, look at: SCOPE

Of the many **SCOPEs** we have available to us, a few play important roles in our lives, directly or indirectly. **FluoroSCOPEs** can help locate hairline fractures; **microSCOPEs** are invaluable in medical laboratories; **spectroSCOPEs** are useful for producing and observing a spectrum of light or radiation; **radarSCOPEs**, the viewing screens of radar equipment, are indispensable to the airline industry; and **teleSCOPEs** provide scientists with information that affects our daily lives.

PeriSCOPEs are important to the crew of a submarine; **kaleidoSCOPEs** provide hours of entertainment for children as well as ideas for designers; **horoSCOPEs**, which are charts rather than instruments, are scanned daily by those who believe that our lives are influenced by heavenly bodies; and the **kinetoSCOPE**, an early motion-picture device invented by Thomas Edison, was instrumental in the development of our modern movie projectors.

To telescope an object is to compress or shorten the image of it; years ago there were two-part suitcases with that name that could expand as one part got more than full. To telescope a piece of writing is to summarize or epitomize it. A **microscopic** object is miniscule, infinitesimal, imperceptible, and minute.

The **SCOPE** of an individual is his or her range, vision, grasp, reach, and knowledge. The scope of a piece of property is its area, span, or spread. A creative person who needs a wide scope should be given elbow room, freedom, and latitude. To scope something out is to look it over. (The speaker scoped out the audience as she waited at the head table for her cue.)

A **bishop** is an overseer, watching over the flock, scoping it out. **Episcopal** comes from scope by way of bishop, for an **episcopate** is the order or body of bishops that governs the church that Episcopalians belong to.

☞ *But not: cope* [F *couper*, to strike], manage; *epistle* [Gk *epistole*, message], a letter.

☞ *Combining forms: bi-*, over; *eido-*, shape; *epi-*, upon; *fluoro-*, fluorescence; *horo-*, hour; *kal-*, beautiful; *kineto-*, moving; *micro-*, small; *peri-*, around; *radar-*, locating device; *spectro-*, spectrum; *tele-*, far off.

Antonyms: microscopic — macroscopic; *telescope* — extend, lengthen, amplify, flesh out.

Both Greek and Latin have given us words meaning sun, but the Latin derivatives are more often in everyday use. People build **SOLarized** houses that utilize **SOLar** energy, and they have **SOLariums** for their plants and their own winter comfort. Women sometimes carry colorful **paraSOLs** on hot days, particularly to fashionable gatherings.

On June 21 and again on December 22 ("the darkest evening of the year," as Robert Frost says in his poem, "Stopping by Woods on a Snowy Evening"), the **SOLstice** occurs, and we tend to think of Old **SOL** as turning around, which, of course, it doesn't do at all, anymore than it rises and sets. The bleaching or drying of an object in the sun is called **inSOLating**. To expose to the sun is to **inSOLate**, and the process is called **inSOLation**. (The Scout troop is learning to insolate certain fruits such as apples, currants, and bananas.)

Helios was the Greek sun god; the Latin-derived word **giraSOL** is the same as the Greek **HELIOtrope**. They both refer to a plant that turns toward the sun, which is what sunflowers do, and the girasol is a sunflower. The tubers of the girasol plant, lightly sautéed in margarine or oil or mashed like a potato, are recommended by nutritionists. If we grew our own, we would most likely call them jerusalem artichokes, but if we shopped for them at the market, we might find them labeled sunchokes. A fire opal, which reflects sunlight in a bright luminous glow, is also known as a girasol.

HELIOcentric describes our solar system: having the sun at the center. **HELIOtherapy** is the use of the sun's rays for medical treatment, and the glass-enclosed rooms at some hospitals — solariums — are used for that purpose. A **HELIOgraph** is a signaling device using sunlight reflected by a mirror, and **helium** is a non-explosive gas used in balloons.

But not: helicopter [GK *helico*, spiral], aircraft; *insole* [*solea*, sandal], the inner sole of a shoe; *insolent* [*solere*, to be accustomed], rude, impertinent; *resolute* [*solvere*, to loosen], firm; *solo* [*solus*, alone], unassisted; *solon* [after *Solon*, c. 639–c. 558 B.C., Athenian statesman and wise lawgiver], member of a legislative body.

At some point during our grammar school days we learn that a few words have multiple personalities, that is, they can function as all four parts of speech. *Last*, for example: A shoemaker works on a last; I came in last; That's my last cent; These flowers will last. **SOLo** is another: I love that piano solo; Sam will solo today at Brice Field; There's a part here for solo clarinet; Sis never jogs solo.

SOLitude is seclusion, isolation, withdrawal, loneliness, privacy, sequestration; it is, wrote Octavio Paz, the Mexican poet who won the Nobel Prize for Literature in 1990, "the profoundest fact of the human condition. Man is the only being who knows he is alone." A **SOLitudinarian** is a recluse, hermit, ascetic; it is a word that does and does not describe Henry David

*SOL [L],
HELIOS [Gk],
sun: SOL, HELIO*

*SOLUS,
alone: SOL*

Thoreau; true, he sought solitude, but he often walked the railroad tracks into town.

DeSOLate is double-edged as both adjective and verb: deserted, uninhabited, isolated, barren, cheerless, and bleak. (That area is so desolate, you think you're at the end of the world.) Also: forlorn, dejected, pitiable, lonesome, friendless, and bereft. (JoJo was desolate when Bud's unit was called up.) And as a verb: ruin, ravage, destroy, wreak havoc, and devastate. (The hurricane **deSOLated** the fishing village.) Also: depress, sadden, dishearten, grieve, and crush. (We were desolated when we got the news of the explosion.) **DeSOLation** is destruction, dreariness, loneliness, and misery. (And in the midst of all this desolation, the guy says to me, "Have a nice day!" Jeez!)

A **SOLfidian** is a person who believes that faith is the **SOLe** requirement necessary for salvation. **SOLipsism** is the theory that nothing is real or exists but the self; it is also what may lie beneath a case of ultimate egocentricity, egomania, or narcissism. A monologue is a **SOLiloquy**, a long discourse in which one is or appears to be talking to oneself. (Dr. Garret's annual lecture on Shakespeare's soliloquies inevitably draws a big audience.) But no matter what manner of speech — apostrophe, sermon, oration, disquisition, tirade, diatribe, address — poor speakers often begin **SOLiloquizing** and the audience dozing.

A **SOLitaire** is a single large, sparkling diamond set in a ring, as well as the name of a card game for one player. Something that is **SOLitary** is alone, unattended, forsaken, deserted, unique, singular. (Not one solitary soul from our department showed up at the ceremony.) Hardened, unruly prisoners are placed in solitary confinement.

All this solitude and loneliness can make one **sullen**, glum, melancholy, morose, depressed, crabby, and in the dumps. The remarkable Samuel Johnson put it nicely in a letter to James Boswell, his biographer: "Are you sick, or are you sullen?" The symptoms are quite similar.

- *Once uPUN a time* a professor of American literature observed that Henry David Thoreau had committed himself to solitary refinement for two years.

- *But not:* sole [*solea*, sandal], European flatfish; *solecism* [Gk *soloi*, after a city in which a corrupt form of Greek was spoken], an ungrammatical usage; *solicitous* [*ciere*, to arouse], anxious, concerned.

- *Combining forms: de-*, completely; *-fid*, faith; *-ips*, self; *-loquy*, talk.

- *Antonyms: desolate* — inhabitated, populated, bustling, cheerful, joyous; cultivate, develop, hearten, encourage; *desolation* — fruitful, productive; happiness; *sole* — shared, divided, joint; *solitary* — sociable, companionable, gregarious, several, many, multiple, popular, included, well-traveled, busy; *solitude* — conviviality, participation, sociability, gregariousness; *solo* — communal, group; *sullen* — animated, enthusiastic, jovial, joyous, vivacious, buoyant, merry, bright.

New Year's **reSOLUtions**, someone has said, are like promises and piecrusts, made to be broken. One who is **irreSOLUte**, that is, lacking resolution, is short on determination, **reSOLVe**, tenacity, and perseverance. (I was big on goals, but I lacked the **abSOLUte**, unqualified, unadulterated, and unequivocal resolution to reach them.) Resolution is also the outcome, end, **SOLUtion**, or result of a conflict or problem. (Worrying about the resolution of the contract dispute caused Marti considerable stress, but she remained adamant, firm, and **reSOLUte**.)

Persons who are **disSOLUte** are immoral, depraved, licentious, and debauched. They may eventually wish to seek **abSOLUtion** and thus be **abSOLVed** of their sins.

The **disSOLUtion** or **disSOLVing** of a partnership or union — however **indisSOLUble** it may have appeared to be — brings it to an end, to its termination and extinction. Some substances, problems, and partnerships are, of course, more **SOLUble** than others and may come to an end more quickly.

Someone who is **abSOLUtely**, definitely, indubitably, positively, and utterly without means of support is **inSOLVent**, bankrupt, penniless, impecunious, straitened, and just plain broke. For one to become **SOLVent** again may be a problem that is **inSOLUble, unSOLVable**, and incapable of being **SOLVed**.

But not: solunar [blend of *solar* and *lunar*], a listing of the rising and setting times of the sun and the moon, moon phases, eclipses, etc.

Combining forms: ab-, from; *dis-*, apart; *in-*, not; *ir-*, not; *re-*, again.

Antonyms: absolute — conditional, partial, contingent, provisional, fragmentary, conjectural; *absolutely* — reasonably, approximately, probably; *absolve* — accuse, blame, condemn, prosecute; *dissolute* — chaste, virtuous, austere, puritanical; *insolvent* — sound, solid, prosperous, flush; *irresolute* — steadfast, firm, fixed; *resolute* — weak, changeable, aimless; *resolution* — uncertainty, indecision, inconstancy; *solvent* — risky, unreliable.

In Italian the word **SONnet** means "little song." In form a sonnet is a fourteen-line poem, usually on one idea, sentiment, or thought, sometimes in two groups, eight lines and six, sometimes in three quatrains and a final couplet. It was introduced to England early in the sixteenth century and has been a popular form ever since. Elizabeth Barrett Browning's *Sonnets from the Portuguese* contains a sequence of forty-four love poems, among them the much anthologized "How do I love thee? Let me count the ways."

A **SONata** is a musical composition most frequently for the piano or another instrument with piano accompaniment and usually in three movements.

The public speaker who has a **SONorous** style has one that can also be called flamboyant, grandiose, florid, and impressive, and if the style is accompanied by a sonorous voice, it will be loud, full-toned, rich-**SOUNDing**, and reverberating. A voice or noise that **reSOUNDs** fills the air, rings, peals, booms, and echoes, ("Lean your body forward slightly to support the guitar against

SOLVERE,
to loosen:
SOLU, SOLV

SONARE,
to sound:
SON, SOUND

your chest, for the poetry of the music should resound in your heart,'' Andrés Segovia). And it is said to tintinabulate, too, having the **SOUND** of ringing bells, (The valley resounded with the tintinabulations of the church bells). **ReSOUNDing** means echoing, plangent, ringing, but it is also used in the sense of emphatic. (The Cats scored a resounding victory over their archrivals the Ponies yesterday.) A **reSONant** voice is one that is thunderous, booming, tumultuous, deafening, stentorian, and orotund. No amplifiers are needed. Sound bites are brief, attention-getting statements that candidates for political office make in hopes they will be repeated on the evening news broadcasts.

AsSONance is also called ''vowel rhyme.'' ''Free as a breeze,'' ''high as a kite,'' and ''mad as a hatter'' are examples. Alliteration, on the other hand, is the repetition of initial **conSONant** sounds as in ''dead as a doornail,'' ''fit as a fiddle,'' and ''pretty as a picture.'' As an adjective, consonant means in accord or in agreement. (As an applicant for the position of headmistress, Jeanette hoped that her views were consonant with those of the trustees.) In addition to being a rhyming device, **ConSONance** means harmony, agreement, and concord. (The school nurse felt that the child's recent behavior pattern was quite out of consonance with his usual comportment.)

Jarring, harsh, grating, clashing sounds are **disSONant**. (The dissonant noises from the band room forced us to close the windows.) Theories or groups or individuals that are at variance with one another can also be dissonant. (The mayor hopes the dissonant factions will settle their differences.) **DisSONance** is discord, strife, contention. (In the early days of their marriage they seemed to be in **uniSON** on many matters, but before long the relationship dissolved into dissonance.)

SONics is the branch of science dealing with the applications of sound. The adjective **SONic** pertains to a speed of approximately 738 miles per hour at sea level. A sonic boom is a loud noise from a shock wave caused by an aircraft moving at **superSONic** speed, that is, a speed greater than that of sound. **TranSONic** speed is between 700 and 780 miles per hour.

☞ *But not: son* [AS *sunu*], male child; *song* [AS *sang*], lyric; *sound* [AS *gesund*], healthy; *sound* [OF *sonder*, to plumb], to measure the depth of water; *sound* [AS *sund*, act of swimming], body of water.

☞ *Combining forms: as-*, to; *con-*, together; *dis-*, away; *re-*, again; *super-*, over; *trans-*, through; *uni-*, one.

☞ *Antonyms: consonance* — dissonance, disparity, conflict; *consonant* — opposed, contrary, inconsistent, discordant; *dissonant* — harmonious, euphonious, tuneful, compatible, congruent, uniform; *resounding* — slight, faint; *sonorous* — weak, tinny, plain, unadorned.

SOROR,
sister: SORO

Several kinds of women's clubs or societies have taken their names from this Latin root. The **SOROrities** that are perhaps best known are found on certain college campuses, usually employing letters from the Greek alphabet as their names and primarily social in nature. But other women's groups, social, professional, and honorary, also call themselves sororities. A **SOROsis** is another generic name given to women's societies or clubs, the first one in America being incorporated in 1869. The **SOROptimist** Club, an international organization of business and professional women, is primarily devoted to welfare work.

SOROal means sisterly; to **SOROize** is to associate with other women as sisters, being analogous to *fraternize*; **SOROrate** is the marriage of a man to his wife's sister, usually after his first wife's death; and **SOROcide** is the killer and killing of one's sister. **Cousin** also comes from **soror**, but in a somewhat roundabout way: *cou-*, together; *sobrinus*, belonging to a sister.

The English *sister* was *sweoster* when the Anglos and Saxons dominated the island. It may be of interest to note that the Indo-European word for sister was *swesor* and that "s" is the initial letter of the word in many languages today: *Schwester* [G], *sesu* [Lith], *soeur* [F], *sorella* [It], *svasar* [Skt], *sestrá* [Russ], and *syster* [Swed].

When political candidates hit the campaign trail these days, they often cast **aSPERsions** on their principal rivals, sprinkling them with slander, calumny, libel, mudslinging, vilification, and impugnment. To **aSPERse**, then, is to malign, slander, vilify, impugn, denigrate, traduce. (Claiming that his reputation had been hopelessly **aSPERsed**, the incumbent dropped out of the race.)

But if an **aSPERsion** takes place in a church, it is a sprinkling of a much different nature: it is a baptism. In the Roman Catholic church the rite or ceremony is known as **ASPERges**, the vessel that holds the holy water is an **aSPERsorium**, and the brush or perforated globe for sprinkling is an **aSPERgillum**.

To **interSPERse** is to scatter or place here and there. (The speaker interspersed her talk with fascinating anecdotes. The book was interspersed with drawings.) To **diSPERse** is to scatter, dissipate, break up, disseminate, spread. (The police dispersed the unruly crowd. The wind dispersed the smoke. The press conference dispersed knowledge of the crisis. The **diSPERsion** of the troops lessened the risk of casualties.) Things that are **sparse** are thin, scanty, spare, meager, skimpy (". . . the sparse shade of one willow tree," Eudora Welty). **Sparsely** means thinly, scantily. (It was a forlorn area, sparsely populated.)

But not: asperity [*asperitas*, rough], irritability; *vesper* [*vesper*, evening], the evening star, Venus.

Combining forms: as-, to; *dis-*, away; *inter-*, between; *-orium*, place for.

Antonyms: asperse — commend, praise, extol, laud, eulogize; *aspersion* — compliment, commendation, encomium, plaudit; *disperse* — combine, collect, assemble, converge, gather; *sparse* — dense, crowded, thick, plentiful, populous.

SPARGO, to scatter, besprinkle: SPER

SPONDERE,
to pledge:
SPOND, SPONS

The society pages of our newspapers often refer to marriage or wedding ceremonies as *nuptials*; **espousals** and **spousals** are synonyms, but today they are considered a bit old-fashioned. **Spouse** remains with us, however, especially since more and more women have opted for public life. Not too long ago it was acceptable to write, "Congressmen and their wives are invited," but today that might be worded, "Representatives [or Congresspersons] and their spouses [or guests] are invited."

In earlier times **espouse** meant to become married, to unit in marriage; today its principal meaning is to champion, support, adopt, advocate, promulgate, embrace, tout, or boost a cause. (The committee voted to espouse the recycling program.)

When one's letter to one's beloved is returned with a note of rejection, one **deSPONDs**, losing heart, hope, and happiness. One becomes **desPONDent**, dejected, and depressed and slowly sinks into a state of **deSPONDency**, despair, and desperation.

A **SPONSor**, being a patron, an angel, a supporter, a backer, or a cereal company that wants to increase the sales of its new Fig and Raisin Bran Breakfast Food, is an **espouser**, too.

One who **reSPONDs** is one who answers, replies, retorts, or acknowledges. A **reSPONDent** is one who replies; it is also the defendant in a law suit, especially a divorce case. As such, his or her **responses** may determine the outcome of the dispute, depending on how **reSPONSive** the jury is to the attorney's argument.

A **reSPONSible** person is reliable and mature (Christine's our candidate for the job; she's a responsible gal); accountable and liable (You are responsible for any damages), important and demanding (Sol has a very responsible position). An **irreSPONSible** person is immature and undependable, one who cannot be trusted to cope with the duties, obligations, and **reSPONSibilities** that come with the job.

To **correSPOND** is to be in agreement with or similar to something else. (Binnerd's words do not always correspond to his actions. Their Parliament corresponds to our Congress; they are **correSPONDing** legislative bodies.) It is also to write letters, to carry on a **correSPONDence** with someone; a letter writer is a **correSPONDent**, as is a person who reports the news from a distant place.

☞ ***But not:*** *spontaneous* [*sponte*, of one's own accord], natural.

☞ ***Combining forms:*** *cor-*, together; *des-*, away; *ir-*, not; *re-*, back.

☞ ***Antonyms:*** *correspondence* — dissimilarity, incongruity, discordancy; *despond* — aspire, anticipate, hope; *despondency* — elation, optimism, courage; *despondent* — cheerful, buoyant, spirited, happy, upbeat; *espouse* — reject, spurn, shun, disown, repudiate; *irresponsible* — dependable, thoughtful, careful, conscientious; *responsible* — unaccountable, fickle, irrational, *non compos mentis*; *responsive* — inert, passive, cold, unfriendly, insensitive, aloof, distant, unapproachable.

To dodo, greak auk, and passenger pigeon are **extinct** birds. The dodo died because it was slow, flightless, and dumb; the last extant, or living, great auk was **extinguished** a century and a half ago; and the **extinction** of the last of several billion passenger pigeons occurred in the Cincinnati Zoo in 1914.

It did not matter that they, like all creatures, had an **inSTINCTive** will to survive; the survival **inSTINCT** was no match for the Dutch settlers in search of food on the dodo's island of Mauritius, or for the men who clubbed the last great auk to death, or for the guns of the pigeon hunters. Today many species are protected from such **extinguishers**, and the whooping crane has the **diSTINCTion** of being one of those on the comeback trail.

Many birds have **diSTINCT** markings and sounds. The crested head and bright red of the male cardinal is **diSTINCTive**. It is easy to **diSTINGUish** the mourning dove's slow, moaning *coo-ah-coo-coo* from the call of the whippoor-will, and to make a **diSTINCTion** between the roadrunner or chaparral and any other bird on the run; this two-foot-long bird has been clocked at fifteen miles per hour.

To the untrained eye, some birds are **indiSTINGUishable** from certain others. The principal markings of many sparrows are **indiSTINCT**, for example, but such a renowned ornithologist as the **diSTINGUished** Roger Tory Peterson could tell one from another at a glance.

But not: *stint* [AS *styntan*, to make blunt], to be frugal; a period of time; *tincture* [*tingere*, to dye], a solution, as tincture of iodine.

Combining forms: *di-*, apart; *ex-*, completely; *in-*, in, not.

Antonyms: *distinct* — obscure, vague, attached, merged; *distinctive* — common, ordinary, anonymous, conventional; *distinguished* — mediocre, ordinary, second-rate, commonplace; *extinct* — thriving, flourishing, active, extant; *indistinct* — clear, defined, evident; *instinctive* — learned, acquired, premeditated, calculated, considered.

To **conSTRUCT** is to build, form, erect, devise, fashion, frame, fabricate, shape. ("Since wars begin in the minds of men, it is in the minds of men that the defenses of peace must be constructed" from the constitution of UNESCO, the United Nations Educational, Scientific, and Cultural Organization.)

A **conSTRUCTion** is a building, erection, formation, invention, or creation. It is also the process of building or erecting. (The construction of the bridge took two years.) However, when King Duncan used the word in Shakespeare's *Macbeth*, it meant makeup, composition, form, meaning: "There's no art / To find the mind's construction in the face . . . ." To **deconSTRUCT** is to dismantle, dissect; hence, the **deconSTRUCTion** of a literary text is a method of analysis or dissection of it.

Something that is **conSTRUCTive** is affirmative, helpful, positive, practical, handy, beneficial. (I don't mind criticism if it's constructive.)

STINGUERE,
to quench, pierce:
STINCT,
STINGU

STRUERE,
to construct:
STRU, STRUCT

When we **conSTRUe** something, we interpret, explain, analyze, render, or explicate it. In his first inaugural address President Abraham Lincoln said, ''I take official oath to-day with no . . . purpose to construe the Constitution or laws by any hypercritical rules.'' To **misconSTRUe** is to misunderstand, misinterpret, or mistake; literary critic Carlos Baker warned that, ''The reader should be on guard against misconstruing the intention of a given passage.''

To **destroy** is to obliterate, eradicate, decimate, demolish, devastate, or annihilate. (''It became necessary to destroy the town to save it,'' U.S. Army officer referring to the Vietnamese town of Ben Tre during the Vietnam War.) A **destroyer** is a fast warship smaller than a cruiser.

At the opening of each episode of an old TV series called *Mission Impossible*, government agents would receive a tape-recorded message outlining their assignment. It always ended with the warning, ''This tape will **self-deSTRUCT** in five seconds,'' at which time it would automatically destroy itself, expire, perish, terminate. In a tongue-in-cheek poem about whether the world would eventually be destroyed by fire or ice, Robert Frost wrote, ''I think I know enough of hate / To say that for **deSTRUCTion** ice / Is also great / And would suffice.'' Destruction is also havoc, ruin, extermination, wreckage, obliteration. Nathaniel Lee, a seventeenth-century English playwright, had a character say, ''Man, false man, smiling, **deSTRUCTive** man''; synonyms are harmful, injurious, detrimental, ruinous, devastating. ''The Constitution, in all its provisions,'' Salmon P. Chase, U.S. Supreme Court Chief Justice, wrote in 1868, ''looks to an **indeSTRUCTible** Union composed of indestructible states'': that is, enduring, permanent, imperishable, everlasting, infrangible.

To **inSTRUCT** is to enlighten, teach, inform, direct, school, apprise; the French playwright Molière offered this advice in *The School for Husbands*, ''I maintain, in truth, / That with a smile we should instruct our youth.'' **InSTRUCTion** is teaching, indoctrination, enlightenment, edification, and pedagogy. In his book *Operating Manual for Spaceship Earth*, R. Buckminster Fuller, inventor, mathematician, and philosopher, claimed the trouble with earth ''is that no instruction book came with it.'' ''Experience,'' an anonymous author has written, ''furnishes very **inSTRUCTive** lessons''; such lessons would be informative, explanatory, edifying, perceptive, hortatory, and, especially, heuristic.

The English author Samuel Butler once said, ''Life is like playing a violin solo in public and learning the **inSTRUment** as one goes on.'' Instruments are tools, devices, implements, utensils, mechanisms, and contrivances; they are also agencies, agents, means, mediums, intermediaries, and expediters. (Police and firefighters are necessary instruments in every community.) Anything that is **inSTRUmental** is useful, essential, vital, crucial, conducive, and utiliarian. And so it means in this quote from *Hamlet*: ''The head is not more native to the heart, / The hand more instrumental to the brain, / Than is the throne of Denmark to thy father.''

''No Parking — Do Not **ObSTRUCT** Traffic'' means do not hinder, impede, delay, stall, or thwart it. Obstruct also means to hide, obscure, screen, block, or close off, as, for example, a view. (The lady's hat obstructed my view of the stage.) An **obSTRUCTion** is an obstacle, barricade, hindrance, blockage, impediment; in his book *The Monarchy*, Walter Bagehot wrote, "Throughout the greater part of his life George III was a kind of 'consecrated obstruction.'" An **obSTRUCTionist** is a person who impedes or thwarts an action. (You, sir, are an obstructionist who is trying to kill this amendment with your delaying tactics.)

In *My Early Years*, Sir Winston Churchill wrote of how he escaped learning Latin and Greek because he was not clever enough to qualify for such courses, thus "I was taught English [and] got into my bones the essential **STRUCTure** of the ordinary English sentence — which is a noble thing." As Churchill used the word it means organization, arrangement, design, pattern, composition. A structure is also a building or edifice, and as a verb it means to put together, plan, organize, assemble, design. (This course has been structured to appeal to everyone who is interested in good writing.) **STRUCTural** pertains to structure; the structural details of a house, for instance, are the floor joists, wall studs, rafters, etc. The footing or foundation of a building is its **subSTRUCTure**, and the part above it is the **superSTRUCTure**. The **infraSTRUCTure** of a country is its basic, underlying framework, notably its communication and transportation systems, power plants, and schools.

*But not: abstruse [*ab-*, away + *trudere*, to push], difficult to understand, recondite; *nostrum* [*nostrum*, our own, sold by the maker, from *noster*, ours], quick-fix scheme; quack medicine; *rostrum* [*rostrum*, beak, a ship's bow, from using the bows of captured enemy ships as decorations on the speakers' platform at the Forum in ancient Rome], raised platform for speakers.

*Combining forms: con-, together; *de-*, down; *in-*, in, not; *infra-*, below; *mis-*, wrong; *ob-*, before; *sub-*, below; *super-*, above.

*Antonyms: construct — destroy, dismantle, demolish, raze, tear down; *constructive* — useless, unhelpful, adverse, negative, inimical; *destroy* — create, construct, make, save, preserve, conserve, found, institute; *destructible* — durable, stable, abiding, permanent, protracted; *destruction* — renewal, creation, restoration, recovery; *destructive* — beneficial, positive, wholesome, good, helpful; *indestructible* — delicate, brittle, crumbly, flimsy; *instructive* — baffling, befuddling, ambiguous, confusing, unfathomable; *instrumental* — negligible, insignificant, inconsequential, useless, ineffectual; *obstruct* — clear, open, unblock, unveil, abet, aid, benefit, promote, facilitate, expedite, further, spur; *obstruction* — assistance, clearing, freeing, furtherance, encouragement, opening, aid.

To be **STUPified** is to be dazed, bewildered, flabbergasted, rattled, amazed, and astounded. (The sign of the little green creatures floating down from the flying soupbowl stupified Grandma.) Something **STUPendous** is overwhelming, prodigious, colossal, immense, and humongous. (The landing was the

STUPERE,
to be stunned:
STUP

most stupendous event that ever happened in our town.) A **STUPor** is a condition in which one's senses are dulled, and one experiences numbness, grogginess, lethargy, lassitude, and languor. It can be caused by drugs or shock. (Poor Grandpa! He lay there as if in a drunken stupor; the **STUPefaction**, the overwhelming amazement of the landing was just too much for him.)

From that it was just a step to **STUPid**, a word meaning dull, slow-witted, dim-witted, foolish, inane, senseless, and irritating, ("A word to the wise ain't necessary — it's the stupid ones who need advice," Bill Cosby, *Fat Albert's Survival Kit*). A **STUPidity** is a senseless, asinine, dopey, idiotic act or statement; it is also the condition of being dull-witted, obtuse, moronic, and puerile. **STUPe** is a slang word for a stupid person.

☛   *But not:* stoop [AS *stupian*], a small porch; to crouch, to lower onself.

☛   *Combining forms:* -faction, -fy, to make.

☛   *Antonyms:* stupendous — tiny, puny, diminutive, minuscule; *stupid* — alert, bright, clever, quick-witted, vigilant, sensible; *stupidity* — acumen, discernment, keenness, intelligence.

T

Sir William Osler, a renowed physician and professor of medicine who the fifteen edition of the *Encyclopaedia Britannica* said was "probably the most famous and beloved physican in the English-speaking and perhaps the whole world," once offered this advice to medical students: "Things cannot always go your way. Learn to accept in silence the minor aggravations [and] cultivate the gift of **TACITurnity** . . . ." Such is the gift of being reserved, restrained, even silent in conversation, of accepting small annoyances **reticently**, silently, **TACITurnly**.

During a valedictory address, however, he himself did not observe the **reticence**, reserve, **TACITness**, or silence that he had advocated when he spoke of "the uselessness of men above sixty years of age," suggesting that if they all stopped work at that age the result would be of "incalculable benefit." An outcry followed, and one newspaper headline screamed, "Osler Recommends Chloroform at Sixty." "To Oslerize" became a byword. When he died in 1919, he was regius profession of medicine at Oxford University in England — and seventy years old!

Reticent and **TACITurn** people are diffident, retiring, uncommunicative, close-mouthed, tight-lipped, and secretive. Something that is **TACIT** is implied, implicit, understood, unspoken, undeclared, and unstated. (Everyone on our block is in tacit agreement that we watch out for any suspicious strangers. The way the good doctor looked at me **TACITly** assured me that he approved of my plan.)

But not: retina [perh. *rete*, net], eyeball part; *retinue* [*tenere*, to hold], aides or servants accompanying a VIP; *Tacitus*, Publius Cornelius, Roman historian, A.D. c. 55–c. 120.

Combining form: re-, again.

Antonyms: reticent — bold, aggressive, outspoken, opinionated, voluble, expansive, frank, open; *tacit* — explicit, spoken, spelled out; *taciturn* — talkative, loquacious, vociferous, garrulous, chatty, verbose, outgoing.

TACERE,
to be silent:
TACIT

The withholding of sunlight from a plant will **reTARD** or slow down its growth. The economic and social progress of a country will be retarded or delayed by continuing uprisings. Malnutrition and a turbulent home life will retard or hinder the academic progress of a child, often resulting in the **reTARDation** of a year or more in the child's schooling.

A **reTARDate** or **reTARDee** is a person whose educational or mental development is abnormally slow or has ceased. A **reTARDed** person is handicapped or disabled in such ways. Fire-**reTARDant** materials are mandatory in the construction of public buildings and recommended for all others.

Flabby joggers lag behind, library books become overdue, buses run late, dawdlers fall behindhand in their bills, and orders don't get shipped because

TARDUS, slow:
TARD

clerks are dilatory. But the ten o'clock scholar who now comes at noon is **TARDy**, glaciers and income-tax refunds move **TARDily**, and constant **TARDiness** is a demerit on one's record.

☞ *Once uPUN a time* a somewhat absent-minded man was puzzled when he turned the page on the calendar and saw the word ''retardate'' penciled in. ''What's this mean?'' he said to his wife. ''Why, this is the day,'' she reminded him, ''when the roofers are coming to fix the leak with hot tar.''

☞ *But not: taradiddle* [?], fib, pretentious nonsense.

☞ *Combining form: re-*, again.

☞ *Antonyms: retard* — hasten, expedite, move ahead, rush, speed; *retardation* — acceleration, advancement; *tardy* — quick, speedy, fleet, punctual, prompt, on time.

TEMNEIN [Gk],
to cut:
TOM, TOMY

An **aTOM** is very small; it is something that has been cut into iotas, specks, bits, pieces, jots, whits, mites, and scintillas — and you just can't get any smaller than those. When one squeezes the bulb on an **aTOMizer**, the contents are reduced to a fine spray. When certain materials are blown apart by an explosure such as an **aTOMic** bomb, they are **aTOMized** into atoms, particles, or fragments.

An **epiTOMe** is a condensation of synopsis or digest of a book; it has been cut. A person can be an epitome, too, one who is most representative of a particular quality or characteristic. (Lori is the epitome of honesty.) Hence, to **epiTOMize** something is to be typical of it. (Lori epitomizes that entire group of fine young people.)

A **dichoTOMY** is something that has been divided or split into two parts. (Because of the recent dichotomy of our party, we can say goodby to any chance our candidates might have had in the election.) Its adjective forms mean divided. (The **dichoTOMous** state of affairs that previously weakened our town is over at last.)

The **anaTOMY** of an animal or plant is its structure, hence a skeleton and, informally, the human body. William Harvey, the English physician who discovered the circulation of the blood, wrote, ''I profess both to learn and teach anatomy, not from books but from dissections.'' That was long before the 1901 publication of (Henry) *Gray's Anatomy*, an exhaustive study of the human body, a **TOMe** of nearly 1,300 pages and more than 800 drawings. Anatomy also means any thorough analysis or examination. (The committee was commissioned to draw up an anatomy of the community's structure.) An **enTOMologist**, a person knowledgeable in the branch of zoology dealing with insects, would be familiar with the anatomy of such creatures.

The names of many surgical operations calling for the removal of a body part end in *-tomy*: **appendecTOMY** (appendix), **gastrecTOMY** (stomach), **hysterecTOMY** (uterus), **mastecTOMY** (breast), **mastoidecTOMY** (mastoid), **tonsillecTOMY** (tonsils), and **vasecTOMY** (vas deferens).

But not: pantomime [Gk *pantomimos*], dumb show; *ptomaine* [Gk *ptoma*, corpse], poison sometimes caused by food bacteria.

Combining forms: *a-*, not; *ana-*, up; *dicho-*, in two; *en-*, in; *epi-*, upon; *-logy*, the study of.

TEMPERARE, to regulate: TEMPER

To be out of **TEMPER** or to lose one's temper can lead to unpleasantness. (The boss sure lost her temper this morning. I mean, she had a tantrum like no storm that I've even seen.) If a steel blade or axe head loses its temper, it loses some of its hardness. (Ah, ah, ah! Don't sharpen that good knife on your electric grindstone; it will get so hot, it will lose its temper.) To temper is to moderate, soften, or mitigate. (That's one of Judge Barr's strong points: he always tries to temper justice with mercy.) An even-**TEMPERed** person is usually easy to get along with.

A person's **TEMPERament** is his or her disposition, nature, makeup, personality, spirit. (It seemed to the board that Dr. Stoke's temperament was not a really good match for the job.) A **TEMPERamental** person tends to be high-strung, excitable, volatile, mercurial, and histrionic. (Val said it was okay for her to be temperamental, for she was, after all, an artist.) An ill-**TEMPERed** person is inpatient, irritable, irascible.

A **TEMPERate** climate is a mild, balmy, soft, clement, moderate one. A temperate response to an antagonistic remark is controlled, calm, stable, cool-headed, and unexcited. A person of temperate habits will be controlled, restrained, prudent, sensible, and sober.

One who is **inTEMPERate** is undisciplined, unrestrained, unbridled, prodigal, and excessive. **TEMPERance** is self-restraint and self-control. (The assembly speaker listed the cardinal virtues as fortitude, justice, prudence, and temperance.) To many the word means teetotaling, abstinence, abstemiousness, sobriety, and prohibition as regards the use of alcohol. (The Women's Christian Temperance Union was founded in 1874 in opposition to the consumption of alcohol.) **InTEMPERance** in this regard is thought to be synonymous with alcoholism and dipsomania.

DisTEMPER is a virus that often affects dogs. In another field it is a technique of decorative painting; **TEMPERa** is a painting technique that employs an emulsion in which pigment is mixed with egg yolk, etc. **Tempura** is a Japanese dish in which vegetables and seafood are dipped in batter and deep-fried.

TEMPERature is a measure of coldness or heat. (The patient insisted that he had no temperature, but we knew he wouldn't be alive if that were true.) To **tamper** with something is to meddle, fiddle, fool, tinker, or monkey around with it. (Will you quit tampering with the antenna? Now we haven't got a picture at all!)

But not: tempest [*tempus*, time], violent storm or commotion; *template* [*templum*, temple], a mold or pattern, orig. *templet*.

Combining forms: *dis-*, away; *in-*, not.

☞ ***Antonyms:** intemperate* — moderate, reasonable, restrained, pleasant; *temper* — weaken, aggravate, stir, increase; *temperamental* — easy-going, unexcitable, unflappable, dependable, reliable; *temperate* — inordinate, irrational, hotheaded, frenzied, inclement, harsh, severe, passionate.

TEMPUS, time: **TEMP**

An antihero in literature is a protagonist who lacks the qualities that make for a truly heroic figure. Willy Loman (low man?) is such a character in Arthur Miller's play *Death of a Salesman*. Willy appeals to his older brother Ben to tell him about the father he never knew; Willy had been but a baby when their father left the family, and he never had a chance to talk with him. That's when he says to Ben, ''I still feel — kind of **TEMPorary** about myself.''

A municipal official who in the mayor's absence takes over his or her duties **TEMPorarily** is known as mayor **pro tem** (short for *temporare*), meaning for the time being. (Council member E.W. Blandings was chosen mayor *pro tem* during this morning's session.)

Earthly life is **TEMPoral** rather than eternal, the length of that stay perhaps being determined to some extent by the **TEMPo** of our life-pace. If our sojourn here is **TEMPestuous**, violent, turbulent, stormy, raging, furious, and **TEMPest-tossed**, it may well be brief indeed. Of course, we may **TEMPorize**, attempting to draw matters out for days, weeks, or years in order to gain time, but it would be a dicey ploy at best. (The pressure was on Walz, and his only chance to salvage his program was to temporize with the opposition; unless he came to terms with them, it was curtains. This, he knew, would mean **exTEMPorizing**, but he was a past master at that, having often spoken for an hour or two without a note. The reporters didn't call him Dr. Ex — for **exTEMPoraneous** — for nothing. He may have had copious notes scribbled on three-by-five cards in his pockets, but no one ever saw him peek at one.)

ConTEMPorary furniture is modern, of the present time; it is sometimes shortened to **conTEMPo**. Abraham Lincoln, Walt Whitman, and the Civil War were **conTEMPoraneous** (or contemporary or **conTEMPoraries**).

Tempus fugit means ''time flew.'' Oops, wrong verb **tense**: ''time flies.''

☞ ***Once uPUN a time** Ike said to Mike, ''What'd you do at camp?''
To which Mike replied, ''I timed flies.''
''You what?'' Ike said. ''You timed flies? What you mean is —.''
''What I mean is,'' said Mike to Ike, ''they are *fast*!''
''I think,'' said Ike, ''that you have got the wrong word or the wrong tense.''
''That's impossible,'' said Mike. ''The tense were numbered, and I always slept in No. 6.''

☞ ***But not:** temperate* [*temperare*, to exercise restraint], moderate; *temple* [*templum*, sanctuary], house of worship; *tempt* [*tendere*, to stretch], to entice; *tense* [*tendere*, to stretch], taut, high strung.

☞ ***Combining forms:** con-*, together; *ex-*, out; *fugit*, flies; *pro-*, for.

Antonyms: contemporary — out-of-date, former, old-fashioned, historical, past; *extemporaneous* — prepared, planned, premeditated, memorized, rehearsed, formal, set; *tempest* — quiet, calm, tranquility, serenity; *tempestuous* — unruffled, even, tranquil, relaxed, unagitated, cool-headed, disinterested, smooth, serene; *temporal* — lasting, durable, permanent, religious, spiritual, godly; *temporary* — fixed, tenured, settled; *temporize* — act, confront, decide, expedite, execute.

TORQUERE,
to twist:
TOR, TORT

Ages ago when one wanted to see what kind of bear was messing around outside the cave, one needed a **TORch**. What to do? Easy, in retrospect, anyway; you take a few dozen long, dried grass stems, twist them together, dip one end into the home fire, and violà! there it is! Today in Great Britain the torch is our flashlight.

ConTORTionists get all twisted up on purpose, often in **conTORTed** postures that to those of us less agile, lithe, and nimble seem like pure **TORTure**. And sometimes people **conTORT** their faces when they scowl or sneer or go trick-or-treating without a mask on.

Our fingers might become **disTORTed** from arthritis, and our facts might become distorted when we twist them to suit ourselves. (The poor soul certainly has a distorted view of life as a result of his tragedy. The **disTORTion** of the TV picture was caused by the nearby electrical storm.)

An **exTORTionist** attempts to twist or **exTORT** money or information from someone by using threats or violence. **ExTORTion** and blackmail are kin. **ExTORTionate** means grossly excessive. (The price of meat has become extortionate recently.)

When one is **TORTured** by force, pain, or memories, it is like being twisted; ditto **TORment**. A **TORTuous** road twists and winds and turns and meanders; so does a tortuous answer to a question, as does a devious explanation of one's actions. **TORsion** is the act of twisting, and **TORque** (tork) is the force that produces or tends to produce rotation or torsion. As a verb, torque means to rotate or twist. (The mechanic told me that if I didn't use a torque wrench, I'd be apt to snap those bolts in two.)

TORToises and **turtles** owe their names to their twisted feet and the **nasturtium** to its pungent taste and odor ("to twist the nose"). Several bread names are said to come from **torquere**, but where the twist factor is in a **TORTe**, **TORTellini**, or **TORTilla** is not clear. It is clearer in **reTORT**, a quick, sharp, witty comeback, reply, rejoinder, or riposte, and in its namesake, the bent tube found in the chem lab.

A **TORT** is a wrongful act for which a civil suit can be brought. A **truss** is a girder, brace, or support, and as a verb it means to bind or tie. A **tart** is both a small open pie with a sweet filling and a fallen woman, sometimes referred to as a harlot, strumpet, wench, or hooker.

But not: exhort [*hortari*, to urge], to plead, appeal to; *tart* [AS *teart*, sharp], sharp or bitter; *torpedo* [*torpere*, to be numb], an explosive; *torrent* [*torrere*, to burn], violent stream or downpour of rain; *torso* [Gk *thyrsos*, stem], the trunk of the body.

☛ *Combining forms: con-*, together; *dis-*, apart; *ex-*, out; *nas-*, nose; *re-*, back.

☛ *Antonyms: contort* — align, straighten, smooth, rectify, untangle, unbend; *torment* — joy, ease, comfort, delight; please, soothe, amuse, assuage, allay; *tortuous* — direct, straight, upright, reliable, straightforward, simple; *torture* — comfort, relieve, charm, coax, wheedle; bliss, rapture, gratification, happiness, ecstasy.

TORRERE,
to parch:
TOAST, TORR

Besides the slice of bread that got stuck in the **TOASTer** and burned and the piece that slipped off the plate and fell to the floor, buttered-side down, there is the **TOAST** that is pledged with a drink in honor of someone. The word is so used because of the piece of spiced toast that on festive occasions in days of yore was dropped into the glass of wine or the tankard of beer.

Handed down from the reign of King Charles II of England is a story about an admirer who offered a toast to a noted beauty with a glass of water taken from her bath (!), to which another hopeful cried out, ''You can have the drink, sir; I'll take the lady!'' With that, the **TOASTee**, the lady to whom the pledge was being drunk, may have wished that she was back in her **TOASTy** tub where it was cosily quiet.

The person at the head table who introduces the after-dinner speakers (among them, no doubt, the toast of the town) is called a **TOASTmaster** or **TOASTmistress** or Master or Mistress of Ceremonies. The clever ones brush up for the event by making notes from the book *Toasts for All Occasions.*

TOASTing forks are essential tools for toasting weiners and marshmallows over an open fire; slender willow twigs make excellent ones. On such outings, one must be careful not to **TORRefy** the food, for scorched weiners sometimes have a bitter taste. Too often, however, the weather is uncooperative and a **TORRential** rain puts a damper on both the fire and the outdoor spirit — or, worse, turns the babbling brook that one drove over earlier into an impassable **TORRent**.

Heat-seeking people who live in regions resembling the Arctic Circle might consider moving south to the **TORRid** zone, the global band between the tropics of Cancer and Capricorn, where it is hot year-round.

☛ *Antonyms: torrent* — drizzle, mist, shower, sprinkle; *torrid* — cool, chilly, mild, indifferent, spiritless, serene, apathetic, lethargic.

U

The advertisement in the magazine you just looked at boasts that the new Cosmos sedan is the **ULTimate** in luxury; that is, the Cosmos is beyond anything else in the automotive world; it is, friends, the Very End! The ad says that it is the grand prize in an exciting new contest.

ULTRA,
beyond: ULT

When you read the fine print that contains the rules of the contest, you discover that it, too, is far out, beyond the bounds of belief. You see that it is an **outrage**, an offense, and an insult. You are so **outraged** and shocked that you decide to write a letter to the editor to tell the world what an **outrageous** scam it is.

How did two words so different in appearance come from the same parents? At one time in French *ultrage* meant "to push beyond limits," the "l" exited and an "o" entered. (In France, *outrage* eventually became **outré**, meaning bizarre, eccentric, freakish, and kooky.)

ULTra means excessive, extreme. It is most often used as a prefix attached to almost any base; thus we have extremes such as ultracold, ultrahot, ultralarge, and ultrasmall.

A person who has an **ULTerior** motive is hiding something. (When Suzzi hung on to Bobby Bigbucks all evening, you knew she had an ulterior motive.) An **ULTimatum** is a final, no-nonsense demand or proposal. (Only when Mother Bigbucks issued an ultimatum — "Get lost or else!" — did Suzzi back off.)

Even though ultimatums are supposed to be the one, the only, and the final warning, sometimes the words are not sufficiently backed up. Let's say that it took Mother Bigbucks three tries to convince Suzzi that she meant what she said. The next to last warning would be the **penULTimate** one; the one before that would be the **antepenULTimate**. Or, to put it another way, in a series of ten, eight is the antepenultimate and nine the penultimate.

*But not: rage [*rabere*, to rage], anger, fury.

*Combining forms: ante-, before; *pen-*, almost.

*Antonyms: outraged — calmed, soothed, pacified; *outrageous* — fair, just, reasonable, moderate; *outré* — ordinary, typical, familiar; *ulterior* — obvious, open, manifest; *ultimate* — least, minimum, first, beginning.

UMBRAge, a word meaning offense, resentment, pique, displeasure, antipathy, and bitterness can be felt (I was insulted, and I felt umbrage), given (I am sorry if I have given umbrage to anyone), and, most commonly, taken (You don't blame me, do you, for having taken umbrage at his contemptuous remarks?). A person who is **UMBRAgeous** is inclined to take offense, tending to be belligerent and resentful. (Because we had been warned that Sam was sometimes umbrageous, we were always wary of his hair-trigger temper.)

UMBRA,
shadow: UMBRA

Umbrageous also means shady, but the two words are not always interchangeable. Umbrageous cannot be substituted for *shady* in this sense: "We'd better watch that guy. He looks like a real shady character to me." The appropriate synonyms of that *shady* are suspicious, slippery, and fishy. However, a large leafy oak, shaped much like an **umbrella**, can create an umbrageous setting for one to rest and cool off in.

An **UMBRA** is shade or shadow; it can also be, hence, a phantom or ghost. But it is in the field of astronomy that we most often see umbras and **penUMBRAs**; they have to do with the shadows of sunspots and planets and lunar eclipses.

To **adUMBRAte** is to foreshadow, to hint, portend, augur, presage, or herald. (As I look back on it now, I can see that the problems at the office adumbrated the eventual breakdown of the organization.)

An **umble** is a characteristic of certain flowering plants, and **umber** is a kind of natural earth used as a pigment, as in raw umber and burnt umber.

In one of her many mystery stories Dorothy Sayers wrote, "The bellchamber was **somber** and almost menacing," thus dark (as if in shade), gloomy, mournful, sepulchral, and funereal. And, not surprisingly, the large, broad-brimmed straw or felt hat that offers shade to wearers in Spain, Mexico, and the southwestern United States is called a **sombrero**.

☛ ***But not:*** *umble pie*, var of *humble pie* [*humilis*, lowly, on the ground], humiliation.

☛ ***Combining forms:*** *ad-*, toward; *pen-*, almost.

☛ ***Antonyms:*** *umbrage* — amity, cordiality, sympathy, good will, harmony.

V

Toward the end of a long day on the road, weary **VACationing** travelers often begin to look for "**VACancy**" signs on the fronts of motels. On holiday weekends their search for a **VACant** room might be in **vain**. They might be well advised to **aVOID** motels whose signs flash "**VACuity**," a **vanity** word sometimes used to impress others. If such a sign existed, it would probably mean an extra $20 per night.

To **vaunt** is to boast about, strut, flaunt, show off, gasconade. (Must Skilmut continue to vaunt his promotion?) **Vaunted** is an adjective meaning boasted about, praised to the skies; Marjorie Kinnan Rawlings spoke of "the vaunted Southern hospitality." A **vain** person is conceited and smug, stuffed with **vainglory**, vanity, arrogance, egotism, and narcissism.

A vacuity is also an empty, **VACuous** remark, a platitude, cliché, banality, truism, chestnut, the **aVOIDance** of which often requires turning a deaf ear. "Have a nice day" and "Hot enough for you?" are empties that seem almost **unaVOIDable** in daily life. A **VACuum** is an unfilled or unoccupied space; Bishop Desmond Tutu of South Africa once explained that he had become "a leader by default, only because nature does not allow a vacuum." Because he stepped into the **VOID** and furthered the cause of peace, he was awarded the Nobel Prize in 1984.

We **VACate** the apartment when we move and **eVACuate** the area when we hear floor warnings; we are then **eVACuees**.

As adjectives, **deVOID** and void are usually interchangeable. The latter, however, is also a noun (When Ma left, Pa felt a great void in his life) and a verb (The judge voided their licenses; they were then null and void.)

*But not: vaccine [vacca, cow], inoculation virus; vacillate [vacillare, to sway to and fro], to waver.

*Combining forms: a-, out; de-, from; e-, out; un-, not.

*Antonyms: avoid — meet, face, confront, pursue, incur, welcome, accept, approach, solicit; devoid — full, fraught, replete; vacancy — profusion, fullness, plenitude; vacant — occupied, alert, intelligent, replete, full; vacation — work, labor, routine, daily grind, rat race; vacuity — fullness, content, brains, intelligence, gray matter; vacuous — bright, attentive, knowledgeable; vacuum — substance, matter; vain — humble, modest, diffident, self-effacing, effective, practical, productive; vanity — humility, modesty, diffidence, self-effacement; vaunt — disparage, detract, conceal, repress, suppress; void — complete, occupied, valid, viable, validate, uphold, fill, ingest.

VACARE,
to be empty:
VAC, VOID

177

VARIUS, bent,
crooked, diverse,
manifold,
speckled,
changeable: VARI

As you can see, this Latin root has **VARIous** meanings. But whether that results in a great **VARIety** of words is open to question. Let's look.

Back in the Middle Ages, in the lands and times dominated by dukes and duchesses and kings and queens, spotted animal fur was the trim of choice on the elaborate ceremonial robes the royals wore. The fur came from ermines or weasels and was called *miniver*, the "mini" growing out of *menu*, small, and the "ver" from **vair**, fur. The pattern of spots on spotted animals always **VARIes** from one to another. That's just the way they develop their coats, **VARIable** little beasts that they are.

To **preVARIcate** is to lie. (Wesley always looked down on the members of the Liars' Club, preferring the more prestigious **PreVARIcators'** Pack. A question on their application form asked, "Do you **inVARIably** think of the word **preVARIcation** when you bend the truth?" If one answered "Yes," it meant an automatic "Okay, you're in!")

Let's not forget those **VARIcolored** or **VARIegated** houseplants, the ones that are higher priced because their leaves have streaks or specks of white or yellow in them. They are **VARIants**, deviations from the normal, **unvarying**, all-green leaves.

A **VARIation** is a change, modification, departure, alteration, innovation, metamorphosis. (The poor chap needs a bit of variation in his life.) **VARIance** is used to express the degree of difference (a daily variance of ten degrees centigrade) or an official permit to do something usually forbidden (We got a variance to put up a large sign). To be **at variance** is to be in disagreement (Everything we did was at variance with the rules).

Now: as we look back on the *varius* family, we see that aside from "miniver" and "prevaricate," the words are not very **VARIed**, nor do they vary very much in meaning.

☛ ***But not:*** *varicose* [*varix*, swollen vein], swollen, as a vein; *varmint* [var. of *vermin*], objectionable animal or obnoxious person; *varsity* [shortened and altered form of *university*], first-string of a school team.

☛ ***Combining forms:*** *-gate*, to do; *in-*, not; *pre-*, before; *ver*, fur, from *varius*, speckled, partly colored.

☛ ***Antonyms:*** *invariably* — irregularly, inconsistently, hardly ever, never; *prevarication* — truth, veracity, verity, fact, reality; *variable* — fixed, predictable, immutable, rigid; *variance* — similarity, correspondence, congruity, accord, unison, agreement; *variant* — original, basic, intrinsic, preferred, archetype, prototype, model; *variation* — uniformity, permanence, sameness; *varied* — standardized, homogeneous, uniform; *variegated* — monotone, monochromatic; *variety* — homogeneity, uniformity, conformity; *various* — identical, alike, same.

VERBUM,
word: VERB

Sam Goldwyn, the legendary Hollywood producer, is reported to have once said, "A **VERBal** contract isn't worth the paper it is written on." Since verbal means oral, spoken, expressed, or stated, it isn't written, which was Mr. Goldwyn's point. Remarks like that won him a place in the quotation books.

To **VERBalize** is to say something in words. (I've got a picture in my mind of what I want this invention to look like, but I just can't verbalize it.) **VERBiage, VERBosity**, and **VERBality** mean wordiness, long-windedness, blather, prolixity, loquacity, garrulity, hot air. (Poor Dr. Stanger. He doesn't realize that he's suffering from a case of acute verbiage.) Someone who is **VERBose** is long-winded, wordy, loquacious, vociferous, garrulous, effusive, voluble, and gabby. (It was an amusing and quite simple story, but the mayor was so verbose that most of us lost the point.) To **VERBigerate** is to babble, repeating meaningless words and phrases endlessly. (The deposed dictator pathetically verbigerated ideas that had lost their meaning years before.) A **VERBalist** is skilled in the use of words but often at the expense of ideas and reality. To speak (or act) with **verve** is to be animated, vigorous, and enthusiastic.

VERBatim means word for word, literal, in exactly the same words. (At work, Ed always gives us a verbatim report of everything his kids said at dinner the night before.) If that seems boring, consider *verbatim et literatim*, word for word *and* letter for letter.

An **adVERB** is a word that will fit either one of these blanks: He turned his radio _____ (on/off/up/down/around/often/upside down/over/toward the window); He showed the car to me _____ (Tuesday/later/alone/anyway/everyday/hastily/uncertainly/by candlelight/at noon). **VERBs** denote being or action. ("God . . . / is a verb / not a noun, / proper or improper," Buckminster Fuller.) A **pro-VERB** is a word that can substitute for a verb, similar in function to a pronoun. "Do" acts as a pro-verb in the following sample: Our neighbors never mow their lawn, but we do.

A **proVERB** is a short, popular saying, sometimes expressing wisdom. It is also called an adage, maxim, saw, axiom, aphorism, apothegm, epigram, and a few more. Dorothy Parker's "Men seldom make passes / At girls who wear glasses" is a modern (1920s) proverb, although the invention of the contact lens diminished some of its punch. The book of Proverbs of the Bible contains wisdom that still packs a wallop, to wit: "Where there is no vision, the people perish." **ProVERBial** is used when expressing something that has been the subject of a proverb. From the proverb "Too many cooks spoil the broth" comes our example: The officials were like the proverbial cooks: because there were too many of them milling around, they spoiled the pageant. Proverbial also refers to something that has become common or legendary. (The boss lost his proverbial temper once again.)

But not: vernacular [*verna*, native], common, everyday language (as opposed to the literary).

Combining forms: ad-, to; *-gerate*, to carry on; *pro-*, before.

Antonyms: verbalize — suppress, inhibit, contain, repress; *verbatim* — inexact, imprecise, garbled, distorted; *verbiage, verbosity* — terseness, precision, concision, laconism; *verbose* — concise, laconic, terse, succinct, pithy, curt, reticent, brusque; *verve* — apathy, inertia, laziness, lethargy, torpor, sloth.

VESTIS,
garment: VEST

Today's **VEST** is commonly a close-fitting, sleeveless, waist-length item of clothing, but three hundred years ago in England the vests men wore were similar to the long cassocks or **VESTments** worn by members of the clergy. The latter are customarily kept in a room called a **VESTry**, which in the Episcopal church is also the name of a committee elected by the congregation. **VESTure** is clothing or anything else that covers; James Baldwin said in his *Notes of a Native Son*, ''The making of an American begins at that point where he himself . . . adopts the vesture of his adopted land.''

When we **inVEST** money in a business venture, we hope that it will prove to be a profitable **inVESTment**. When we become seriously involved in a charitable project, we invest our time and energy in it. When we are installed in an office or position, we are **inVESTed** with certain powers and responsibilities. (The president is invested with the power of veto by the Constitution.)

The ceremony of being installed in an office or of receiving a distinguished honor is called an **inVESTiture**, and it is often a formal and elaborate affair. A **diVESTiture**, however, is not usually a happy occasion, for to **diVEST** people of their property or rights is to strip them away. (The court ordered him divested of all his stock holdings.)

A **VESTed** interest is one in which a person has a personal stake. (Would Bromide like to see the biology textbooks changed? You better believe he would. With all the stock he owns in Bio-Sci Publishers, Inc., he has a vested interest. And I don't mean a mere **VEST-pocket** interest, either. I'm talking overcoat-pocket.)

A **transVESTite** is one who wears the clothing of the opposite sex. Columnist Jimmy Breslin alluded to some **transVESTites** he mingled with one night in New York, when he wrote ''Precious was one of a large number of people on the street, many of whom appeared to be women; some, like Precious, actually were.'' A **traVESTy** is sometimes in good fun. (The *Saturday Night Live* travesty of a presidential candidate trying to milk a cow and kiss a baby at the same time was hilarious.) But it can also convey a sense of shame. (The poor migrant workers' treatment by the county attorney was a travesty of justice.)

☞ ***But not:*** *investigate* [*vestigium*, footprint], look into; *vestibule* [*vestibulum*], entrance hall; *vestige* [*vestigium*], trace.

☞ ***Combining forms:*** *di-*, from; *in-*, in; *tra-*, over; *trans-*, over.

☞ ***Antonyms:*** *divest* — confer, empower, sanction, dress, clothe, cover; *invest* — withdraw, deny, withhold; *vest* — unfrock, divest, expose, uncover, lay bare; *vested* — contingent, occasional, provisional.

VETerinary medicine is the branch that treats animals, small and large, but usually domesticated. **VETerinarians**, however, often specialize, those in metropolitan areas generally treating cats and dogs and other household pets, while those in or around smaller towns may take in large farm animals as well. Some of these restrict their practices to horses.

To **VET** is to examine or treat, as a medical doctor or a veterinarian; others may vet, verify, check, or appraise something for accuracy, authenticity, or validity. (The sports editor vetted the young reporter's story. We suggested that our attorney vet the deed just to make sure.) A vet may be a veterinarian or a **VETeran**; however, there is no record of a veterinarian who is a veteran insisting on being called a vet-vet.

An **inVETerate** liar is a pathological, deep-rooted, habitual, ineradicable, confirmed, hopeless prevaricator. Something that goes on and on and on, such as a disease or habit or feeling can be called inveterate, too, but "chronic" works just as well.

Combining forms: in-, in, with the sense of very.

Antonyms: inveterate — sporadic, occasional, irregular, transitory, curable, rare; *veteran* — novice, neophyte, beginner, tyro, green, inexperienced, unschooled, raw.

VETUS, old, long-standing: VET

When we travel from one place to another **VIA** a third place, we are going "by way of." (They flew from Chicago to Copenhagen via the North Pole.) But in an Italian city most of the streets are called **Via** or **VIAle**. (In Rome we walked down Viale Manzoni to where it intersects Via Marulana.) This road can be traced twenty-three hundred years to the time the Romans built the *Via Appia*, the "queen of long-distance roads," extending from Rome south to Brindisi, a distance of some 350 miles.) The road that Jesus took to Calvary is known as the *Via Dolorosa* (from *dolorous*, sorrowful); without the capital letters the phrase means any painful, mournful course of events. A **via media** is a mean between two extremes, a middle course. (The mediation board was determined to find the via media.)

Scholars in the Middle Ages felt that there was a "fourfold way" to knowledge: arithmetic, astronomy, geometry, and music [*quadrivium*, four ways], and a "threefold way" to eloquence: grammar, logic, and rhetoric [*trivium*, three ways]. *Trivium* also meant crossroads, an intersection or junction of three roads where people met to discuss the latest news and to catch up on the current gossip and neighborhood **triVIA**. It is **obVIOus** that much of it was **triVIAl**, petty, inconsequential stuff, the trifles and **triVIAlities** that we sometimes call small change, small potatoes, and small talk.

PerVIOus soil is absorbent, permeable, and porous. **ImperVIOus** material is sealed, impenetrable, and waterproof; a person who seems impervious to aging or criticism is immune to, unaffected by, or protected against either or both.

VIA, way, road: VIA, VIO

To **deVIAte** is to wander, differ, digress, defect. (By the time she had finished her first college semester, Vi had deviated completely from her parents' lifestyle.) **DeVIAnt** social behavior is that which departs from the accepted norm. (The dean told the freshmen that their deviant conduct would not be tolerated, and he called them both deviants and deviates.) A **deVIAtion** is, **obVIOusly**, a departure from a standard. (Deviations from the rules will be dealt with severely.) **DeVIOus** methods are dishonest, deceitful, sly, tricky, shifty, wily, and foxy, whether in business, politics, law, or evangelism. A person who has had **preVIOus** encounters with the likes of con men will be in the best position to **obVIAte** another such scam.

To **convey** a message is to tell, relate, or communicate. (Kindly convey my best wishes to your family.) To convey a package is to transport, carry, or move it. (The oil is **conveyed** here by pipeline.) To convey a title to a piece of property is to grant, bequeath, or transfer. (I hereby convey to you my golf sox, shoes, and tees.) The **conveyor** is the person or instrument that does the **conveying**, the **conveyance** is the method of communication or transportation.

If it is merchandise, the **invoice** may be attached. If it is the transfer of an army unit to another post, the vehicles may form a long **convoy**. If it is to be shipped by freighter to an **envoy** at an overseas embassy, it should be readied for a long **voyage**. If it is to go by rail, it will travel across a number of **VIAducts**.

☞ *But not: trivet* [*tri-*, three + *pes*, foot], three-legged vessel or plate; *viable* [*vita*, life], practicable.

☞ *Combining forms: con-*, together; *de-*, from; *-duct*, to lead; *en-*, on; *im-*, not; *in-*, on; *ob-*, before; *per-*, through; *pre-*, before; *tri-*, three.

☞ *Antonyms: deviate* — follow, conform, comply, adhere, stick to, continue; *devious* — forthright, truthful, reliable, honest, direct, straightforward, aboveboard, open, frank; *impervious* — vulnerable, susceptible, exposed, open, prone, sensitive, liable, penetrable; *obviate* — necessitate, compel, make essential, cause, entail, permit, bring on; *obvious* — obscure, indistinct, ambiguous, abstruse, hidden, concealed, unapparent; *previous* — later, following, subsequent, ensuing, consequent, succeeding, posterior, opportune, timely; *trivia* — basics, essentials, fundamentals, vitals, substance; *trivial* — momentous, vital, crucial, weighty, important, unusual, appreciable, exceptional.

VICIS, change, instead of: VIC

In the Church of England **VICars** are persons serving as parish priests in place of the rector; in essence, they are deputies or substitutes. In a larger sense, they are called "God's vicars on earth," as, in the Roman Catholic church, the pope is referred to as the "vicar of Christ." The vicar lives at the **VICarage**, a residence that in other churches might be called a parsonage, manse, rectory, or presbytery.

The combining form **VICe-** also means instead of, deputy, or substitute; thus we have vice-admirals, -chairpersons, and -presidents, and viceroys (the latter stemming from *royalty*).

When we use the term **VICe versa**, we are saying in effect, in the opposite order, the other way around, in reverse order from the stated, three good reasons to be thankful for being able to write simply ''v.v.'' (I would like my soup before my salad, if you please, and not vice versa.) That other vice, the one that is a sin, comes from the Latin *vitium*,a fault.

The **VICissitudes** of life are the changes, the ups and downs, the variations in one's fortune. (Despite the extraordinary vicissitudes of their married lives, the two stayed in love and together for more than fifty years.)

When Emily Dickinson, the nineteenth-century poet who spend most of her life secluded in her father's Massachusetts home, wrote, ''I never saw a Moor — / I never saw the Sea — / Yet know I how the Heather looks / And what a Billow be,'' she demonstrated what a **VICarious** experience is: she knew of the moor, the sea, the heather, and the billow through the eyes and other senses of people who *had* seen them. When we read a story or watch a play or movie, we are participating in the experiences of one or more of the characters **VICariously**.

*But not: vicennial [vicen, twenty], occurring once every twenty years; vicinity [vicinus, near], neighborhood; vicious [vitium, fault], malicious; vise [vitis, vine], mechanism for holding things firmly (named for the spiral of the screw).

*Combining form: versa, turn.

*Antonyms: vicarious — direct, firsthand, personal, own, proper; vicissitudes — stability, constancy.

About two hundred years ago an Irish judge named John Curran said, ''The condition upon which God hath given liberty to man is eternal **VIGilance**.'' That means heed, care, concern, caution, prudence, attention, and being on guard. Like the sentry at the gate, those who prize liberty must be **VIGilant**, watchful, alert, wary, circumspect, attentive, and on the *qui vive* [F who goes there?].

VIGILARE, to watch: VEIL, VIG

But that assumes one works within the law. **VIGilantes** take the law into their own hands, often in avenging a wrong, and what is known as vigilante justice is sometimes violent and without warning. Vigilante committees terrorized blacks and abolitionists in the South before and during the Civil War, as well as establishing their own kind of justice in the rough and tumble era during the westward expansion. In many respects the iniquities were reminiscent of what happened — legally — during the reign of terror in Salem, Massachusetts, in and before 1692, in which more than 150 people, mostly women, were charged with witchcraft; twenty were executed.

SurVEILlance is a form of vigilance, tailing, tracking, and trailing. (The suspects were kept under surveillance on an around-the-clock schedule.) **SurVEILlant** guards must keep every watchful and maintain their **VIGil**. Vigil candles are kept burning in churches in front of icons and shrines, and in some churches vigils are services on the eve of a festival. The vigil flame over the grave of John Fitzgerald Kennedy is never allowed to go out. Today's yellow ribbons are much like the vigil lights of a previous era.

ReVEILle is the military signal of awaken, to assemble; once awake, the personnel are expected to remain vigilant.

☛ *But not: revelry* [*rebellare*, to rebel], merrymaking; *veil* [*velum*, a salt], cover.

☛ *Combining forms:* re-, again; sur-, over.

☛ *Antonyms: vigilance* — negligence, carelessness, laxity, inattention; *vigilant* — remiss, unwary, preoccupied, trusting, heedless, slack.

VILLA,
farmhouse:
VILLA

Yesteryear's simple, rustic farmhouse is today's country estate, often kept as a retreat by a wealthy person; such is how the meaning of **VILLA** has changed from the days of feudalism in medieval Europe.

Back then serfs were **villeins**, some of whom were free, some of whom were bound in service to a lord, and some of whom occupied a middle ground. As members of the lower classes, the villeins were, of course, looked down upon by people of means. Over the years both the spelling and the attitudes changed, and the simple villeins of the past were undeservedly and unwittingly transformed into the the **VILLAins** and **VILLAinesses** of the present. Had this alteration been a deliberately **VILLAinous** act, one might have accused the perpetrators of **VILLAiny**, but etymological changes are neither intentional nor wicked, sinful, criminal, vicious, or diabolical; it's just an evolutionary process.

As the villas multiplied, they consolidated into **VILLAges** and eventually qualified for Zip Code numbers. The name of the folk who populated the communities kept its meaning through the centuries, and yesteryear's **VILLAgers** are today's, too.

☛ *But not: Villa*, Pancho (Francisco Villa, 1877–1923), Mexican bandit and revolutionary hero.

☛ *Antonyms: village* — city, metropolis, megalopolis; *villain* — prince, hero, idol, protagonist, leading man, worthy, champion, nice guy; *villainous* — heroic, saintly, moral, virtuous, righteous, humane; *villainy* — virtue, benefit, boon, good deed.

VIR,
a man: VIR

Even a brief study of the Latin root *vir* throws considerable light on our social history. For starters let's put the spotlight on **VIRtue**: Alexander Pope wrote in *An Essay on Man*, "Know then this truth, enough for man to know, / 'virtue alone is happiness below.' " Benjamin Franklin followed that up with this advice in *On Early Marriages*: "Be in general **VIRtuous**, and you will be happy." What is of interest here is that our word for this most esteemed quality stems from *man*, almost as though it can be possessed by him alone.

Next, we find that virtue's blood brother (see?) is **VIRility**, that much sought-after property of machismo, force, vigor, and a stalwart brawniness that saves a proper male from the dreaded wimpism. For to be **VIRile** is to be macho, muscular, masculine, mighty, masterful, manful, male, and manly.

What else? Hmmm. A **VIRtuoso** is a male artist, genius, prodigy, whiz, wizard, and master (!), particularly in the performing arts. Male? Yes. A female is a **VIRtuosa. VIRtuosity**, however, is a star that members of either sexual persuasion can reach for.

That covers **VIRtually** all of it. However one adds it all up, it amounts to more than a mere **triumVIRate**, a threesome; it's a **VIRtual** mantle of maleness.

No room at the inn for the fairer sex? Ah, yes, there is this: **VIRilism** is a female disorder that results in, among other undesirable masculine features, a deep voice; and a **VIRago** is a woman like Dame Van Winkle, Rip's "termagant wife," a loud-voiced, ill-tempered, scolding shrew to whom Rip was "an obedient henpecked husband." So there you have it. The history of *man*unkind, as the poet e.e. cummings put it.

But not: *virgin* [*virgo*, a maiden], pure, chaste, person who has never had sexual intercourse; *viridity* [*viridis*, green], greenness; *virulent* [*virus*, slime, poison], noxious, lethal.

Combining form: *trium-*, three.

Antonyms: *virile* — spineless, weak, impotent, effeminate; *virtual* — direct, express, explicit, emphatic, definite; *virtue* — sin, error, curse, weakness, evil, vice, immorality, promiscuousness, promiscuity; *virtuosity* — mediocrity, ineptness, amateurishness, dullness; *virtuoso* — tyro, beginner, neophyte, novice, greenhorn, novitiate; *virtuous* — immoral, wicked, corrupt, unchaste, loose, dishonorable, sinful, venal.

VOCARE,
to call:
VOX, voice:
VOC, VOK

In his poem entitled "Two Tramps in Mud Time," Robert Frost says, "[My] object in living is to unite / My **aVOCation** and my **VOCation** / As my two eyes make one in sight." It's a sunny but chilly April day in New England, and the poet is chopping firewood when two "hulking tramps" not long out of the lumber camps come by. They want to do for pay what the poet is doing out of love, uniting what had to be done with what he really enjoys doing, combining his hobby with his job.

When he turns down the men's offer, he may well **proVOKe**, anger, irritate, vex, rile, or nettle them; they may think that he "had no right to play / With what was [their] work for gain." But it is not, it seems, sufficient **proVOCation** (challenge, cause, goad, spur, or stimulus) to **eVOKe**, arouse, summon, call forth, or induce anger. They are not, after all, **proVOCateurs**, that is, agitators or troublemakers. Nor does their brief exchange of words become clamorous, noisy, or **VOCiferous**, with one side or the other **VOCiferating** at the tops of their **voices**.

"Two Tramps" is a **proVOCative** piece of writing, stimulating and challenging. People who have enjoyed splitting wood for a winter's fire feel that "Two Tramps" is an **eVOCative** poem, as it calls forth such memories. To **conVOKe** is to call together, as an assembly or **conVOCation**. **InVOKe** means to beg, appeal, or pray for something (The condemned man invoked God's mercy), to put into effect (The president invoked the veto again), to call forth (The widow of Houdini, the great magician, tried in vain to invoke his spirit). An **inVOCation** is a prayer.

To **reVOKe** a driver's license is to cancel it. If such a **reVOCation** is for a short period, it is annoying and bothersome. If it is declared **irreVOCable**, not reversible or alterable, it is, for many, calamitous and disastrous. If the decision is to be appealed, one should engage a competent **adVOCate** from a reliable law firm to advocate one's innocence. It would also help to be **avouched** or **vouched** for by **vouchers** (character witnesses) who do not **equiVOCate** but, instead, declare him or her to be honest and upstanding in clear, absolute, and **unequiVOCal** language. It could help to have **vox populi** ("the voice of the people") on one's side; authorities tend to show respect for popular opinion.

A study of our **VOCabulary** often turns up oddities such as the words *abstemiously*, meaning moderately or sparingly in eating and drinking, and *facetiously*, meaning in jest, humorously. Strange? Well, sort of. They both contain all our **vowels** — in order. Of course this is spotted more easily when one sees the word; if it is presented as a **voiced, VOCal,** or **VOCalized** word, it is more difficult to catch.

☛ ***Once uPUN a time***, way back when a pun was also known as a *paronomasia* as well as — take your choice — an **equivoque** or **equiVOKe**, one fine day a young punster was asked to define the word *convocation*. After a moment's thought, the budding pundit declared, "It's a job in a prison."

☛ ***But not:** invoice* [*in-*, in + *via*, way], itemized bill; *ouch* [G *autsch*], expression of pain; *vow* [*vovere*, to vow], to pledge, promise.

☛ ***Combining forms:*** *a-*, away; *ad-*, to; *con-*, together; *e-*, out; *equi-*, equal; *-fer*, to carry; *in-*, on; *ir-*, not; *pro-*, forth; *re-*, back; *un-*, not.

☛ ***Antonyms:*** *advocate* — oppose, counter; opponent, adversary; *equivocal* — precise, definite, explicit, clear; *irrevocable* — changeable, variable; *provocative* — dull, boring, meaningless, unstimulating, uninteresting; *provoke* — calm, ease, please, assuage, mollify, propitiate; *unequivocal* — ambiguous, enigmatic, obscure, noncommital; *vocal* — speechless, mute, dumb, silent, inarticulate; *vocation* — distraction, diversion, leisure pursuit; *vociferous* — quiet, muted, hushed, reticent; *voice* — speechlessness; keep silent, be quiet, stifle, suppress.

VORARE, to devour: VOR

One may **devour** books by the dozens, delighting in them, soaking them up, feasting on them, and thoroughly enjoying and appreciating them; one can also drink in and devour the beauty of the sunrise on a spring morning. If you're really hungry, you may devour your food by wolfing it down, stuffing it in, gobbling it up, or attacking it as if it might try to escape.

A **VORacious** eater might be greedy, hoggish, and piggish. A voracious business competitor might be avaricious, grasping, and covetous. A voracious lover might be intemperate, uncontrolled, and unappeasable. But a voracious reader of historical novels or collector of old bottles or seashells will not be likely to offend or harm anyone. Some folks even have a voracious love of life.

CarniVORous animals are meat-eating. Bears, cats, dogs, seals, and weasels make up the order of **carniVORes**. **HerbiVORous** animals, such as deer and cattle, eat plants; **insectiVORous** ones, such as moles, eat insects and ignore the poison some gardeners place in their runs; **pisciVORous** creatures eat only fish. **OmniVORous** beings have broad appetites; they eat both animals and plants and will read just about any kind of book they can get a hold of.

*But not: vortex [*vertere*, to turn], a whirlpool.

*Combining forms: carni-, meat; *de-*, down; *herbi-*, plants; *omni-*, all; *pisci-*, fish.

*Antonyms: voracious — fussy, delicate, satisfied, moderate, undemanding, temperate.

THE WORLD'S BIGGEST ICE CREAM BASH!

X

XENOS [Gk],
foreign, strange:
XENO

A **XENOphobe** is a person who distrusts, fears, and hates foreign cultures, customs, and people, right along with anything that has another country's label on it. **XENOphobia** is that distrust and, therefore, a fanatical nationalism.

A **XENOphile** is one who is attracted to whatever a xenophobe is repelled by. **XENOphilia** is the attraction to things foreign. **XENOmania** is an abnormal, irrational, extreme, inordinate attraction to everything foreign, usually at the expense of and distaste for all things domestic. People so afflicted are sometimes accused of being snobs and elitists.

XENOn is a chemical element discovered in 1898 by Sir William Ramsay; he gave the gas its "strange' name.

 Combining forms: -mania, enthusiasm that is often extreme and not long lasting; *-philia,* a strong and often unnatural attraction; *-phobia,* a fear, dread, or aversion.

Z

A person who is **JEAL**ous is possessive, suspicious, watchful, obsessed with, wary. ("When I told my missus once I should never dream of being jealous of *her*, instead of up and thanking me for it, she spoilt the best frying-pan we ever had," W.W. Jacobs.)

JEALousy is suspicion, resentment, hostility, intolerance, distrust. ("Jealousy is all the fun you think they had," Erica Jong.)

ZEAL is enthusiasm, gusto, fervor, verve, passion, fanaticism, vehemence, devotion. ("Like fire, [zeal] wants both feeding and watching," W.G. Benham. [It's] what we do which in a calmer condition we would not have done," Robert Zwickey.)

A **ZEAL**ot is a fanatic, partisan, enthusiast, believer, devotee, ideologue, extremist, bigot, crank, nut. ("For forms of government let fools contest; / Whatever is best administered is best: / For modes of faith let graceless **zealots** fight; / His can't be wrong whose life is in the right," Alexander Pope.)

Someone who is **ZEAL**ous is enthusiastic, fervent, fervid, eager, ardent, devoted, monomaniacal, rabid. ("A zealous blacksmith died of late, / And did arrive at heavengate, / He stood without and would not knock, / Because he meant to pick the lock," epitaph for a locksmith in an English graveyard.)

Antonyms: jealous — trusting, open, tolerant, easy-going, generous, indifferent, uncaring; *jealousy* — trust, confidence, faith, security, assurance, openness; *zeal* — apathy, coolness, detachment, nonchalance, listlessness, languor, torpor; *zealot* — cynic, unbeliever, disparager, detractor, depreciator, knocker; *zealous* — bored, lazy, uninterested, torpid, languorous, dispassionate, lackadaisical, lackluster, low-key.

ZELOS [Gk],
ardor:
JEAL, ZEAL

Index

Note: not all the featured words in the book are listed in this index. Instead, it is designed to give the reader access to their related forms by way of keywords. For example, *age* is the keyword for such forms as *aged*, *ageism*, *ageless*, *agemates*, *age-old*, and *ages*, all of which are listed in the unit on the Latin root *aevum*.

BIPEDS, pes
BISCUIT, coquere
BISECT, secare
BISHOP, skopein
BOAR, porcus
BONA FIDE, bonus
BON AMI, bonus
BONHOMIE, bonus
BOSS, bos
BOUNTY, bonus
BOVINE, bos

C

CABARET, kamara
CACHE, agere
CADET, caput
CALM, kaiein
CALUMNY, calvi
CAMARADERIE, kamara
CAMERA, kamara
CANARY, canis
CAP, caput
CAPITAL, caput
CAPSIZE, caput
CARDIOLOGY, logos
CARESS, carus
CARNIVOROUS, vorare
CASTIGATE, agere
CATALOG, legein
CATEGORY, agora
CATTLE, caput
CAUSTIC, kaiein
CAUTION, cavere
CAVALIER, caballus
CAVEAT, cavere
CENSOR, censere
CENTIPEDE, pes
CENTRIFUGAL, fugere
CERTIFY, facere
CHAFE, facere
CHALLENGE, calvi
CHAMBER, kamara
CHAPEL, caput
CHAPTER, caput
CHARITY, carus
CHENILLE, canis
CHERISH, carus
CHISEL, caedere
CHRONIC, chronos
CHRONOLOGY, chronos
CIRCUMFERENCE, ferre
CIRCUMLOCUTION, loqui
CITADEL, civis
CIVILITY, civis
CLARIFY, facere
CLASSIFY, facere
CLAUSE, claudere
CLOISTER, claudere
CLOTURE, claudere

COAGULATE, agere
COALESCE, alere
COARSE, currere
COEVAL, aevum
COGENT, agere
COGITATE, agere
COGNATE, nasci
COGNITIVE, gnoscere
COLANDER, colare
COLLATE, latus
COLLEAGUE, legare
COLLEGE, legare
COLLOCATE, locare
COLLOQUIAL, loqui
COLLUSION, ludere
COMEDO, edere
COMFIT, facere
COMMAND, mandare
COMMEND, mandare
COMPARE, par
COMPATRIOT, pater
COMPEER, par
COMPETE, petere
COMPUNCTION, pungere
COMRADE, kamara
CONCHOLOGY, logos
CONCISE, caedere
CONCLUDE, claudere
CONCOCT, coquere
CONCOURSE, currere
CONCRETE, crescere
CONCUR, currere
CONDIGN, dignitas
CONFECTION, facere
CONFER, ferre
CONFETTI, facere
CONFLUENCE, fluere
CONFRERES, frater
CONGREGATE, gregare
CONGRESS, gradi
CONIFEROUS, ferre
CONJECTURE, jacere
CONJUGATE, jugum
CONJURE, jurare
CONNOISSEUR, gnoscere
CONNOTE, notare
CONSANGUINEOUS, sanguis
CONSCIENCE, scire
CONSCRIPT, scribere
CONSONANCE, sonare
CONSTRUCT, struere
CONSTRUE, struere
CONTEMPORARY, tempus
CONTORT, torquere
CONVEY, via
CONVOKE, vocare
CONVOY, via
COOK, coquere
COPIOUS, copia
COPY, copia
CORPORAL, caput, corpus

CORRELATE, latus
CORRESPOND, spondere
CORRIDOR, currere
CORRODE, rodere
CORSAGE, corpus
CORSAIR, currere
CORSET, corpus
COSMOLOGY, logos
COSMOPOLITAN, polis
COULEE, colare
COUNTERACT, agere
COUNTERFEIT, facere
COUNTERMAND, mandare
COURIER, currere
COUSIN, soror
COVER, aperire
COVETOUS, aperire
CREDIT, crescere
CRESCENT, crescere
CRIMINOLOGY, logos
CRISIS, krinein
CRITERIA, krinein
CRITIC, krinein
CRONY, chronos
CRUCIFY, figere
CUISINE, coquere
CULINARY, coquere
CULPABLE, culpa
CULPRIT, culpa
CUM LAUDE, laudare
CURRENT, currere
CURRICULUM, currere
CURSIVE, currere
CURSORY, currere
CYNIC, canis
CYNOSURE, canis

D

DAINTY, dignitas
DAUB, albus
DEBASE, bassus
DEBONAIR, bonus
DECALOGUE, legein
DECAPITATION, caput
DECATHLON, athlon
DECIDE, caedere
DECONSTRUCT, struere
DECREASE, crescere
DEFACE, facere
DEFAMATORY, fama
DEFEASANCE, facere
DEFEAT, facere
DEFECT, facere
DEFER, ferre
DEFICIT, facere
DEFLECT, flectere
DEFUNCT, fungi
DEGRADE, gradi
DEGREE, gradi

DEIFY, facere
DEJECT, jacere
DELECTABLE, lacere
DELEGATE, legare
DELI, lacere
DELICACY, lacere
DELIGHT, lacere
DELIVER, liber
DELUDE, ludere
DEMAGOGUE, plebes
DEMAND, mandare
DEMERIT, merere
DEMOCRACY, plebes
DEMONOLOGY, logos
DERIDE, ridere
DERIVE, rivus
DERMATOLOGY, logos
DESCRIBE, scribere
DESOLATE, solus
DESPONDENT, spondere
DESTROY, struere
DEVIATE, via
DEVOID, vacare
DEXTERITY, dexter
DIAGNOSE, gignoskein
DIAL, dies
DIALECT, legein
DIARY, dies
DICHOTOMY, temnein
DIET, dies
DIFFER, ferre
DIFFICULT, facere
DIGNITY, dignitas
DIGRESS, gradi
DILATE, latus
DILATORY, latus
DILETTANTE, lacere
DIOCESE, oikos
DISAFFECT, facere
DISAPPEAR, parere
DISASTER, astron
DISCLOSE, claudere
DISCOMFIT, facere
DISCOURSE, currere
DISCOVER, aperire
DISCURSIVE, currere
DISDAIN, dignitas
DISEASE, jacere
DISFEATURE, facere
DISILLUSION, ludere
DISLOCATE, locare
DISLOYAL, lex
DISMAL, dies
DISPARAGE, par
DISPERSE, spargo
DISSECT, secare
DISSEMINATE, semen
DISSOLUTE, solvere
DISSOLVE, solvere
DISTEMPER, temperare
DISTINCT, stinguere

DISTORT, torquere
DIURNAL, dies
DIVAGATE, agere
DIVERSIFY, facere
DIVEST, vestis
DOXOLOGY, logos
DROMEDARY, dromein
DU JOUR, dies
DYSLEXIA, legein

E

EASE, jacere
ECHELON, scala
ECLECTIC, legein
ECOLOGY, oikos
ECONOMY, oikos
EDIBLE, edere
EDIFICE, facere
EDIFY, facere
EFFACE, facere
EFFECT, facere
EFFICIENT, facere
EFFLUENT, fluere
EFFRACTION, frangere
EGREGIOUS, gregare
EGRESS, gradi
EJACULATE, jacere
EJECT, jacere
ELATE, latus
ELECTRIFY, facere
ELICIT, lacere
ELOQUENCE, loqui
ELUCIDATE, lucere
ELUDE, ludere
EMBELLISH, bellus
EMEND, mendum
EMOLUMENT, molere
ENACT, agere
ENAMOR, amare
ENCLOSE, claudere
ENCYCLOPEDIA, pais
ENDEMIC, plebes
ENEMY, amicus
ENNUI, odium
ENSEMBLE, simul
ENTOMOLOGY, logos
ENVOY, via
EPIDEMIC, plebes
EPILOGUE, legein
EPISCOPAL, skopein
EPISODE, hodos
EPISTEMOLOGY, logos
EPITOME, temnein
EQUIVOCATE, vocare
ERODE, rodere
ESCALATE, scala
ESCAPE, caput
ESCARGOT, edere
ESCRITOIRES, scribere

ESCULENT, edere
ESPRIT DE CORPS, corpus
ESSAY, agere
ETERNAL, aevum
ETHNOLOGY, logos
ETYMOLOGY, logos
EUCHARIST, eus
EUGENICS, eus
EUPHEMISM, eus
EUPHORIA, eus
EUTHANASIA, eus
EVACUATE, vacare
EVANGELIST, angelus
EVOKE, vocare
EXACT, agere
EXAMINE, agere
EXCISE, caedere, censere
EXCLUDE, claudere
EXCOGITATE, agere
EXCULPATE, culpa
EXCURSION, currere
EXEMPLIFY, facere
EXIGENT, agere
EXIGUOUS, agere
EXOBIOLOGY, logos
EXODUS, hodos
EXPATRIATE, pater
EXPEDITE, pes
EXPIATE, pius
EX POST FACTO, facere
EXPUNGE, pungere
EXPURGATE, agere
EXTEMPORANEOUS, tempus
EXTINCT, stinguere
EXTINGUISH, stinguere
EXTORT, torquere

F

FABLE, fari
FACADE, facere
FACILE, facere
FACSIMILE, facere
FACT, facere
FACULTY, facere
FAME, fama
FAMILIAR, familia
FASHION, facere
FATE, fari
FEASIBLE, facere
FECKLESS, facere
FELICIFIC, facere
FERTILE, ferre
FETIPAROUS, parere
FETISH, facere
FEVERFEW, fugere
FIX, figere
FLEX, flectere
FLUENT, fluere
FLUORIDE, fluere

FORECLOSE, claudere
FORFEIT, facere
FRACAS, frangere
FRAGILE, frangere
FRATERNITY, frater
FUGACIOUS, fugere
FUNCTION, fungi
FUSTIGATE, agere

G

GARNER, granum
GENEALOGY, logos
GENOCIDE, caedere
GENUFLECT, flectere
GEOLOGY, logos
GIRASOL, sol
GIST, jacere
GLOSS, glossa
GNOSTIC, gignoskein
GRADATION, gradi
GRADE, gradi
GRADIENT, gradi
GRADUATE, gradi
GRAIN, granum
GRANDILOQUENCE, loqui
GRANITE, granum
GRATIFY, facere
GRAVY, granum
GREGARIOUS, gregare
GRENADE, granum
GRESSORIAL, gradi
GYNECOLOGY, logos

H

HACIENDA, facere
HAGIOLOGY, logos
HANDICAP, caput
HANDKERCHIEF, caput
HELIOTROPE, sol
HEMATOLOGY, logos
HEPTATHLON, athlon
HERBIVOROUS, vorare
HERPETOLOGY, logos
HIDALGO, quid
HIERARCHY, arkhein
HIPPODROME, dromein
HISTOLOGY, logos
HOLOCAUST, kaiein
HOMICIDE, caedere
HOMOLOGOUS, logos
HOMO SAPIENS, sapere
HONORIFIC, facere
HOROLOGY, logos
HOROSCOPE, skopein
HOSPITALITY, hospes
HOSTEL, hospes
HOSTILE, hostis
HYPERACTIVE, agere
HYPOCRISY, krinein
HYSTERECTOMY, temnein

I

ICHTHYOLOGY, logos
ICON, eikon
IDÉE FIXE, figere
IDENTIFY, facere
IDEOLOGY, logos
IGNOBLE, gnoscere
IGNORANCE, gnoscere
ILLEGAL, lex
ILL-FAMED, fama
ILL-FATED, fari
ILLIBERAL, liber
ILLITERATE, littera
ILLOGICAL, logos
ILLUMINATE, lucere
ILLUSION, ludere
ILLUSTRATE, lustrare
IMMEDIATE, medius
IMMOLATE, molere
IMMORTAL, mors
IMPEACH, pes
IMPECCABLE, peccare
IMPEDE, pes
IMPERFECT, facere
IMPERVIOUS, via
IMPETUOUS, petere
IMPIETY, pius
IMPLACABLE, placare
IMPOLITIC, polis
INAMORATA, amare
IN CAMERA, kamara
INCISIVE, caedere
INCIVILITY, civis
INCLUDE, claudere
INCOGNITANT, agere
INCOGNITO, gnoscere
INCOMPARABLE, par
INCOMPETENT, petere
INCORPORATE, corpus
IN COURSE, currere
INCREASE, crescere
INCULPABLE, culpa
INCUR, currere
INDECISIVE, caedere
INDESCRIBABLE, scribere
INDESTRUCTIBLE, struere
INDIFFERENT, ferre
INDIGNANT, dignitas
INDISSOLUBLE, solvere
INDISTINCT, stinguere
INEFFABLE, fari
INEFFACEABLE, facere
INEXACT, agere
INFAMY, fama
INFANT, fari
INFECT, facere
INFER, ferre
INFERTILE, ferre
INFIX, figere
INFLEXIBLE, flectere
INFLUENCE, fluere

INFRACTION, frangere
INFRINGE, frangere
INGRAINED, granum
INGREDIENT, gradi
INHOSPITABLE, hospes
INIMICAL, amicus
INJURE, jurare
INJUSTICE, jurare
INNATE, nasci
INNOCENT, nocere
INOCULATE, oculus
INSCRIBE, scribere
INSECT, secare
INSECTIVOROUS, vorare
INSEMINATION, semen
INSIPID, sapere
INSOLATE, sol
INSTINCT, stinguere
INSTRUCT, struere
INSUFFERABLE, ferre
INSUFFICIENT, facere
INSULATE, insula
INTEMPERATE, temperare
INTENSIFY, facere
INTERCOLLEGIATE, legein
INTERCOURSE, currere
INTERFACE, facere
INTERJACENT, jacere
INTERJECT, jacere
INTERLOCUTOR, loqui
INTERLUDE, ludere
INTERLUNAR, luna
INTERMEDIATE, medius
INTERNATIONALIST, nasci
INTERREGNUM, rex
INTERSECT, secare
INTERSPERSE, spargo
INTRANSIGENT, agere
INVARIABLE, varius
INVEIGLE, oculus
INVEST, vestis
INVETERATE, vetus
INVOCATION, vocare
INVOICE, via
INVOKE, vocare
IRRESOLUTE, solvere
IRRESPONSIBLE, spondere
IRREVOCABLE, vocare
ISLE, insula
ISOGLOSS, glossa
ISOLATE, insula

J

JEALOUS, zelos
JESS, jacere
JET, jacere
JOIST, jacere
JOURNAL, dies
JUGULAR, jugum

JUNIOR, juvenis
JURIDICAL, jurare
JURISPRUDENCE, jurare
JURY, jurare
JUS, jurare
JUST, jurare
JUVENILE, juvenis

K

KALEIDOSCOPE, skopein
KAPUT, caput
KENNEL, canis
KERCHIEF, caput
KEYNOTE, notare
KILN, coquere
KINETOSCOPE, skopein
KITCHEN, coquere

L

LACKLUSTER, lustrare
LAISSEZ FAIRE, facere
LA SCALA, scala
LATERAL, latus
LATITUDE, latus
LAUD, laudare
LEGACY, legare
LEGAL, lex
LEGISLATE, lex
LEGITIMATE, lex
LEPRECHAUN, corpus
LETTER, littera
LEVIGATE, agere
LEXICOLOGY, logos
LEXICON, legein
LIBERAL, liber
LIEU, locare
LIQUIFY, facere
LITERAL, littera
LITIGATE, agere
LIVERY, liber
LOCAL, locare
LOCATE, locare
LOCUS, locare
LOCUTION, loqui
LOYAL, lex
LUCID, lucere
LUCUBRATE, lucere
LUDICROUS, ludere
LUMINOUS, lucere
LUNACY, luna
LUSTROUS, lustrare

M

MAGNA CARTA, magnus
MAGNA CUM LAUDE,
magnus
MAGNATE, magnus
MAGNITUDE, magnus
MAJESTIC, magnus

MALAISE, bene
MALADJUSTED, bene
MALEDICTION, bene
MALFUNCTION, bene
MALICE, bene
MALLEABLE, malleus
MALPRACTICE, bene
MANDATORY, mandare
MANUFACTURE, facere
MANUSCRIPT, scribere
MAP, mappa
MARTYROLOGY, logos
MASTECTOMY, temnein
MATERNAL, mater
MATRIARCH, arkhein
MATRICIDE, caedere
MATRICULATE, mater
MATRIX, mater
MAUL, malleus
MAXIM, magnus
MAYOR, magnus
MEA CULPA, culpa
MEAN, medius
MEDIEVAL, aevum
MEDIOCRE, medius
MEGALOPOLIS, polis
MELLIFLUOUS, fluere
MEMENTO MORI, mors
MENDACIOUS, mendum
MERIDIAN, dies
MERIDIEM, dies, medius
MERITRICIOUS, merere
METEOROLOGY, logos
METHOD, hodos
METROPOLIS, mater
MICROBE, mikros
MILIEU, locare, medius
MILLENNIUM, annus
MINIVER, varius
MISANTHROPE, misein
MISCHIEF, caput
MISCONSTRUE, struere
MISFEASANCE, facere
MISOGAMY, misein
MITIGATE, agere
MODIFY, facere
MONARCH, arkhein
MONOCLE, oculus
MONOLOGUE, legein
MONSIGNOR, senex
MOP, mappa
MORTAL, mors
MORTGAGE, mors
MORTIFY, mors
MULTIPAROUS, parere
MYCOLOGY, logos
MYSTIFY, facere
MYTHOLOGY, logos

N

NAIF, nasci

NAIVE, nasci
NAPKIN, mappa
NASCENT, nasci
NASTURTIUM, torquere
NATION, nasci
NATURE, nasci
NAVIGATE, agere
NECROLOGY, nekros
NEE, nasci
NEOLOGY, logos
NEPHEW, nepos
NEPOTISM, nepos
NESCIENT, scire
NEUROLOGY, logos
NICE, scire
NIECE, nepos
NOBLE, gnoscere
NOCUOUS, nocere
NOEL, nasci
NOISOME, odium
NONDESCRIPT, scribere
NON PAREIL, par
NONPROFIT, facere
NOSTRUM, struere
NOTA BENE, notare
NOTABLE, notare
NOTCH, secare
NOTICE, gnoscere
NOTORIETY, gnoscere
NOXIOUS, nocere
NULLIFY, facere
NUMEROLOGY, logos

O

OBESE, edere
OBJECT, jacere
OBJURGATE, agere
OBLATE, latus
OBLIGATE, agere
OBLITERATE, littera
OBLOQUY, loqui
OBNOXIOUS, nocere
OBSTRUCT, struere
OBVIOUS, via
OCCLUDE, claudere
OCCUR, currere
OCULIST, oculus
ODOMETER, hodos
OFFER, ferre
OFFICE, facere
OLFACTORY, facere
OLIGARCHY, arkhein
OMNISCIENCE, scire
OMNIVOROUS, vorare
ONCOLOGY, logos
ONTOLOGY, logos
OPHTHALMOLOGY, logos
OPINION, opinari
ORIFICE, facere
ORMOLU, molere
ORNITHOLOGY, logos

OROLOGY, logos
ORTHOPEDIC, pais
OSSIFY, facere
OUTRAGE, ultra
OVERT, aperire
OVIPAROUS, parere

P

PACIFY, facere
PADRE, pater
PAIR, par
PALEONTOLOGY, logos
PALINDROME, dromein
PALL MALL, malleus
PANACHE, penna
PANDEMIC, plebes
PANEGYRIC, agora
PARALEGAL, lex
PARALLEL, allos
PARAMOUR, amore
PARASOL, sol
PAREGORIC, agora
PARENT, parere
PARI-MUTUEL, par
PARISH, oikos
PARITY, par
PARLAY, par
PAROCHIAL, oikos
PARTURITION, parere
PATERNAL, pater
PATHOLOGY, logos
PATRIARCH, arkhein
PATRIOT, pater
PATRON, pater
PATTERN, pater
PAWN, pes
PECCADILLO, peccare
PEDAL, pes
PEDANT, pais
PEDESTAL, pes
PEER, par
PELLUCID, lucere
PEN, penna
PENINSULA, insula
PENNANT, penna
PENOLOGY, logos
PENTATHLON, athlon
PENULTIMATE, ultra
PENUMBRA, umbra
PEON, pes
PER CAPITA, caput
PERCOLATE, colare
PER DIEM, dies
PEREGRINATION, ager
PERENNIAL, annus
PERFECT, facere
PERFUNCTORY, fungi
PERIOD, hodos
PERISCOPE, skopein
PERJURE, jurare

PERK, colare
PERPETRATE, petere
PERSONIFY, facere
PERT, aperire
PERVIOUS, via
PETITION, petere
PETRIFY, facere
PETULANT, petere
PHARMACOLOGY, logos
PHRASEOLOGY, logos
PHYSIOGNOMY, gignoskein
PHYSIOLOGY, logos
PIEDMONT, pes
PIETA, pius
PILGRIM, ager
PINNACLE, penna
PINOCHLE, oculus
PIONEER, pes
PISCIVOROUS, vorare
PITEOUS, pius
PITIFUL, pius
PITTANCE, pius
PIVOT, pungere
PLACATE, placere
PLEBISCITE, plebes, scire
PLEBEIAN, plebes
P.M., medius
PODIATRIST, pes
POIGNANT, pungere
POINT, pungere
POLICE, polis
POLITICAL, polis
POLYGLOT, glossa
POMEGRANATE, granum
PONTIFF, facere
PORCELAIN, porcus
PORTCULLIS, colare
POST-MORTEM, mors
POSTNATAL, nasci
POSTPARTUM, parere
POSTSCRIPT, scribere
POUNCE, pungere
POWDER, pulvis
PRECAUTION, cavere
PRECIPICE, caput
PRECIS, caedere
PRECLUDE, claudere
PRECOCIOUS, coquere
PRECOGNITION, gnoscere
PRECURSOR, currere
PREFACE, fari
PREFECT, facere
PREFER, ferre
PREFIX, figere
PREGNANT, nasci
PRELATE, latus
PRELUDE, ludere
PRENATAL, nasci
PRESCIENCE, scire
PRESCRIBE, scribere
PREVARICATE, varius

PREVIOUS, via
PRIMEVAL, aevum
PRIVILEGE, lex
PRO BONO, bonus
PRODIGAL, agere
PRODROME, dromein
PROFICIENT, facere
PROFIT, facere
PROGNOSIS, gignoskein
PROGRESS, gradi
PROJECT, jacere
PROLEGOMENON, legein
PROLIFERATE, ferre
PROLIFIC, facere
PROLOGUE, legein
PROPITIOUS, petere
PROSCRIBE, scribere
PRO TEM, tempus
PROVERB, verbum
PROVOKE, vocare
PSEUDODROME, dromein
PSYCHOLOGY, logos
PTOMAINE, temnein
PUN, pungere
PUNCTILIOUS, pungere
PUNCTUAL, pungere
PUNY, nasci
PURGE, agere
PUTREFACTION, facere

Q

QUADRUPED, pes
QUAINT, gnoscere
QUALIFY, qualis
QUANTITY, quantus
QUANTUM, quantus
QUASI, quam
QUIBBLE, qui
QUID PRO QUO, quid
QUINCENTENNIAL, annus
QUINSY, canis
QUIP, quid
QUONDAM, quom
QUORUM, qui
QUOTA, quot
QUOTE, quot
QUOTIDIAN, quot

R

RADARSCOPE, skopein
RADIOLOGY, logos
RATIFY, facere
REACT, agere
READJUST, jurare
REAPPEAR, parere
RECAP, caput
RECENSION, censere
RECLUSE, claudere
RECOGNIZE, gnoscere

RECOMMEND, mandare
RECONNAISANCE, gnoscere
RECOOK, coquere
RECOURSE, currere
RECOVER, aperire
RECRUIT, crescere
RECTIFY, facere
RECUR, currere
REDACT, agere
REENACT, agere
REFECTION, facere
REFER, ferre
REFLECT, flectere
REFLEX, flectere
REFRACTION, frangere
REFUGE, fugere
REGAL, rex
REGICIDE, caedere
REGNANT, rex
REGRESS, gradi
REGULUS, rex
REIGN, rex
REJECT, jacere
REJUVENATE, juvenis
RELATE, latus
RELEGATE, legare
RELOCATE, locare
RENAISSANCE, nasci
REPEAT, petere
REPERTOIRE, par
REPETITION, petere
RESOLUTE, solvere
RESOLVE, solvere
RESOUND, sonare
RESPOND, spondere
RETARD, tardus
RETICENCE, tacere
RETORT, torquere
RETROACTIVE, agere
RETROGRESS, gradi
REVAMP, pes
REVEILLE, vigilare
REVOKE, vocare
RIANT, ridere
RICOTTA, coquere
RIDICULE, ridere
RIPARIAN, ripa
RISIBLE, ridere
RISK, secare
RISQUE, secare
RIVAL, rivus
RIVER, ripa
RIVULET, rivus
RODENT, rodere
ROOKIE, crescere
ROSTRUM, struere
ROYAL, rex

S

SAGE, sapere

SALUBRIOUS, salus
SALUTE, salus
SANCTIFY, facere
SANG-FROID, sanguis
SANGUINARY, sanguis
SAPIENT, sapere
SATISFY, facere
SAVOIR FAIRE, sapere
SAVOR, sapere
SAVVY, sapere
SCALE, scala
SCHEDULE, skhizein
SCHISM, skhizein
SCHIZY, skhizein
SCIENCE, scire
SCIOLISM, scire
SCISSORS, caedere
SCOPE, skopein
SCRIBBLE, scribere
SCRIPT, scribere
SECANT, secare
SECLUDE, claudere
SECTOR, secare
SEGMENT, secare
SEGREGATE, gregare
SEISMOLOGY, logos
SELENOGRAPHY, luna
SELF-CONSCIOUS, scire
SELF-IMMOLATION, molere
SEMIANNUAL, annus
SEMINARY, semen
SENATE, senex
SENESCENT, senex
SENILE, senex
SEÑOR, senex
SESQUICENTENNIAL, annus
SESQUIPEDALIAN, pes
SICKLE, secare
SIMPLIFY, facere
SIMULCAST, simul
SIR, senex
SOCIOLOGY, logos
SOJOURN, dies
SOLAR, sol
SOLE, solus
SOLILOQUY, solus
SOLIPSISM, solus
SOLITUDE, solus
SOLO, solus
SOLSTICE, sol
SOLUBLE, solvere
SOLVENT, solvere
SOMNILOQUY, loqui
SONIC, sonare
SONNET, sonare
SOPORIFIC, facere
SORORITY, soror
SOUND, sonare
SPARSE, spargo
SPECTROSCOPE, skopein
SPELEOLOGY, logos

SPOUSE, spondere
SQUAT, agere
STRUCTURE, struere
STULTIFY, facere
STUPOR, stupere
SUBJACENT, jacere
SUBJECT, jacere
SUBJUGATE, jugum
SUBLUNARY, lunar
SUBSCRIBE, scribere
SUBSTRUCTURE, struere
SUBTERFUGE, fugere
SULLEN, solus
SUMMA CUM LAUDE, laudare
SUPERFICIAL, facere
SUPERFLUOUS, fluere
SUPERJACENT, jacere
SUPERLATIVE, latus
SUPERSCRIPT, scribere
SUPERSONIC, sonare
SUPERSTRUCTURE, struere
SURFACE, facere
SURFEIT, facere
SURVEILLANCE, vigilare
SYLLOGISM, logos
SYNC, chronos
SYNDROME, dromein
SYNOD, hodos

T

TACIT, tacere
TAMPER, temperare
TARDY, tardus
TART, torquere
TAUTOLOGY, logos
TECHNOLOGY, logos
TELESCOPE, skopein
TELEVANGELIST, angelus
TEMPER, temperare
TEMPEST, tempus
TEMPO, tempus
TEMPORARY, tempus
TEMPUS FUGIT, tempus
TENSE, tempus
TERMINOLOGY, logos
THEOLOGY, logos
TINCTURE, stinguere
TOAST, torrere
TOME, temnein
TONSILLECTOMY, temnein
TORCH, torquere
TORQUE, torquere
TORRENT, torrere
TORT, torquere
TOXICOLOGY, logos
TRAJECTORY, jacere
TRANSACTION, agere
TRANSCRIBE, scribere
TRANSFER, ferre
TRANSFIXED, figere

TRANSGRESS, gradi
TRANSLATE, latus
TRANSLUCENT, lucere
TRANSONIC, sonare
TRANSPARENT, parere
TRANSVESTITE, vestis
TRAVELOGUE, legein
TRAVESTY, vestis
TRIATHLON, athlon
TRILOGY, logos
TRISECT, secare
TRIUMVIRATE, vir
TRIVET, pes
TRIVIA, via
TRUSS, torquere

U

ULTERIOR, ultra
ULTIMATUM, ultra
UMBRAGE, umbra
UMBRELLA, umbra
UMPIRE, par
UNAFFECTED, facere
UNAMBIGUOUS, agere
UNAVOIDABLE, vacare
UNCHARITABLE, carus
UNCIVIL, civis
UNCONSCIONABLE, scire
UNCOVERED, aperire
UNDECIDED, caedere
UNDERCOVER, aperire
UNDERCURRENT, currere
UNDIGNIFIED, dignitas
UNEQUIVOCAL, vocare
UNFAMILIAR, familia
UNFASHIONABLE, facere
UNICAMERAL, kamara
UNIFY, facere
UNIPAROUS, parere
UNISON, sonare
UNJUST, jurare
UNNATURAL, nasci
UNOFFICIAL, facere
UNPROFITABLE, facere
UNQUALIFIED, qualis
UNRIVALED, rivus
UNSAVORY, sapere
UNSCIENTIFIC, scire
UNSOLVABLE, solvere
UNVARYING, varius
UPSCALE, scala

V

VACANCY, vacare
VACUITY, vacare
VAIN, vacare
VANITY, vacare
VARIABLE, varius
VARIEGATED, agere

VARIETY, varius
VASECTOMY, temnein
VAUNT, temnein
VENTRILOQUIST, loqui
VERBAL, verbum
VERBIAGE, verbum
VERBOSE, verbum
VERIFY, facere
VERVE, verbum
VESTIGE, vestis
VET, vetus
VIADUCT, via
VICARIOUS, vicis
VICE, vicis
VICEROY, rex
VICISSITUDES, vicis
VIGIL, vigilare
VILLAIN, villa
VIPER, parere
VIRAGO, vir
VIRILE, vir
VIRTUE, vir
VIVIFY, facere
VIVIPAROUS, parere
VOCIFEROUS, vocare
VOICE, vocare
VOID, vocare
VORACIOUS, vorare
VOUCH, vocare
VOX POPULI, vocare
VOYAGE, via

X

XENOPHOBIA, xenos

Z

ZEAL, zelos
ZOOLOGY, logos